The Translations of Valery Larbaud

The Translations of
Valery Larbaud

A Model of Literary Exploration

Allison Connell

Chapel Street Editons

Copyright © 2019 by Allison Connell
All rights reserved

Published by
Chapel Street Editions
150 Chapel Street
Woodstock, New Brunswick E7M 1H4
www.chapelstreeteditions.com

ISBN 978-1-988299-21-1

Library and Archives Canada Cataloguing in Publication
Title: The translations of Valery Larbaud : a model of literary exploration / Allison Connell.
Names: Connell, Allison, author.
Description: Includes bibliographical references.
Identifiers: Canadiana 20190143835 | ISBN 9781988299211 (softcover)
Subjects: LCSH: Larbaud, Valéry, 1881-1957—Criticism and interpretation. | LCSH: Translating and interpreting.
Classification: LCC PQ2623.A65 Z678 2019 | DDC 843/.912—dc23

Book design by Brendan Helmuth

Dedication

To the memory of
Laeta Pons

Contents

Introduction 1
Part I: Translations from English: Apprenticeship 15
   Chapter 1: Coleridge 17
   Chapter 2: Landor 29
   Chapter 3: Whitman 35
Part II: Translations from English: The Master Translator 49
   Chapter 4: Butler: Introduction 51
   Chapter 5: Butler: *Erewhon* 59
   Chapter 6: Butler: *The Way of All Flesh* 73
   Chapter 7: Butler: *Life and Habit* 89
   Chapter 8: Butler: *Life and Habit*—Further Considerations . . . 103
   Chapter 9: Butler: *Erewhon Revisited* 153
   Chapter 10: Butler: *Note-Books* 161
   Chapter 11: Butler: *Note-Books*—Further Considerations 169
   Chapter 12: Other Authors Writing in English: Joyce and Sitwell . . 177
Part III: Translations from Other Romance Languages 187
   Chapter 13: Translations from Spanish 189
   Chapter 14: Translations from Italian 195
   Chapter 15: Translations from Portuguese 199
   Chapter 16: Conclusion 203
Bibliography 207
About the Author 215

Introduction

The publication in 1961 of the Pléiade edition of the original work of Valery Larbaud (1881–1957)[1] was the recognition of a major humanist of the twentieth century who was not merely a model writer but a virtuoso of the French language. The select but ever-growing Pléiade series of the work of major French writers thus put Larbaud's creative work on the same shelf as Montaigne's.

In his much more recently published complete diary (*Journal*), Larbaud provides a picture of a "specimen day" (Whitman's expression) in his life on the Mediterranean coast of Spain near Alicante.[2] (This four-year sojourn in Spain, 1916–1920, was the longest of his various sojourns abroad.) After a walk near his villa in May, 1917, at the age of thirty-five, he comments:

> There are many fine and very old olive trees, and almost all the plants common to Morocco and Algeria. All this makes me think often of my long walks up and down Warwickshire in the year 1909....I have translated a little more than one page a day of *The Way of All Flesh*; besides I have been going on with the rereading of *The Origin of Species* and have begun another of Miró's books: *Del Vivir*.[3]

Larbaud's program for the day thus includes the continuing translation of Samuel Butler's major novel, *The Way of All Flesh*, into French, a further rereading of Darwin's *The Origin of Species* resulting from his work on evolution theory in order to fully appreciate Butler's particular contribution to it, and reading a recent novel by his Alicante friend, the prolific Spanish novelist Gabriel Miró:

> My timetable is this: get up before seven; breakfast; when well enough out for a walk; working between ten and lunch time (1:30 or 2:00); stay for about an hour in the garden after lunch; then work and read till tea time; after tea going to one of the

---

1 Paris: Gallimard, 1961.
2 Paris: Gallimard, 2009.
3 op. cit., pp. 219–220; Sunday, May 13, 1917.

> two great *tertulias* there are here...where there are a lot of nice girls and children; then dinner; and after sitting up for about two hours in the drawing room with the ladies, bed time.[4]

In this evocation of his working day, nothing at all exceptional appears at first to be related. However, Larbaud's walks in Warwickshire and near Alicante may be understood as an important expression of his cosmopolitan ideal. They will be resumed in other places, such as the vicinity of Vaduz in Liechtenstein, for example, so that, symbolically, he walks Europe, discreetly living out his opposition to extreme nationalism and his fervent support of a future united Europe. Even his interest in botany could be seen as a manifestation of his implicit commitment to the cause.

He then draws attention to his work as a translator: on this particular day his translation from English into French of Samuel Butler's classic novel *The Way of All Flesh* is only slowly progressing, since it is competing with his "rereading" of Darwin. His understanding of Darwin's conception of evolution had to be thorough in view of his forthcoming translation of Samuel Butler's major work in the evolution field, *Life and Habit*, in which Butler develops a number of important reservations concerning Darwin's theory. Such activities are always considered pleasurable and blend into such other pleasurable activities as the parties ("*tertulias*") to which he refers.

At the international level, Pascale Casanova's work *La République Mondiale des Lettres*[5] and its English translation, *World Republic of Letters*,[6] demonstrate how the work of Larbaud may be seen, by its very nature, as an antidote to extreme nationalism. The situation that prevailed just before the First World War, when nationalism was the order of the day, had created a political and social climate that seemed to make the cosmopolitan ideal untenable. Larbaud's fictitious character A.O. Barnabooth, whose *Oeuvres complètes* were published in 1913, was born in South America and writes in French from such countries as Italy, Russia, and Denmark—a gesture that might easily have been interpreted as provocative at the time, although there is little evidence that it caused a reaction from the then very vocal French right wing.

That was possibly because Larbaud did not engage directly in debating such issues: there is no editorializing on them in his work. It is the very nature of his work that is "universalist," as, for example, the fact that in his critique he is often presenting work written in languages other than French, such as English, Spanish, Italian, and Portuguese. As Pascale Casanova sums it up:

---

4 Ibid., p. 220.
5 Paris: Editions du Seuil, 1999
6 M.B. De Bevoise, transl. Cambridge, MA: Harvard University Press, 2004.

> Valery Larbaud...souhaitait l'avènement...d'une petite société cosmopolite qui ferait taire les préjugés nationaux...en favorisant la libre circulation et la reconnaissance des grands textes de l'avant-garde littéraire du monde entier.[7]
>
> Valery Larbaud...foresaw the advent of a small, cosmopolitan, enlightened society that would silence national prejudices by recognizing and promoting the free circulation of great works of avant-garde literature from all over the world.[8]

Thus Larbaud implicitly saw himself as a man with a mission: the advocacy of a united Europe through the medium of Europe's literatures.

Sometimes he expresses this cause in terms of a metaphorical "conquest." The activity of translation is one of several ways in which this conquest is carried out because it integrates works in other languages into the maternal language of the translator, and, on rare occasions, the reverse. Translation, as understood by Larbaud, is an uncompromising dedication of the translator's own time and resources to a cause that he or she feels to be just because of the new insights and pleasures being "translated," that is, "given," to fortunate readers in their own language.

He is often remembered as a prodigious traveller, although he much preferred to be considered a resident of the various countries in which he sojourned, participating in their cultural activities while acquainting his own country with the new works, which, as an indefatigable literary prospector, he had discovered in his new surroundings. Thus his actual *oeuvre* extends far beyond the limits of the Pléiade edition of his work and, importantly, includes his extensive literary criticism and translations.

Enthusiastic studies were one means of communicating his new discoveries. However, when he had become impressed with important works not yet translated into French, he generously invested valuable time in the craft and art of translation.

Larbaud's sojourns abroad took place in Spain, England, and Italy, although he famously visited many other countries and regions as well: North Africa, Portugal, Switzerland, Belgium, Holland, Germany, Denmark, Sweden, Russia, Greece, the Dalmatian coast, and Albania.

His "grand tour" with his tutor at the age of seventeen had taken him as far as St. Petersburg and Constantinople. Such dimensions of his life were

---

7 op. cit., p. 237.
8 op. cit., transl., p. 172.

projected in 1913 into his major novel, *A.O. Barnabooth*.[9] Barnabooth's poetry has been reprinted as a separate work and is well known. A young South American multi-millionaire, Barnabooth experiences Europe as a single nation, which was possibly the most important point, especially in times when national sentiment was dangerously strong.

Throughout Larbaud's work, language learning is always viewed as one of life's greatest pleasures. From childhood he learned ancient Greek and Latin, and later mastered Spanish, English, and Italian while acquiring a working knowledge of German as well. Later, in his early forties, he undertook to learn Portuguese, a process he describes in an essay entitled "Divertissement Philologique." (It is noteworthy that Larbaud lived in the time of philology. Although the science of Linguistics was already being developed in the universities, such as in the work of Ferdinand de Saussure at the Sorbonne, its principles had not yet influenced major writers.)

What is by far the most significant recent contribution to Larbaud studies is the publication in 2009 of his complete diaries under the title *Journal*, mentioned above. It is now evident that less than half of his diaries had appeared during his lifetime as volumes nine (1954) and ten (1955) of the *Oeuvres Complètes*, published by Gallimard. The present critical edition of *Journal*, a model of the genre, was a major event, providing answers to innumerable questions which had previously gone unanswered. A great deal of detailed information has thus been made available on his life near Alicante.

Since a major preoccupation at that time was the translation of five of Samuel Butler's works into French, the *Journal*, which he soon began keeping very regularly, represents a particularly important documentation of the interaction of the translations with the creation of his original work and critique.

Nonetheless, a number of earlier studies of Larbaud's work remain relevant. We find that the first major monograph was Georges Jean-Aubry's *Valery Larbaud: Sa Vie et son oeuvre: La Jeunesse 1881–1920*.[10] There had been several much shorter, but often excellent, presentations before Jean-Aubry's work appeared. However, it supersedes them for purposes of research. It is a very detailed and well-researched literary biography and still an essential reference, since it represents the final result of a long-term collaboration between Jean-Aubry and Larbaud himself.

---

9 Larbaud, *A.O. Barnabooth Ses Oeuvres Complètes c'est-à-dire un Conte, ses Poésies et son Journal Intime* (Paris: NRF, 1913).

10 Monaco: Rocher, 1949.

Their correspondence shows that they worked together in a spirit of mutual respect. After the debilitating stoke suffered by Larbaud in August 1935, which left him unable to write or even dictate, Jean-Aubry continued to enjoy access to his manuscripts, correspondence, and a vast amount of documentation. It was also largely as a result of Jean-Aubry's initiative that the portion of Larbaud's works intended for publication but still uncollected in volumes was edited and published in its definitive form. Thus it was Jean-Aubry who brought about the publication of *Aux Couleurs de Rome* in May 1938 and *Ce Vice impuni la lecture: Domaine Français* in June 1941. In 1946 Jean-Aubry also published Larbaud's *Sous l'Invocation de St. Jérôme*, which contains various studies on the subject of literary translation.

Georges Jean-Aubry later established the first three volumes of Larbaud's ten-volume *Oeuvres Complètes* (1950–1955), which were completed by Robert Mallet and Vincent Milligan, but with continuing dependance on Jean-Aubry's notation, up to and including volume eight.

Jean-Aubry was a musicologist as well,[11] being able to count among his friends Debussy, Roussel, Dukas, and Ravel. From 1919 to 1940 he was the editor in England of the somewhat forgotten journal of music studies, *The Chesterian*. This was a major undertaking, published in London by J. & W. Chester Ltd., with contributors from twenty-two countries.

Jean-Aubry died in 1950 before the proposed second volume of the Larbaud biography could be produced. He did, however, leave notes on the period to be included in it, most of which may be found in the Pléiade edition of Larbaud's work. He was himself a remarkable *homme de lettres* whose career in many respects paralleled Larbaud's. Like Larbaud, he greatly admired London and would frequent certain "*coteries*" such as the one that sometimes assembled in the salon of Louise (Harding) Alvar, where, besides famous composers and conductors, he met Eliot, Bennett, and Paul Valéry. Again, like Larbaud, he was a remarkable traveller whose itinerary included Poland, Sweden, Denmark, Germany, and Argentina.[12]

His best-known work is probably his authoritative *Vie de Conrad* (1947), which has remained a primary reference for Conrad scholars. Jean-Aubry was also a Jules Laforgue specialist, producing the first edition of Laforgue's complete works. Above all, like Larbaud, he was a dedicated translator, translating thirteen of Conrad's works from English into French and, in the process, often consulting Conrad himself. These translations have more recently

---

11 Cf. Philippe Rodriguez, Presentation of G. Jean-Aubry in *Cahiers Maurice Ravel* 8, 2004.

12 Ibid.

appeared, along with all other French translations of Conrad, in the Pléiade edition of Conrad's complete work, in which a number of Jean-Aubry's Conrad translations have undergone further revision (often the work of Professor Sylvère Monod, the well-known Dickensian) for this definitive edition.

As he points out in his brief Introduction to *Valery Larbaud: Sa Vie et son oeuvre*, Jean-Aubry became interested in Larbaud's work from the time of the latter's first publications, and he had known him personally since their collaboration on Jean Royère's literary journal *La Phalange*, one of the predecessors of *La Nouvelle Revue Française*. Their correspondence begins in 1920. Jean-Aubry's research in view of his monograph on Larbaud was well underway in May 1933, as seen in a letter from Larbaud to his publisher in Holland, A.A.M. Stols:

> G. Jean-Aubry...avec qui je suis resté en contact depuis 1910 et qui est un des meilleurs érudits lettrés que je connaisse, a entrepris spontanément une "Bibliographie Raisonnée" de tous mes ouvrages....De plus il accompagne cette bibliographie de renseignements biographiques très minutieux.[13]

Given that Larbaud's translations of five of Samuel Butler's works represent his most significant achievement as a translator, a parallel becomes evident between Larbaud's literary partnership with Jean-Aubry and Butler's with the indispensable Henry Festing Jones, which, in turn, was sometimes compared with the Johnson–Boswell relationship. Besides assisting Butler with various publication projects, Festing Jones eventually produced his model biography of Butler.[14] In fact, Larbaud, during his sojourn in London following the return from Spain, was present at the time when this famous literary biography was about to appear.

However, the parallel between Jean-Aubry's collaboration with Larbaud and Henry Festing Jones's with Butler requires further clarification, since the Johnson–Boswell analogy is applicable only in part. Boswell was both Johnson's secretary and his "portrait painter," creating a series of vivid scenes through which the reader comes to know Johnson the man. That is true also of Festing Jones in his biography of Butler. Jean-Aubry, however, was obliged to confine himself strictly to his role as secretary, as seen in his chief concern

---

13 Valery Larbaud–A.A.M. Stols, *Correspondance* (Paris: Edition de Cendres, 1986), vol. 1, p. 285. Lettre du 4 mai, 1933.

14 *Samuel Butler Author of "Erewhon": A Memoir* (2 vols.) (London: MacMillan & Co. Ltd., 1920).

to make appropriate use of the abundance of documents at his command, including correspondence.

This could be explained by the circumstance that Jean-Aubry's study of Larbaud's work was carried out and published during Larbaud's lifetime, creating a need for discretion. Another reason may well be found in Larbaud's views concerning literary studies in general. In an essay first published in 1923 entitled "Pour l'Inauguration d'une nouvelle ligne," Larbaud makes a clear distinction between literary criticism and literary history, referring to scholars who tended to display literary pretensions when writing literary history: "Ce que je leur reproche, c'est de mêler l'histoire littéraire, qui est science, à la critique, qui est art."[15]

Jean-Aubry, indeed, understands his biography as contributing strictly to literary history. (In making this distinction, Larbaud is referring in particular to university theses: the purpose of these, like articles in an encyclopedia, being essentially to inform.) Classifying Larbaud's own critique in this way, however, is somewhat problematic, as it often consists of presentations of writers and their work in which there can be an almost complete identity with his subject.

Although these presentations do make enduring contributions to literary history, this creative identification means that they must be seen as belonging essentially to criticism. This is especially true of the critical monographs in the two volumes *Ce Vice impuni la lecture: Domaine Anglais* and *Ce Vice impuni la lecture: Domaine Francais*.

In Larbaud's *Domaine Français*, these concern the work of Héroet, Scève, Jean de Lingendes, Racan, D'Ablancourt, Patru, Mérimée, Dondey de Santeny, Mirbeau, Charles-Louis Philippe, Marguerite Audoux, Edouard Dujardin, Valéry, Fargue, St. John Perse, and Henry J.-M. Levet, and in *Domaine Anglais* that of Butler, Hardy, Digby Dolben, Henley, Conrad, Francis Thompson, Arnold Bennett, Poe, Whitman, Faulkner, James Stephens, Joyce, and Wyatt.

Actually these "domains" extend far beyond the limits of the two volumes, as shown by Béatrice Mousli in her edition of the latter[16] and by the translations into French from Spanish by Martine and Bernard Fouques of Larbaud's articles in the Buenos Aires daily *La Nacion* on French literature.[17] Thus Larbaud, although essentially a critic, is also participating in a significant revision of literary history.

---

15 Cf. "Technique." In *Oeuvres Complètes de Valery Larbaud*, Tome 8, "Sous L'Invocation de Saint Jérôme" (Paris: Gallimard, 1953), p. 293.

16 Paris: Gallimard, 1998.

17 Larbaud, *Du Navire d'Argent* (Paris: Gallimard, 2003).

Larbaud's published correspondence with Jean-Aubry[18] makes it possible to find these two *hommes de lettres* working together in an *atelier des muses*. Thus, in a letter to Larbaud of October 28, 1934, Jean-Aubry refers to his work in progress, the translation into French of Conrad's late novel *The Rescue*. He seeks Larbaud's assistance in the rendering of two challenging passages, and in his reply of October 31, Larbaud makes very detailed suggestions. To quote only the first passage, which concerns the translation of the title of the sixth and last part of the novel, "The Claim of Life and the Toll of Death," Jean-Aubry writes:

> Je cherche en vain quelque chose qui fasse "titre," avec rythme et brièveté; et je patauge. Avez-vous une idée; je crois qu'il faudrait supprimer les articles et même le "et," mais je ne trouve rien de satisfaisant.[19]

Larbaud replies:

> La vie et la mort / la tombe / le tombeau...demandent / exigent / réclament / reprennent...leur droit, leurs droits, leur bien, leur dû....La vie réclame...exige...son bien...ses droits... et la mort son tribut.[20]

This example of a Conrad translation in progress, in which Jean-Aubry brings together the authors of the two works for whose promotion he had dedicated so much if his time, demonstrates his commitment to his task, admirable with respect to Conrad in that he had chosen a particularly challenging *oeuvre* in his desire to see Conrad properly appreciated in the French-speaking world. One has only to remember some of Conrad's great scenes, such as the storm in Chapter Three of *The Nigger of the Narcissus* (which Jean-Aubry did not translate), to be made aware that Conrad's English has unusual qualities, such as the "poetic" resonance of many words. Conrad is in love, as it were, with the English language, and often uses words which take us far beyond mere denotation. A translator is therefore challenged to an unusual degree. However Jean-Aubry's long experience as an editor clearly served him well.

Not all of his Conrad translations present such challenges. In *The Rover*, the scene is on the Mediterranean coast of France near Toulon in the early 1800s

---

18   Valery Larbaud–G. Jean-Aubry *Correspondance* 1920–1935. Introduction et notes de Frieda Weissman (Paris: Gallimard, 1971).

19   Jean-Aubry, op. cit., p. 180 (28 octobre 1934).

20   Ibid., p. 181 (31 octobre 1934).

and, for the sake of local colour (often reminiscent of Maupassant), Conrad sometimes uses French phraseology and syntax for arranging English words. It is clear, however, that such passages do not necessarily render the French translation less challenging. (Conrad recognized Jean-Aubry's translations by dedicating *The Rover* to him.)

Following the chronological order of other major studies of Larbaud's work, it may be noted that Ortensia Ruggiero's *Valery Larbaud et L'Italie*,[21] a published thesis, established Larbaud's relations with Italian writers as well as Italian influences on his own work, such as those of Croce and De Sanctis. This is precisely the sort of thesis Larbaud had been advocating.

A number of important critical editions of Larbaud's correspondence appeared in the 1970s, many of which illuminate the very active period of the 1920s, thus compensating to some degree for the absence of a second volume to Jean-Aubry's biography and also for the absence of diary entries between 1921 and 1931.

Of particular significance was the publication in 1972 of Larbaud's correspondence with the Mexican writer and diplomat Alfonso Reyes.[22] Paulette Patout's notes reveal the vast network of relations Larbaud maintained with writers in Latin America, some of whom he met in Paris. Several were translators who discussed translation projects with him. This was true of Alfonso Reyes himself, who may be understood as a colleague as well as a friend.

Larbaud's correspondence with his close friend Marcel Ray, also a diplomat, appearing in three volumes in 1979–1980, makes it possible to trace the origins and early development of Larbaud's literary activities.[23] In the earlier letters we find the young Larbaud "prospecting" classical American literature shortly after his discovery of Whitman. Although he was later to prove himself a Whitman specialist, in 1899–1900 he was still under the impression that it might be possible to bring to light another poetic work equal to Whitman's. (At the time, Emily Dickinson's had not yet been published, although it was being prepared for publication.)

Larbaud's earliest translations (which remain unpublished) are mentioned in this correspondence—translations of Dobson, Thackeray, Hawthorne, Shelley, and Meredith. One important matter taken up in the third volume

---

21 Paris: Nizet, 1963.
22 Valery Larbaud–Alfonso Reyes *Correspondance* 1923–1952. Introduction et notes de Paulette Patout (Paris: Didier, 1972).
23 Valery Larbaud–Marcel Ray *Correspondance* 1899–1937. Introduction et notes de Françoise Lioure. Paris: Gallimard. Vol. 1: 1899–1909 (1979); Vol. 2: 1910–1920 (1980); Vol. 3: 1921–1937 (1980).

of this correspondence with Marcel Ray is his position on "committed" literature ("*la littérature engagée*"). He is adamantly opposed to the notion of the subordination of literature to a "message." However, he acknowledges that certain philosophical positions may be inherent in the work itself, so that we arrive at the notion of two kinds of commitment: explicit and implicit. His own work does, on occasion, express certain implicit commitments. This matter is broached toward the end of the correspondence, especially in his letter of April 11, 1935, with respect to the work of Samuel Butler.

The publication of John L. Brown's study of 1981,[24] a presentation of Larbaud and his work in English, also raises the question of implicit commitment. Brown points out that Larbaud clearly favoured the concept of a European union long before its present evolving realization, and that he looked forward to a time when nation states would grant autonomy to those of their components which had historically played independent roles. Thus Larbaud's tribute to his native Bourbonnais, *Allen*, draws attention to the time just before the formation of nation states as understood today, that is, the early sixteenth century, when Bourbonnais could ally itself with the Austrian Empire in opposition to the King of France, with no consideration of "treason."

A Rabelaisian style of humour is the order of the day in Larbaud's published correspondence with his close friend the poet Léon-Paul Fargue,[25] in which there is a great play of fantasy, as for example in their signatures: Larbaud signs "Potame," "Dépotame," "Papotame" and "Hipparion," etc., referring to Fargue's amused impression, apparently based on a well-known photo portrait of Larbaud, that there was something "hippopotamic" about his friend, which, with Larbaud, became a private cult, even inducing him to visit hippopotami in the zoos of Paris and Lisbon.

Another important document that makes it possible to reconstruct many of Larbaud's activities in this decade that is missing in his diaries is *Lettres à Adrienne Monnier et à Sylvia Beach (1919–1933)*.[26] As is well known, these two remarkable ladies each operated a bookstore on the Rue de l'Odéon. Adrienne Monnier's was called La Maison des Amis des Livres and it was there that Larbaud gave his public lecture on the work of Samuel Butler on November 3, 1920, and another, a year later, on the work of James Joyce (December 7, 1921). This correspondence takes the reader backstage during the momentous translation of Joyce's *Ulysses* into French, to which Larbaud devoted much

---

24 John L. Brown, *Valery Larbaud* (Boston: G.K. Hall & Co., Twayne Publishers), 1981.
25 Léon-Paul Fargue–Valery Larbaud. *Correspondance* 1910–1946 (Paris: Gallimard, 1971).
26 Larbaud, op. cit. Correspondance établie et annotée par Maurice Saillet (Paris: Institut Mémoires de l'Edition Contemporaine, 1991).

time as a very important member of a team of translators. It also contains information on the superb literary journal *Commerce*.

Larbaud was the most active member of its editorial board as well as being a regular contributor. (The other two members of the board were Paul Valéry and Léon-Paul Fargue.) Its title was inspired by a fragment of *Anabase*, the epic poem by St. John Perse: "Ce pur commerce de mon âme." *Commerce* provides considerable insight into the literary activities and projects of Larbaud at the peak of his career, including his translations.

A special number of *Les Cahiers de l'Herne* on Valery Larbaud, edited by Professor Anne Chevalier and published in 1992,[27] responded to the need to bring Larbaud to a new generation and a broader readership. This is done through an attractive presentation of parts of Larbaud's diaries and correspondence which had remained unpublished, and selections from work that had appeared in periodicals but had not been included in the *Oeuvres Complètes*. (Larbaud uses the word *casuel* with respect to work he wouldn't have allowed to be published except in "un recueil anecdotique et de curiosité.") However, Larbaud's major essay on translation ("De la Traduction") is also reprinted here among the many other reprints. This number of *Les Cahiers de l'Herne*, by immersing the reader in the "real world" of Larbaud, is possibly the best introduction to his work. However, the formula was actually pioneered by Bernard Delvaille in his well-illustrated and excellent "Essai sur Valery Larbaud" in 1963.[28]

The distinction between what is formal and what is not was very important to Larbaud, whose published work has a first class polish not always to be found in the "raw material" from which it sometimes evolved. The great virtue of this number of *Les Cahiers de l'Herne* is that it is able to present the latter, so that we often have a "close up" view of Larbaud and his work. The then unedited parts of his diary concerning the Montpellier region of coastal Languedoc (Sète-Mèze) are, in this respect, of particular interest and stand comparison with the already mentioned explorations in Warwickshire which were published as *Le Coeur de l'Angleterre*.[29]

Montaigne had also once used the informal, colloquial style, that is, the style of "letters home," for his account of his long and arduous tour of Italy, as Samuel Butler had likewise done in his *Alps and Sanctuaries of Piedmont and the Canton Ticino*. (1881).

---

27 *Cahiers de l'Herne* 61 (Paris: Editions de l'Herne, 1992).
28 In the series *Poètes d'Aujourd'hui* 100 (Paris: Seghers, 1963).
29 Paris: Gallimard, 1971.

In 1998 a new edition of *Ce Vice impuni la lecture: Domaine anglais*[30] appeared with an introduction and notes by Béatrice Mousli. A very large new section entitled "*Pages retrouvées*" more than doubles the contents of the 1936 edition with reprints of studies and articles which had originally appeared in periodicals. These provide further insight into Larbaud's study of English Literature, including the literatures of Ireland and North America in the English language.

Béatrice Mousli's thoroughly researched *Valery Larbaud*[31] appearing in the same year, is a full-length and seemingly definitive account of Larbaud's life and work. Here the respectful formality of Jean-Aubry's biography is replaced by the informal style which has more recently become *de rigueur*. The book is visibly designed for a very broad reading public. Being well structured and indexed it may clearly be considered a significant reference for future research.

The well chosen quotations from Larbaud's huge correspondence, much of it previously unpublished, as in the example of the lively exchanges with his famous Parisian publisher, Gaston Gallimard, are a further reminder of the well organized facilities of the Fonds Larbaud at the Municipal Library in Vichy. This work also contains many references to Larbaud's translations and, like Mousli's edition of *Ce Vice impuni la lecture: Domaine Anglais*, it puts them into perspective. Mousli also published *Valery Larbaud Le Vagabond Sédentaire* with colour illustrations and *textes choisis*, in 2003.

A significant reprint of 2001 was Larbaud's *Lettres de Paris pour le "New Weekly"* (March–August 1914).[32] These are translated into French by Jean-Louis Chevalier but the original letters were written directly in English and designed to inform English readers of contemporary works in France.

This was a bold gesture of literary cosmopolitanism at a moment of increasing national tension in both countries, through its assumption that literature cannot be classed by nationality but only by language.

In the 1920s Larbaud had made a similar but much more visible gesture through an arrangement with his Argentine friend, the novelist, poet and *estanciero* Ricardo Guiraldes, well known as the author of the "gaucho" novel *Don Segundo Sombra*. Larbaud had agreed to contribute articles written directly in Spanish on various subjects in French literature, to the Buenos Aires daily *La Nacion*. It has often been assumed that this was merely journalism. Their actual significance to the history of French literature has only been fully

---

30 Paris: Gallimard, 1998.
31 Paris: Flammarion, 1998.
32 Larbaud, *Lettres de Paris* (*mars–août 1914*) (Paris: Gallimard, 2001).

understood in recent years and particularly as a result of their publication in French by Martine and Bernard Fouques in 2003 in a volume entitled *Du Navire d'Argent*.[33] Here Larbaud writes in a very direct manner, even giving his readers in Argentina a glimpse of the atmosphere of his summer home in Bourbonnais (Valbois) near St. Pourçain sur Sioule, where he discovers an old theatre and "Café du Théâtre." He is concerned with the poetry and prose of the early baroque and classical periods of French literature and then with the work of "precursors" of his own time (Banville, Laforgue, Corbière, John-Antoine Nau, Elémir Bourges and Edouard Dujardin.) The later articles highlight many poets who were also his friends: Jammes, Claudel, Valéry, Fargue, St.-John Perse, Jules Romains. His article on Vildrac and the "Poètes de l'Abbaye" is an extended one and he notes that they were conscientious objectors, which he expresses in a sentence he could possibly not have published in France during these years following the First World War. Larbaud implicitly sees the "Poètes de l'Abbaye" as followers of Whitman, just as his South American friends sometimes saw Larbaud as the European Whitman. These articles reveal the full extent of Larbaud's "*Domaine Français.*"

As noted, a major more recent document on Larbaud is the edition of the complete diaries (*Journal*).[34] Much of it, especially with respect to the years spent in Spain, is in English with a French translation. All previous publication of these diaries accounted for only about half of the present text. (This work is also referred to as "*Le Journal Intégral.*") In the detailed notes by Paule Moron we find ample evidence that this edition must be understood as superseding all previous partial publication of these diaries.

As Larbaud had not intended most of the diary for publication during his lifetime, the tone is usually that of an *aide-mémoire* which he is writing to himself, so that the reader is able to follow the candid expression of his feelings and attitudes toward all that came within his experience, whether literary or "real world." The diary is far more detailed on the subject of his translations of Samuel Butler than the parts which had previously appeared in the last two volumes of the *Oeuvres Complètes*. His admiration for Butler's neo-Lamarckian and sometimes anti-Darwinian master work, *Life and Habit*, knows no bounds: "Indeed it seems as if Lamarck, Darwin and all the Evolution writers had been sent only to prepare the way for *Life and Habit...* to announce it and make it possible."[35]

---

33 The Introduction and Notes are by Professor Anne Chevalier.
34 Larbaud, *Journal Edition définitive*. Texte établi, préfacé et annoté par Paule Moron (Paris: Gallimard, 2009).
35 Larbaud, *Journal*, pp. 281–282. December 30, 1917.

The translation of *Life and Habit* into French required a vast commitment to research into the entire field of evolution. Larbaud appears to have read virtually all the relevant works available in his time, in French, English, German, and Italian, before undertaking it. He sometimes compares his translations to a number of others such as those of Auguste-Jean-Baptiste Defauconpret (1767–1843), who, in collaboration with his son Charles Auguste, had translated much of Scott, Cooper, and Dickens into French. Larbaud carefully studied Defauconpret's translation of Scott's *Ivanhoe*. Defauconpret had been notorious for ignoring a great many passages and Larbaud comments:

> About a third part of the text is left untranslated. However, what he translates he translates well, or at least correctly, but he is rather unscrupulous in the way of "arranging," suppressing parts of sentences. I am certainly much more scrupulous and painstaking than Defauconpret but my scrupulousness acts sometimes as a drawback....On the other hand there are no finds, no happy renderings, in Defauconpret's work, while there are a few (not many, though) in mine."[36]

Here Larbaud expresses his own achievement with remarkable modesty. However, his well-earned pride in his work is to be found almost immediately in this same entry: "I should like to translate Butler in such a way that anyone taking any page at random and giving to its translation a good deal of care, could scarcely do better than I did."[37]

---

36 Larbaud, *Journal*, p. 461. Saturday December 8, 1920.
37 Ibid., pp. 461–462.

Part I

Translations from English: Apprenticeship

Chapter 1

Coleridge

To look first at Valery Larbaud's translations from English and beginning with what might be considered the period of his apprenticeship, we find that only one of the early translations to which he refers in his letters to his friend Marcel Ray (of Coleridge, Shelley, Dobson, Meredith, Hawthorne, and Prescott) was actually published: his translation into French of Coleridge's *The Rime of the Ancient Mariner* (1798) as *La Complainte du vieux marin*[1] using the English text of the 1817 edition, which was considered definitive. As there were a number of problems in this translation, it eventually reappeared in a greatly revised edition ten years later.[2]

This second attempt, however, also proved problematic. There is, for example, a problem in the word "rime" in the sense in which Coleridge uses it because that usage was becoming archaic. The same could be said of "ancient." Thus, in 1911, Larbaud translated the title simply as *La Chanson du vieux marin*. This had also been Auguste Barbier's title for the first French translation (1877) which was in prose. Curiously, Samuel Butler comments on Coleridge's title in his *Note-Books*, which Larbaud was later to translate, and in a way that perfectly expresses its problem for a translator: "This poem would not have taken so well if it had been called *The Old Sailor*."[3] Other French translations included one by Alfred Jarry, the famous "*pataphysicien*," in 1921, which has been much admired. Larbaud had heard of this translation through his friend the poet Léon-Paul Fargue, but its publication was greatly delayed: "Coleridge interprété par Alfred Jarry, voilà de quoi intéresser tous les lettrés du monde."[4] Auguste Barbier's translation had been illustrated with Gustave Doré's justly famous engravings which appeared again in the third edition of Henri Parisot's

---

1 Paris: Vanier, 1901.
2 S.T. Coleridge, *La Chanson du vieux marin*. Traduction Nouvelle de Valery Larbaud (Paris: Beaumont, 1911).
3 Samuel Butler, *Note-Books*, London: Fifield, 1912, p. 229.
4 op. cit., p. xxvi.

in 1978. There have been several others but we may take Jacques Darras' very accomplished version of 2005, published in a bilingual format and annotated, in Gallimard's *Poésie* collection (2007), as a model for the purposes of comparison with Larbaud's.[5]

Larbaud's effort to provide an ingenuous but nonetheless "correct" translation in the hope that this would be enough to conjure up the effect of the original, which attempts to be literally "spellbinding" (the term Coleridge himself uses in the marginal notes for stanza 4 of Part One), takes us immediately to the whole question of the translatability of poetry. Larbaud does not yet seem to have pondered this problem. In this instance, the late Romantics' notion of poetry as capable of being the equivalent of a drug, *un divin opium*, which allows the listener or reader to escape into it, is the essential challenge the poem presents to the translator. It would hardly seem surprising that neither the first (1901) nor the second (1911) edition quite succeed at that level.

Larbaud's 1901 translation contains a number of amusing beginners' *contresens*:

> The ship was cheer'd, *the harbour clear'd,*
>
> > 1901: l'eau du port était claire.
> >
> > 1911: Le navire, salué d'acclamations, sortit du port;
>
> Merrily did we drop *below the kirk, below the hill,*
>
> > 1901: le long de l'église, puis au pied de la colline,
> >
> > 1911: Joyeusement nous laissâmes Derrière nous l'église, puis la falaise;[6]

---

[5] Other French translations include J.A. Moisan, *Le Vieux Marin*. Traduction inédite équirythmique. Gravures originales de Noel Santon. Collection "Le Sorbier" (Paris: Corymbe, 1939); G. Guibillion, *La Ballade du vieux marin et autres poèmes* Paris: Hatier,1940); Henri Parisot, *Le Dit du vieux marin, Cristabel et Koubla Khan* (Paris: Corti, 1941, 1947); réédité avec douze lithographies d'André Masson (Paris: Pro Francia, Collection Vrille, 1948 (1975, 1978); Guy Lévis Mano, *La ballade du vieux marin en sept parties* par S.T. Coleridge (Paris: GLM, 1946). Version en prose: Marianne Van Hirtum, *Le Dit du vieux marin*, préfacé par Pierre MacOrlan; illustré de gravures de cuivre par André Collot (Paris: Aux Dépens de bibliophiles amis de l'artiste, 1963).

[6] op. cit. Cf. Coleridge, *La Complainte du Veux Marin*. Texte et traduction de Valery Larbaud. Précédé d'une Notice (Paris: Librairie Léon Vanier, 1901). Also: Coleridge, *La Chanson du Veux Marin;* traduction nouvelle de Valery Larbaud (Paris: Beaumont, 1911).

The particular problem in the 1901 rendering of the latter line is that of the word "below," which continues to be a major one for translators from English into French, as this usage, meaning "farther down the river" (or estuary) is customary mainly on the part of people who live along rivers. It may easily be unfamiliar to those for whom English is a second language. (Larbaud had clearly grasped this distinction when revising his translation for the 1911 edition.) This well-known translator's conundrum arises because English has no direct equivalent for the French *en aval* ("below") the same holding true for *en amont* ("above") referring to positions along a river.

Larbaud discusses the essential effect of a translated text in his major study of translation: *De la Traduction*, which appeared in 1946 among various other essays and writings on the subject of literary translation, in the volume entitled *Sous l'Invocation de Saint Jérôme*.[7] This exposition is particularly relevant to translations of *The Rime of the Ancient Mariner*. As an illustration he improvises his own French version of a part of Francesco De Sanctis' *Studio su Giacomo Leopardi* concerning Leopardi's translation of Virgil into modern Italian as compared with Annibale Caro's:

> Chaque texte a un son, une couleur, un mouvement, une atmosphère qui lui sont propres. En dehors de son sens matériel et littéral, tout morceau de littérature a, comme tout morceau de musique, un sens moins apparent et qui seul crée en nous l'impression esthétique voulue par le poète.[8]

De Sanctis was a major nineteenth-century Italian critic (1817–1883) concerned with the relationship between form and content and is remembered for his *Storia della Letteratura Italiana* (1871). It is remarkable that Larbaud is influenced here not only by a writer of another "linguistic domain" in the traditional manner, but actually takes his inspiration (his "cue") for his own understanding of translation from De Sanctis rather than from French sources. He is thus seeing himself within a European context rather than a narrowly national one, which we might understand as expressing an implicit critique of the notion of national literatures, as well as the essence of his contribution to literary Europeanism. Comparative Literature may be understood objectively as a discipline but to Larbaud it is also internalized and becomes highly subjective because of this intimate identification with the work of writers and critics of various languages.

---

7   op. cit. Chapitre 2, "Droits et devoirs du Traducteur." In: Valery Larbaud, *Sous L'Invocation de St. Jérôme, Oeuvres Complètes,* Tome 8 (Paris: Gallimard, 1953), p. 77.
8   Ibid., p. 85.

De Sanctis here becomes a veritable translator's Toscanini, pointing out that in the first lines of the *Aeneid*, "On se sent soulevé à trois pieds de terre dans cette magnificence du vers,"[9] and that this effect must survive translation. He then calls Caro "ce prosaique accoucheur [qui] n'a produit qu'un avorton."[10] De Sanctis's point can be clarified by thinking of the saying: "He has the words but where is the music?" In this translation of Virgil's Latin into modern Italian it is, according to De Sanctis, precisely the "song" that is missing, the song announced by Virgil himself in the famous first words: *Arma virumque cano*. The specific qualities of this song, whose absence De Sanctis deplores in this passage, are "ce ton solonnel et élevé...ces divines, douces et mélacoliques harmonies...ce flottement d'images, cette fusion des couleurs et des objets."[11] "Ou [sont]...le halètement, la fatigue physique, l'angoisse, l'agonie?"[12]

Thus the essential emotions are absent, according to De Sanctis, and Caro's Italian form is reduced to something dry, prosaic, and even prudishly "bourgeois" as Leopardi, whose own translation of Virgil is greatly admired by De Sanctis, had called it in his earlier critique of Caro's version. Furthermore, the ability to "feel" Virgil does not imply that the translator has recreated him, which De Sanctis claims is what the translator must set out to achieve.[13]

Although Larbaud wonders if De Sanctis is not being excessively demanding here, he nevertheless identifies with these words to the point that in his later career they become the major principle in his own conception of the art of translation. Referring to art in general in terms that apply especially well to translation, Samuel Butler made the observation that "the details must minister to the main effect and not obscure it."[14]

The problem with Larbaud's second Coleridge translation is that the effect is still not achieved, precisely because the details (i.e., the words) do obscure it. The prosaic word *acclamations* (prosaic, that is, in this context) in the passage quoted above, seems to break the spell created by the strong rhythm of the original. Thus Larbaud's early translations (those of his apprenticeship period) do not yet always follow the "De Sanctis principle," which he will later adopt.

The essence of the De Sanctis principle might be stated as the need, in literary translation, to express the content of the original in such a way that its impact survives translation, even if this means that the translator must at

---

9 Ibid., p. 78.
10 Ibid., p. 81.
11 Ibid., p. 82.
12 Ibid., p. 83.
13 Ibid., p. 86.
14 *The Note-Books of Samuel Butler* (London: Fifield, 1912), p. 97.

times depart from the literal (as in the French expression *le mot à mot*) or what was formerly called "the construe level."

The particular point about *The Rime of the Ancient Mariner* is, of course, that the narrator holds the wedding guest under a hypnotic spell and, vicariously, the listener or reader as well. That is the effect of the "atmosphere" of the poem and the peculiar challenge it poses for the translator who must actualize this "hypnotism" in the translated text and also such reactions as the horror which the narrator expresses while the wedding guest is thus transfixed.

In *Les Fondements Socio-Linguistiques de la Traduction*,[15] Maurice Pergnier refers to the distinction made in translation theory between *le contenu* (*le message*) and *le contenant* (*la langue*). Language is the medium of the message and there is the supposition that two (or many more) given languages can mediate the same message. This is a scientific way of reformulating Butler's distinction between "details" and "effect." The success of a translation must be understood within this framework and its implication that the translator need not be bound by the mere words of the original *contenant*.

As we shall see, the problem of translating texts that are very well known in their original version, often known by heart, was one of Larbaud's major challenges in his early translations. Since he did himself possess a huge repertory of quotations in several languages, few translators could have been better equipped for the task. The degree of his success in the *Ancient Mariner* translation could possibly be measured by examining his versions of the well-known stanzas 5 and 9 of Part II:

> The fair breeze blew, the white foam flew,
>
> The furrow followed free;
>
> We were the first that ever burst
>
> Into that silent sea.[16]

> La bonne brise soufflait, la blanche écume volait,
>
> Notre sillage se déroulait librement;
>
> Nous étions les premiers qui fussent entrés
>
> Dans cette mer silencieuse.[17]

---

15 Presses Universitaires de Lille, 1993, pp. 17–19.
16 Coleridge, *The Rime of the Ancient Mariner*. "Poems of Samuel Taylor Coleridge" (London: Folio Society, 1963), p. 24.
17 op. cit. (1911 trans.), p. 18, lines 103–106.

> Water, water, everywhere,
>
> And all the boards did shrink;
>
> Water, water, everywhere,
>
> Nor any drop to drink.[18]

> L'eau, l'eau de toutes parts,
>
> Et toutes nos planches se contractaient de chaleur,
>
> L'eau, l'eau de toutes parts.
>
> Et pas une goutte à boire.[19]

It is clear that what we have here, in Larbaud's version, is usually a form of "rhythmic prose" arranged in stanzas, in an effort to find a means of communicating the horror of this epic, since it relates a cataclysmic ordeal. Unfortunately this solution runs the risk of being unable to convey the effect of Coleridge's internal rhymes, although Larbaud does create internal rhymes in other places. Thus it is evident that it will be virtually impossible to produce the equivalence of the famous alliteration in stanza five, line two, which is another of the means by which the "hypnotic" effect is maintained. Furthermore, the attempt to create rhymes for the ear (parts, boire, etc.) although echoes of the original effect, may seem not quite comparable. Such rhymes may, nonetheless, be taken as a reasonable attempt to convey an impression of the "atmosphere" of the original.

Jacques Darras confronts the same problems in his 2007 version in which these lines of Part Two, stanza 5 are rendered:

> Ecumes aux vagues, faveur du vent,
>
> Sillage libre derrière s'ouvrant,
>
> Dans le silence de cette mer
>
> Nous avançâmes les tout premiers.[20]

Given that the internal rhymes of the original won't work here, he too invents several ingenious rhymes in other stanzas and in this one there is a

---

18 op. cit., p. 25.
19 op. cit. (1911 trans.), p. 18, lines 119–122.
20 Coleridge, *La Ballade du vieux Marin et autres poèmes*. Choix, présentation et traduction de Jacques Darras (Paris: Gallimard, 2007) p. 43.

rhyme between *derrière* and *cette mer*. Like Larbaud, as expected, he finds no means of creating an equivalent for the alliteration in line two of the original, although his French version does have a suggestive and appropriate rhythm and a *rime suffisante* (*vent, s'ouvrant*) in the first couplet.

Similar problems also confront the translator of the equally famous assonance in stanza 15 of Part I, thought to have been inspired by John Davis' account of his searches for the Northwest Passage as published by Richard Hakluyt in *Principal Navigations, Voyages, and Discoveries of the English Nation* (1589):

> The ice was here, the ice was there,
>
> The ice was all around:
>
> It cracked and growled, and roared and howled,
>
> Like noises in a swound! (p. 22)
>
> La glace était ici, la glace était là-bas,
>
> La glace était partout à l'entour;
>
> Elle craquait et criait, et grondait et hurlait,
>
> Comme les bruits qu'on entend lorsqu'on s'évanouit![21]

Darras's version might seem more in the manner of Coleridge:

> La Glace ici, la Glace par là,
>
> Partout autour de nous la glace:
>
> Qui se fendait, grondait, hurlait
>
> Comme rugissements hallucinés.[22]

This is possibly because the repetitions of the French *ou* phoneme in line two correspond to Coleridge's repetitions of the *ou, ow* phoneme in English.

The first line of the next stanza (16) provides a perfect example of a remarkable internal rhyme important for the maintenance of what Coleridge called the "charm," using the word in its strict original meaning in the realm of magic:

---

21 op. cit., p. 12, lines 59–62.
22 op. cit. (Darras trans.), p. 39, lines 57–60.

> At length did cross an Albatross,[23]
>
> Larbaud: Enfin passa un Albatros;[24]
>
> Darras: Enfin survint un Albatros,[25]

Darras's solution represents a definite improvement over Larbaud's, which Larbaud might perhaps have applauded. As Larbaud had published poems in the Parnassian manner at the age of fifteen (*Les Portiques*) which he later renounced, one could well speculate on whether the "sound effects" achieved by Coleridge in stanza fifteen of Part One might not have found a correlative in an emulation of certain poems by Leconte de Lisle. An accomplished poet himself, as *Les Poésies de Barnabooth* demonstrate, Larbaud worked among a number of remarkable poets whose experimentation was bringing about a significant renewal of French poetry at this time: Claudel, Perse, Paul Valéry, Francis Jammes, Léon-Paul Fargue and Apollinaire.

The Parnassians had already "remodelled" the classical alexandrine line, as the Romantics too had done before them, a development which Larbaud and his contemporaries pursued further, so that it is not surprising that the occasional alexandrine appears embedded in his Coleridge translation. Thus in stanza nineteen of Part One we find the line:

> And a good south wind sprung up behind;[26]

This becomes an alexandrine in French and it might be said to succeed in conveying an impression of the rhythm of the original:

> Et un bon vent du sud souffla à l'arrière;"[27]

Again, we have in stanza 2 of Part Four:

> Fear not, fear not, thou Wedding-Guest![28]

Four groups of three syllables each with the expected caesura (*"la césure"*) after the sixth syllable, represent the most familiar form of the alexandrine:

---

23 *Rime*, p. 22, line 63.
24 p. 12, 1ine 63.
25 p. 391, line 61.
26 p. 23, 1ine 71.
27 op. cit. (Larbaud trans.), p. 121, line 71.
28 p. 30.

N'aie pas peur, n'aie pas peur, Invité de la noce,[29]

Finally in stanza 3 of Part Six:

For she guides him smooth or grim.[30]

Larbaud seems, at first sight, to manage an alexandrine almost worthy of Racine:

Car c'est elle qui le guide, qu'il soit calme ou farouche;[31]

A closer examination, however, in view of the absolute necessity, in the classical alexandrine, to be certain that there are precisely twelve syllables (within the definition of Malherbe) quickly reveals that this line contains one syllable too many, given that the pronoun "elle," coming within the *hémistiche*, has two syllables. It seems at first that one is reduced to observing that this line merely reminds one of an alexandrine. However, since in colloquial French one hears only twelve syllables, Larbaud may be experimenting by deliberately rebelling against Malherbe.

We may be sure that Larbaud is experimenting here at a time when experimentation with classical lines was becoming far more radical than in the poetry of Victor Hugo. Another contemporary example might be found in many of the lines of Claudel's *Cinq Grandes Odes* which show the *grandeur* and the equilibrium of the alexandrine even when running into many more syllables.

Thus we have here an example of the kind of experimentation that was occurring in these highly creative years, in music as well as in poetry. The early work of St. John Perse, the significance of whose poetry was revealed for the first time by Larbaud in an article in *La Phalange* of December 20, 1911, experiments with combinations of lines of varying length, so that when an alexandrine does emerge it rings out like a clarion, as in this line of Perse's *Eloges*:

Végétales ferveurs, ô clartés ô faveurs![32]

---

29 p. 30.
30 p. 39.
31 p. 45, 1ine 419.
32 St. John Perse, *Pour Feter une Enfance* (1910) in *Eloges* (Paris: Gallimard, 1948).

Coleridge's alternating tetrameters and trimeters, both familiar to his readers, and which constitute another potent means of maintaining the "hypnotism," thus occasionally find an echo in the well tempered alexandrine in French through Larbaud's effort to create a strong impression of the original. The alexandrine, although it had also been masterfully used in the didactic (Boileau) and mock heroic veins (LaFontaine) has, of course, usually been understood as the appropriate line for tragedy. Larbaud clearly understands the poem as a tragedy waiting to happen and seems to attempt, through the occasional alexandrine, to maintain the appropriate tone.

Another example may be found in Part Five, stanza 1, but again, only as pronounced in colloquial French, abandoning the principles of seventeenth-century prosody. In this instance there would seem to be an echo of the poetry of Racan, one of the artificers of the classical alexandrine who had collaborated with Malherbe. Larbaud later studied Racan in depth in one of the monographs that were collected in his major critical work on French literature: *Ce Vice Impuni La Lecture: Domaine Français.* (This study still remains the best introduction to Racan.) The line in question is:

Louanges en soient rendues à la Reine des Cieux![33]

Since Coleridge's poem was first published in 1798 at the height of Mesmer's popularity in Britain and on the continent, the matter of the relative success of its "mesmeric" effect remains a matter of consequence. Could the use of the alexandrine line in itself be considered to produce an impression of such an effect? Certainly the sheer brilliance of Racine's performance with alexandrines in his tragedies creates such an admiration on the part of the audience that this quality might indeed be described as "mesmeric," as a means of providing a temporary escape from the everyday world.

An alexandrine from Part Six, stanza 1, is suggestive of the motion of the ship:

Qu'est-ce qui fait voguer ce navire si vite?[34]

A variation occurs in stanza 4:

Mais pourquoi ce navire avance-t-il si vite?[35]

---

33 p. 37, line 294.
34 p. 45, line 412.
35 line 422.

There are many other challenges as well. Thus in the first two lines of stanza 3 of Part Four, the challenge is to avoid what is commonplace in the prosaic expression "all alone" (*tout seul*) by attempting to endow it with a sense of the transcendental:

> Alone, alone, all, all alone,
>
> Alone on the wide wide Sea;[36]

This is accomplished by the addition of *absolument* in the first line and then by a bold retention of the English syntax in the second:

> Seul, seul, absolument tout seul,
>
> Tout seul sur une immense, immense mer![37]

The positioning of adjectives in defiance of the "rules" is clearly considered an aspect of translators' "rights" and will become characteristic of Larbaud in his later translations. However, despite this impressive achievement, Larbaud's "last word" on his second Coleridge translation is still an admission of defeat, to be found in a letter of March 12, 1912 to Cyprien Godebski: "Malheureusement il n'est pas possible qu'une traduction fasse justice à ce chef-d'oeuvre, et la mienne n'est pas bonne non plus. Qu'elle puisse donner envie de lire l'original...."[38]

There is, nonetheless, a reference to the last two lines of this translation in Larbaud's full-length novel *A.O. Barnabooth: Ses Oeuvres Complètes* (1913). It occurs near the end of Barnabooth's *Journal Intime*. The young *cosmopolite* is in Copenhagen and struggling with self doubts:

> Je n'étais plus le jeune homme qui avait écrit ces pages; j'avais dépouillé cela:
>
> "plus triste et plus sage."[39]
>
> A sadder and a wiser man,

---

36 p. 31.
37 p. 31, line 232.
38 G. Jean-Aubry, *Valery Larbaud: Sa Vie et Son Oeuvre* 1 "La Jeunesse" 1881–1920 (Monaco: Rocher, 1949), pp. 193–194.
39 In *Oeuvres* (Edition de la Pléiade); (Paris: Gallimard, 1961), p. 282.

> He rose the morrow morn.[40]
>
> Le lendemain matin il se leva Transformé: plus triste et plus sage.[41]

This reference is important since it shows that Larbaud considered his novel a *Bildungsroman*. Coleridge's work is clearly an example of Aristotelian catharsis as experienced by the narrator. This cathartic effect is now also experienced vicariously by Larbaud's protagonist Barnabooth. It also shows how Larbaud's vast readings often become personalized to the point of identity with them.

Despite his admission of the inadequacy of this translation, Larbaud remained devoted to the study of Coleridge throughout his career, and often refers to Coleridge's work in his correspondence and diaries.

---

40 *Rime*, p. 48.
41 p. 58, lines 624–625.

Chapter 2

Landor

An important event in Larbaud's career as a translator was his translation of a fragment of W.S. Landor's *High and Low Life in Italy* (1837–1838) an epistolary novel (*roman par lettres*) first published as a series of instalments in Leigh Hunt's *Monthly Repository*. However, it had never been published as a book. Larbaud may be said to have been the first to have created the book, that is, through the medium of his translation, *Hautes et basses classes en Italie*, which appeared in 1911.[1]

At the time, the work of Landor was a major commitment. Larbaud had devoted a doctoral thesis to Landor and actively collaborated on the production of Stephen Wheeler's edition of the complete works, as acknowledged in the *Cambridge History of English Literature* (1915). This commitment to Landor is indeed remarkable: Larbaud clearly felt that Landor occupied a much more important place in the evolution of English prose than had previously been acknowledged by literary historians and that his work therefore needed to be given due credit through a demonstration of its proper value. T.S. Eliot was later to congratulate Larbaud for drawing attention to Landor's importance as a nineteenth-century *prosateur* and in 1922 invited him to contribute a critical study of Landor to his new journal *The Criterion*.[2] This study seems never to have been published.

Larbaud understood Landor's work as representing a fine example of the creation of Romanticism, pointing out that Voltaire's epic poetry must have influenced both French and English Romantic poets, Landor and Byron being good examples. He saw this work as both satirical (almost Voltairean indeed) and potentially tragic, a perfect example, it would seem, of the famous *mélange des genres*. By putting forward such insights, Larbaud is speaking from within literature, as it were, rather than viewing the phenomenon objectively. Nonetheless, this particular insight could be taken as a source by literary historians.[3]

---

1 Walter Savage Landor (Paris: Beaumont), 1911.
2 *The Letters of T.S. Eliot*, vol. 1 (New York: Harcourt Brace Jovanovich, 1988), pp. 516, 595.
3 *Journal*, p. 700 (August 29, 1919).

The satirical tone of Landor's novel is immediately established in a note that accompanies the title: these letters are said to have been "collected by the late J.J. Pidcock Raikes, Esq.; and now first published by his nephew, Sir Rodney Raikes."[4]

Landor's game in distancing himself from the work by inventing fictitious editors may have influenced Larbaud in his creation of the first *A.O. Barnabooth*, when he invented the fictitious X.M. Tournier de Zamble as the alleged author of the *Biographie de M. Barnabooth*. Thus in Jean-Aubry's *Valery Larbaud: Sa Vie et son oeuvre*,[5] we find Larbaud at work on both *Barnabooth* and Landor in the same period. Landor, indeed, had pursued the game even further by inventing Mr. J.J. Stivers, who is Mr. Raikes's secretary and "first editor" of the work. Stivers's letters to a Lady C. inform the reader of the action at various times, creating an epistolary narrative when needed. Curiously, Landor not only creates in this manner a calculated distance between himself and his work but at one point in the novel goes a step farther in a letter from the chief male protagonist, Edward Talboys, to Mr. Raikes, by inserting a report concerning a certain Mr. Landor who is under a threat of expulsion from Tuscany. (This becomes an edict which is later revoked after an intervention by the French Legation.)[6] A similar incident is later the fate of Talboys as the plot thickens in the dramatic climax of the novel. Talboys's exile is also revoked, this time through the efforts of an influential member of the English community in Florence. Such attempts to distance an author from his work will eventually lead, in the evolution of the novel, to the technique of the "heteronym." Larbaud was clearly interested in this development as a practitioner of the heteronym, given that Barnabooth is, strictly speaking, a heteronym. (Larbaud does not analyze the technique in his critical writings).

In his translation, Larbaud created an adaptation of an important part of Landor's original work by extracting from it a sequence of letters that trace a potentially tragic love story, surrounded by conflicting interests and much scheming. The English protagonist, Edward Talboys, courts the innocent Italian maiden Serena Bruchi. She belongs to the local establishment and her family will soon disapprove of the proposed marriage with him. In some respects Larbaud seems to have viewed Landor as an English Stendhal[7]

---

4 Landor, *The Complete Works of Walter Savage Landor*, edited by T. Earle Welby, vol. 10 (New York: Barnes & Noble Inc., and London: Methuen & Co. Ltd., 1969).

5 op. cit., p. 202.

6 op. cit., pp. 86–89.

7 Especially the Stendhal of *La Chartreuse de Parme*.

in his creation of these complex, melodramatic plots, as well as in his brilliant reconstitution of Italian life. With regard to melodrama, this work could be more properly described as a parody of the melodrama. Certainly the general tone of the work is that of satirical comedy in the manner of Voltaire and occasionally Marivaux. It could be understood as a revival of an eighteenth-century genre, as seen for example in a certain light *badinage* in letters such as one sent by Edward Talboys to Serena containing a *Dialogue Between a Lover and a Canary Bird*. The liberties taken by Larbaud in this translation are relatively slight, designed merely to reinforce what is implicit in the original, as seen in a letter from Edward Talboys to Serena, concerning the canary, in which we have the line:

> He [the canary] is not prouder of his captivity than I of mine although he has many advantages which I must wait for.[8]
>
> Il n'est pas moins fier de sa captivité que je ne le suis de la mienne, quoiqu'il ait sur moi l'avantage de bien des faveurs qu'il me faut attendre.[9]

Here "prouder" becomes "not less proud" in the French of the translation. The English "advantages" is developed as a phrase retaining the cognate word *avantage*.

Serena's English, although the question of whether it is a translation from Italian is not quite clear, is sometimes a little too elliptical. Thus in one of her earlier letters to Edward Talboys, she writes:

> Do canary birds speak in England? I have heard it is the language of birds; we have a proverb that says it; and when you speak I am convinced.[10]

The antecedent of the first "it" is absent but it is, of course, *English*, meaning the English language, which becomes clear in the French translaion:

> Est-ce que les canaris parlent en Angleterre? J'ai entendu dire que l'anglais est le langage des oiseaux; nous avons un proverbe qui le dit et quand vous parlez j'en suis convaincue.[11]

---

8 p. 103.
9 p. 32.
10 Ibid.
11 p. 94.

As the novel later moves swiftly toward its inevitable *dénouement*, brought about by the disapproval of the proposed marriage between Edward Talboys and Serena Bruchi by Serena's parents, another bridegroom, a member of the local establishment, is proposed for Serena.

A letter from Stivers to the mysterious Lady C., relating these events in detail, begins with the words:

> Master is another man.[12]

> On a changé mon maître![13]

Quite apart from the intricacies of the plot, these echoing words may have a significance in themselves because "master" and "man," standing out as they do, may be an allusion to the words of the slave (the "monster") Caliban, in Shakespeare's *The Tempest*:

> 'Ban, 'Ban, Ca Caliban

> Has a new master; get a new man.[14]

If Landor is indeed referring to Caliban, then such words could well imply a further caricature of marriage in the "high society" of the Tuscany of the period, suggesting that it amounts to little more than the relationship of master and slave. However, there is no suggestion of any such cynical interpretation in Larbaud's translation even though Serena's marriage to a Signor Gaddi does turn out to be merely a *mariage de convenance*, as we soon discover in a letter from Serena to Edward after that marriage:

> If you come, tho but four or five times a week, I shall be quite enchanted.[15]

> Si vous venez, ne serait-ce que quatre ou cinq fois par semaine, j'en serai enchantée.[16]

Belonging himself to a similarly rigid and hierarchical society in England, Landor was clearly endowed with special insights into such matters. This is

---

12 p. 158.
13 p. 59.
14 Act 2, Scene 2, lines 188–189.
15 op. cit., p. 155.
16 p. 57.

seen again in the language of modes of address in some of the letters, such as the one in which Serena's mother writes to Edward: "Most Illustrious Signor," followed by the words "Your venerated leaf,"[17] referring to Edward's letter to her. Larbaud avoids an equivalent *préciosité* here: "votre vénérée lettre."[18] Patrick McCarthy in his doctoral dissertation: *Valery Larbaud: Critic of English Literature*, finds in this translation a possible source of the "Angiola Cacace" episode in *A.O. Barnabooth*. In Barnabooth's diary (*Journal Intime*) which takes up much of the novel, Barnabooth relates a conversation with another of the characters, his friend the Marquis de Putouarey, who is something of a "Don Juan," and who, during a sojourn in Naples, arranges to support the seductive Angiola. whose mother agrees to the financial terms and is the *metteur en scène*. Thus this episode is, in essence, a burlesque *comédie de moeurs* of the "boulevard" variety but might nonetheless remind the reader of Landor's piece.[19]

In each work, it is the matriarch who pulls the strings and in each there is a failure to integrate the heroine into a society other than her own. This shows not only Larbaud's understanding of Italian families of two classes and two periods, but also his remarkable versatility. In fact, in his original work, Larbaud writes in virtually every genre except theatre.

In a passage of his "Lettre d'Italie" in *Jaune Bleu Blanc*, Larbaud mentions taking flowers to Landor's tomb in Florence, and again in the equally autobiographical *Une Journée*, with respect to a sojourn on Lake Como, where Landor had lived for three years, we find him "occupé surtout à chercher... les maisons qu'il avait habitées, les plans et les descriptions de la ville telle qu'il l'avait connue...et ce que les archives... contenaient à son sujet." Larbaud continues: "J'avais eu la chance de trouver l'explication de plusieurs points obscurs de sa biographie et quelques lettres inédites de lui en italien très caractéristique de sa manière. bien qu' écrites dans une langue étrangère."[20] Hence the pleasure he takes in his research on Landor becomes the particular manifestation of his pleasure in being in Italy.

We also have here a further example of the extent of Larbaud's identification with Landor, which sometimes manifested itself even in seemingly psychic ways, since his *Journal* reveals that on April 6, 1917, he learned of the death of Landor's son, Charles Landor, whom he had known,

---

17 p. 94.
18 p. 63.
19 *A.O Barnabooth / Ses Oeuvres Complètes* (Paris: Gallimard, 1913; Bibliothèque de la Pléiade, 1958), pp. 170–179. Cf. Patrick McCarthy (Oxford, 1968), p. 44.
20 *Oeuvres* (Paris: Gallimard; Bibliothèque de la Pléiade, 1958), p. 839.

and writes that in the previous two weeks he had frequently thought of another member of the Landor family, Henry Savage Landor: "Et le souvenir des occasions où nous nous sommes rencontrés via Farini et à Paris m'est nettement revenu en mémoire."[21]

---

21 *Journal*, p. 294.

Chapter 3

Whitman

As we have seen, Barnabooth's poetry had revealed in its first (1908) edition[1] that Larbaud was a considerable poet in his own right. This poetry, attributed thus to his "heteronym," had imaginary fictitious sources, explained in the accompanying *Biographie de M. Barnabooth*, and real sources as well. In both we find that these are essentially the French symbolist tradition and Whitman, whose work made a deep impression on Larbaud from the age of eighteen, only seven years after Whitman's death.

Larbaud reminisces about his discovery of Whitman in the course of a lively conversation with his friend the poet Léon-Paul Fargue, which was published by way of an introduction to their edition of the cosmopolitan poems of the diplomat Henry J.-M. Levet.[2] He was looking outside of French literature for something more daring than the work of the most avant-garde French poets of his time. Thus, in 1899, he came upon Whitman:

> Quels horizons n'ouvraient pas ces grands vers plus libres que tous ceux que nous avions vus jusqu'alors, et ce ton nouveau, ce ton d'effusion lyrique, quotidienne et prophétique. Et ce programme *The commonplace I sing*!... je me plongeais dans l'étude de la littérature américaine, pensant y trouver un autre Whitman. Je me trompais. Mais après tout je ne regrette pas trop les journées...que j'ai passées sur ces livres nets, à dos plats, comme des boîtes de cigares...que j'allais acheter chez Brentano.[3]

Thus he relates how his explorations, with a view to discovering other poetic works equal to Whitman's, took him to *Brentano's* on the Avenue de

---

1 *Poèmes par un riche amateur ou Oeuvres françaises de M. Barnabooth* (Paris: Messein, 1908).
2 Henry J.-M. Levet, *Poèmes. Précédés d'une Conversation de Léon-Paul Fargue et Valery Larbaud*. Collection Métamorphoses (Paris: Gallimard, 1943).
3 Levet, p. 16.

l'Opéra many more times and often left him with the illusion of having actually visited Boston or New York. This was clearly a defining moment in his life as a specialist in American literature.

In *Les Poésies de Barnabooth*, there are many lines which intentionally emulate Whitman's *vers libres*, so that recognizing their Whitmanian rhythm might have become a source of interest for readers familiar with Whitman's poetry, although at the time of their first publication (1908), Whitman had not yet been translated into French. Thus Larbaud was able to hail Whitman's translation into Italian before Bazalgette's French translation of *Leaves of Grass* appeared in France in 1912. We may deduce from this that Larbaud was addressing readers of a future time when Whitman would be sufficiently familiar in the francophone world to make it possible to recognize the Whitmanian cadences in Barnabooth's poetry.

Some might see a parody of Whitman in certain lines in Barnabooth's poetry but Larbaud clearly takes it for granted that his character Barnabooth has assimilated Whitman as a natural poetic influence of the period, since, as we have seen, Barnabooth's poetry is situated among many poetic influences, an example of the sort of literary "game" the young Larbaud enjoyed. *Vers libres* had also been practised by such French poets as Francis Viélé Griffin, Gustave Kahn, and Stuart Merrill.

As these and various other eminent French poets of the period, as well as André Gide, who was then the director of *La Nouvelle Revue Française*, later expressed reservations concerning the Bazalgette translations of Whitman's poetry into French, this review decided to publish a new translation that was clearly intended to be less academic. A generous selection of Whitman's poems was translated by Jules Laforgue, Louis Fabulet, André Gide, Valery Larbaud, Jean Schlumberger, and Francis Vielé-Griffin. These were preceded by a very perceptive study by Larbaud which he had begun in 1901 and only finished in 1914, the year in which the book was expected to appear. Due to problems occasioned by the war, however, these new translations were not actually published until September 1918.

Larbaud's major contribution to them was his French version of *The Sleepers* (*Les Dormeurs*), and he also contributed two fine examples of Whitman's prose: selections from *Specimen Days* and *Democratic Vistas*.

It is not surprising, therefore, that Barnabooth's poetry shows a number of Whitmanian features. For example, Whitman's poem *To a Stranger*, from the *Calamus* series, is transposed in Barnabooth's *Images*:

Whitman: Passing stranger! you do not know how longingly I look upon you,

You must be he I was seeking, or she I was seeking, (it comes to me, as of a dream,)[4]

This poem was translated by Louis Fabulet:

Etranger qui passe! Tu ne sais pas avec quelle ardeur je te regarde,

Tu dois être celui que je cherchais, ou celle que je cherchais (Cela me vient comme en rêve).[5]

Larbaud's *Poésies de Barnabooth* are often explicitly "Whitmanian." An example, illustrating the practice of *vers libres*, could be:

Ne sera-t-il jamais possible que cette grande joie me soit donnée,

De les connaître?

Car je ne sais pourquoi, mon Dieu, il me semble qu'avec elles quatre,

Je pourrais conquérir un monde![6]

Thus Barnabooth-Larbaud sings Europe with all the enthusiasm with which Whitman sings "these States," in the mood of optimism that reigned during the latter's youth. Barnabooth's poetry could be described as Whitmanian in its expression of the "cosmic consciousness" that Whitman's Canadian friend, Dr. R.M. Bucke, saw as being at the heart of Whitman's poetic work:

Je chante l'Europe, ses chemins de fer et ses théâtres

Et ses constellations de cités,[7]

Pour moi,

L'Europe est comme une seule grande ville

Pleine de provisions et de tous les plaisirs urbains,[8]

---

4 "To a Stranger," in *Leaves of Grass* (New York: Modern Library), p. 182.
5 Whitman, *Oeuvres choisies* (Paris: Gallimard, 1918), p. 95.
6 Larbaud, *Oeuvres* (Pléiade) (Paris: Gallimard), p. 65.
7 Ibid., *Ma Muse*, p. 60.
8 Ibid., *Europe* III, p. 72.

> Mais quoi! Je sens qu'il faut à ce coeur de vagabond
>
> La trépidation des trains et des navires
>
> Et une angoisse sans bonheur sans cesse alimentée.[9]

Georges Jean-Aubry remarks in his biography that Larbaud was translating Whitman poems shortly after his first discovery of Whitman in 1899.[10] In October 1901, while on a trip to Germany, he was already preparing his study on Whitman.[11] A little later he was working on a lecture entitled *Whitman and the Civil War*, intended for a group of factory workers. Jean-Aubry describes him at that time as "absolument intoxiqué de Whitman."[12] We also find him translating two Whitman poems during a prolonged sojourn in Toulouse in 1904 and writing poems influenced by Whitman while in North Africa in the spring of 1905.[13] It is possible that certain unpublished lines date from this period, such as the very first lines of *Leaves of Grass*:

> One's-Self I sing, a simple separate person,
>
> Je chante un moi, une simple personne séparée,
>
> Yet utter the word Democratic, the word En-Masse.
>
> Et pourtant je dis le mot démocratique, le mot *en masse*.[14]

There are other early unpublished translations of Whitman poems with which Larbaud clearly identified, and which are, at the same time, very close in tone to Barnabooth's poems, as, for example, Part Nine of *Salut au Monde*:

> I see the cities of the earth and make myself at random a part of them,
>
> Je vois les cités de la terre et je m'en fais au hasard un citoyen,[15]
>
> I am a real Parisian,

---

9 Ibid., V, p. 74.

10 Jean-Aubry, p. 56.

11 Ibid., p. 67. Cf. Larbaud, *Journal* (Berlin): "Travaillé sur mon étude sur Walt Whitman" (p. 42).

12 Jean-Aubry, p. 56.

13 pp. 97–98.

14 Fonds Valery Larbaud, Médiathèque de Vichy.

15 Ibid.

> Je suis un vrai Parisien,[16]
>
> I am a habitant of Vienna, St. Petersburg, Berlin, Constantinople,
>
> Je suis un habitant de Vienne, de St. Petersbourg, de Berlin, de Constantinople,[17]
>
> I see vapours exhaling from unexplored countries,
>
> Je vois les vapeurs s'exhalant de contrées inexplorées,[18]
>
> I see African and Asiatic towns,
>
> Je vois les villes d'Asie et d'Afrique,[19]

These early impromptu translations belong to the time of the first creation of Barnabooth's poems, and are clearly among the more important sources of inspiration from which the latter emerged.

Larbaud explains that the prose was translated at Sète in March 1914 and declares himself completely satisfied with these pages, calling them "*vraiment bonnes.*"[20] We may therefore expect his translation of *The Sleepers* to be genuinely "Whitmanian" in French and we are not disappointed. The choice of *The Sleepers* as his contribution to this special collection published by *La Nouvelle Revue Française* is in itself an admirable one because, being the evocation of a vision, there are a number of formidable challenges. The narrator's point of view, for example, is sometimes that of an observer of the dreamers and at other times that of his "presence" in his own dream. The very word "dreamers" is a problem because of its pejorative connotation in both languages:

> I dream in my dream all the dreams of the other dreamers.[21]
>
> Dans mon rêve je rêve tous les rêves des autres rêvants.[22]

Thus he avoids the commonplace "rêveurs" in favour of "rêvants" which, as a noun, is a bit original but perfectly "juste."

---

16 Ibid.
17 Ibid.
18 Ibid.
19 Ibid.
20 Larbaud, *Journal*, p. 581.
21 Whitman, *The Sleepers*, p. 334.
22 Whitman, op. cit., p. 283.

Another challenge is Whitman's occasional use of French words in his English text, but in places where, paradoxically, they might not seem appropriate in French. For example: "An amour of the light and air"[23] becomes "Une intrigue amoureuse entre l'air et la lumière."[24] Almost immediately below is the exclamation "O love and summer."[25] When translated as "O amour, ô été,"[26] it is reminiscent of certain lines in Perse's *Eloges* which Larbaud had discovered before the First World War. Other lines seem inspired by Whitman's experiences with the wounded near the battlefields of the American Civil War, as related in *Specimen Days*, from which Larbaud translated excerpts:

> I go from bedside to bedside, I sleep close with the other sleepers, each in turn.[27]

> Je vais d'un lit à l'autre, je dors tout près des autres dormeurs, chacun à son tour;[28]

A particular challenge in translating Whitman into French is illustrated in Louis Fabulet's translation, in this same collection, of the first words of the first line of *These I Singing in Spring*,[29] which coincide with the title "*Voici chantant au printemps.*"[30]

Just as there are internal rhymes in English when the sound "ing" occurs three times, there is a similar rhyming system in French which corresponds logically (as a "*mot-à-mot*" translation), and yet the French *em an* (the same nasal phoneme) is unable to quite replicate the resounding effect of the original, or in linguistic terms, the "signifier" doesn't fully express the "signiifed," which lies partly in this very effect of the word as well as in its strict denotation. We have here a notable problem in the translation of Whitman, a problem which Larbaud will encounter again in his future translations of James Joyce.

Thus the fundamental challenge in translating *The Sleepers* is brought about by the very nature of the two languages in question. The contrast between English and French has sometimes been viewed as one between ambiguity and

---

23 Whitman, p. 338.
24 p. 289.
25 p. 338.
26 p. 289.
27 *Specimen Days*, p. 334.
28 p. 283.
29 Whitman, p. 96.
30 p. 83.

precision. Larbaud's prose style, like Gide's, has been admired for its clarity. (It is cited in the *Robert* Dictionary.) Voltaire, indeed, is quoted as having said: "*Tout ce qui n'est pas clair n'est pas français.*"

It was this alleged precision of French that was said to have made it appropriate as the language of diplomacy in the eighteenth and nineteenth centuries when it was even known as "*la langue universelle.*"

This aspect of French has more recently been invoked by Claude Hagège in *Contre la Pensée Unique*[31] in a somewhat provocative reaction against what he calls the English of neoliberalism. He is calling for a revival of the traditional understanding of the role of French in the world, which the *philosophes* of the eighteenth century had once made into a language of the Enlightenment.[32] Thus we have in Larbaud's translation of Whitman's *The Sleepers* an apparently "ambiguous" work expressed in a language famous for its precision. (Whitman's poem has also been called "surrealistic.") How then can it be rendered into French?

A closer examination of Whitman's language in this poem reveals that the ambiguities are not as frequent as might be assumed. For example, the line "I would sound up the shadowy shore to which you are journeying"[33] may seem a little diffuse at first glance. Larbaud translates:

Je voudrais toucher l'obscur rivage vers lequel tu poursuis ton voyage.[34]

Here the original also expresses the concept of making soundings in the sea near the shore. Larbaud avoids this image altogether. However, the translation of "shadowy" by "*obscur*" (dark) does convey the notion of approaching the unknown. Personified darkness, in this poem, a major motif also associated with death, is thus maintained in the translation.

Other lines, however, sing the theme of light so that we then have effects of chiaroscuro:

> It seems to me that everything in the light and air ought to be happy.[35]
>
> Il me semble que tout ce qui est dans l'air et la lumière devrait être heureux.[36]

---

31 Paris: Odile Jacob, 2012.
32 Cf. Robert Gillan, "Review," *The Times Literary Supplement* (July 29, 2012), p. 28.
33 p. 335.
34 p. 285.
35 p. 336.
36 p. 286.

This line also expresses one of Whitman's more important themes. We have here, in the midst of this great "Ode to the Joy of Being Alive" that is *Leaves of Grass*, the essence of the revived humanism to which *La Nouvelle Revue Française*, from the time of its inception, had been striving to lend a voice.

Whitman's language is sometimes naturalistic in an innocent, "pre-Freudian" manner, and in some editions of *Leaves of Grass* there is evidence of censorship and even deliberate falsification. This seems to have been true of the edition Larbaud used, since in the standard Modern Library edition, uncensored, we have the line:

> He whom I call answers me and takes the place of my lover;[37]

"He" is translated here with the feminine form of the pronoun:

> *Celle* que j'appelle me répond, et prend la place de mon amant;[38]

Again, in the first line of Part III, the word "naked" is not translated:

> I see a beautiful gigantic swimmer swimming naked through the eddies of the sea,[39]
>
> Je vois un beau nageur aux formes géantes qui nage à travers les vagues,[40]

In other places, the English points to its own translation with words that had been almost identical historically:

> The head well grown, proportioned and plumb,[41]
>
> La tête s'est développée selon de justes proportions bien d'aplomb;[42]

This line reveals a major challenge in translating Whitman: the difficulty of maintaining the poetic rhythm of the original text—the inherent melody

---

37 p. 335.
38 p. 285.
39 p. 103.
40 p. 336.
41 Whitman, p. 286.
42 p. 339.

in the flow of Whitman's words that makes them poetry. The translation here seems dangerously close to the line between poetry and prose, whereas the original maintains the poetic rhythm.

It is possibly because of matters of this sort that in his *Journal* Larbaud later expressed reservations about his translation of *The Sleepers*, finding it "assez plate et fade."[43] The translations contributed by Louis Fabulet and André Gide are greatly admired and he considers those by the symbolist poet Francis Vielé Griffin the best of all.[44] This critical frame of mind leads him, in the same passage, to conclude that in his own translations he should have been bolder in departing from the original phrasing in order to make them more concise, more idiomatic and sometimes more daring.[45] Larbaud was intrigued by Whitman's occasional use of French words in *Leaves of Grass*. He attributes Whitman's title *Salut au Monde* to a desire to express himself in *la langue universelle* and thinks that the word *ennui* derives from Sir Walter Scott, whose novels Whitman said he had read as a boy. However, Larbaud is perplexed by Whitman's use of the word *camerado*, as it is neither Italian, Spanish, nor Portuguese: "Il l'a peut-être fabriqué de toutes pièces et, si c'est le cas, c'est une preuve de sens artistique."[46]

Larbaud, who, as noted, had already revealed the poetry of Perse for the first time in his now historical article in *La Phalange*[47] seems sometimes to find solutions to translating Whitman's *The Sleepers* through echoes of Perse's *Eloges*, although this could not be easily demonstrated.[48] Conversely, Perse's manner of extending the poetic vocabulary to specialized and esoteric realms could remind the reader of certain of Whitman's lines:

> The consumptive, the erysipalite, the idiot, he that was wrong'd,[49]
>
> Le phtisique, celui qui est atteint d'érésypèle, l'idiot, l'homme à qui on a fait tort.[50]

---

43 Larbaud, *Journal*, p. 643 (November 20, 1918).
44 Ibid., p. 644.
45 Ibid., p. 647.
46 Ibid., p. 645 (December 3, 1918.)
47 December 20, 1911.
48 Cf. "Récitation à l'Eloge d'une Reine," *Nouvelle Revue Francaise*, Avril 1911.
49 Cf. Whitman, op. cit., p. 339.
50 p. 291.

Here the poetic qualities in technical words such as érésypèle could be taken as examples, although it is also the only possible French translation. (In his *Journal* Larbaud notes that there is another correct form for this word: érysipèle.)[51] Given Larbaud's well-known propensity to recite favourite poems by heart and his well documented enthusiasm for the work of both Whitman and Perse, we may conclude that assimilation of this order is a characteristic of his own creativity.

Referring to the reception of his article on Perse's *Eloges* in *La Phalange*[52] in a letter to Gide of February 19, 1912, Larbaud makes the comment: "Je vois qu'on croit un peu que j'ai inventé Léger comme j'ai inventé naguère 'le riche amateur.'"

A psychocritical analysis might possibly reveal, with respect to this juxtaposition, more than a casual remark. Larbaud's work does seem to precede life at times as we could note also regarding Ricardo Guiraldes. Perse was indeed destined to become a kind of "Barnabooth," that is, like Whitman, a poet at the global level, resulting in part from his diplomatic career, so that in this respect, Wilde is vindicated in his famous paradox that "life imitates art more than art imitates life."

David S. Reynolds, in *Walt Whitman's America: A Cultural Biography* (1995), points out that *The Sleepers* is "perhaps the only surrealist poem of the nineteenth century, remarkable in its anticipation of later experiments."[53] It is precisely this quality of evolving experimentalism that clearly appealed to Larbaud, who also admired the "primitive freedom" expressed by Whitman and American culture in general, qualities he could not enjoy in Europe according to Patrick McCarthy in his seminal unpublished thesis, already mentioned, *Valery Larbaud, Critic of English Literature*.[54]

Walt Whitman: Oeuvres choisies concludes with a fifty-one page selection of samples of Whitman's prose (*Specimen Days* and *Democratic Vistas*) translated by Larbaud along with the famous eulogy on the occasion of the assassination of President Lincoln. The passage on Whitman's earliest reading enthusiasms as a boy is one which the translator clearly considered of particular importance:

> For a time I now revel'd in romance reading of all kinds, first *The Arabian Nights*, all the volumes, an amazing treat. Then, with sorties in very many other directions, took in Walter

---

51 Cf. Larbaud, *Journal*, p. 643.
52 Cf. *La Phalange*, 20 décembre 1911.
53 op. cit. New York: Knopf, 1995, p. 275.
54 Oxford, 1968, p. 44.

Scott's novels one after another and his poetry and continue to enjoy novels and poetry to this day.⁵⁵

Pendant quelque temps je m'absorbai dans les récits d'aventures de toutes sortes, d'abord *Mille et une Nuits*, tous les volumes, prodigieux régal. Ensuite, avec des excursions dans beaucoup d'autres directions, je me mis aux romans de Walter Scott et les lus l'un après l'autre, et aussi sa poésie, et jusqu'à ce jour je continue à aimer les romans et la poésie.⁵⁶

Larbaud also appears to have considered Whitman's early life on Long Island ("Paumanok") at a time when it was still relatively pristine, as highly significant:

I have often been out on the edges of these plains toward sundown and can yet recall in fancy the interminable cow processions, and hear the music of the tin or copper bells clanking far and near and breathe the cool of the slightly aromatic evening air.⁵⁷

J'ai souvent été en promenade sur les bords de ces plaines au coucher du soleil, et peux encore revoir en imagination les interminables processions de vaches, et entendre la musique des cloches d'étain ou de cuivre battant près ou loin et respirer la fraîcheur de l'air du soir légèrement parfumé.⁵⁸

The challenge in passages of this sort is that Whitman's prose is still very poetic, imbued with the natural musicality he seems unable to abandon. Larbaud's, on the other hand, runs the risk of being too much within the strict eighteenth-century distinction between prose and poetry. However, the very words, such as "la musique," and their concepts, come to his rescue and we have, finally, a fine example of *la poésie en prose* in the splendid evocation of Long Island as it was at the time of Whitman's youth.

Whitman's particular fascination with the ferries that plied between Brooklyn and New York could be compared with Barnabooth's association

---

55 Walt Whitman, *Complete Poetry and Collected Prose* (including complete prose works). New York: The Library of America. Distributed by Viking Press. 1982, Series: Literary Classics of the United States, p. 699.
56 op. cit., transl., pp. 319–320.
57 op. cit., p. 697.
58 op. cit., transl., p. 320.

with *trains de nuit* and ocean liners. Indeed Larbaud's absolute loyalty to the works of certain writers, and particularly Whitman, takes the form of an unconditional identity, being tantamount to absorbing it into his own *oeuvre*: it becomes an integral part of the same edifice. Thus Whitman writes:

> Indeed I have always had a passion for ferries; to me they afford inimitable, streaming, never failing, poems. The river and bay scenery all about New York island, any time of a fine day—the hurrying, splashing sea-tides, the changing panorama of steamers, all sizes, often a string of big ones outward bound to distant ports—the myriad of white-sailed schooners, sloops, skiffs and the marvellously beautiful yachts.[59]

> Vraiment j'ai toujours eu la passion des bacs, ils sont pour moi d'inimitables poèmes, jaillissants, ininterrompus, vivants. La rivière et la baie, tout autour de l'île de New York, à n'importe quelle heure d'une belle journée, les vagues pressées, éclaboussantes, le panorama changeant des navires de toutes tailles, souvent une file de grands vapeurs en route pour des ports lointains, les myriades de shooners aux voiles blanches, les sloops, les barques, les yachts—merveilleusement beaux."[60]

Specimen Days is clearly autobiographical. *Democratic Vistas*, a much shorter work, might be described as an editorial in which Whitman champions the cause of the democratization of literature both in its creation and its content. Larbaud, although issuing from a very privileged social background, had given a great deal of attention to this very problem in France, or, more precisely, in the central provinces of France and especially his native Bourbonnais. He personally knew Charles-Louis Philippe and the laundress Marguerite Audoux, the author of the novel *Marie-Claire* (who was from the Berry). Larbaud and several of his friends promoted the latter work as well as its English translation by John M. Raphael with a preface by Arnold Bennett.[61]

Whitman states the case with a few well-chosen words:

> Literature, strictly considered, has never recognized the People, and, whatever may be said, does not today....It seems as if so far, there were some repugnance between a literary and professional

---

59 op. cit., p. 701.
60 op. cit., transl., pp. 324–325.
61 Toronto: Musson, 1911, and New York: George H. Doran Company.

life, and the rude rank spirit of the democracies....I know nothing more rare, even in this country, than a fit scientific estimate and revered appreciation of the People...of their measureless wealth and latent power and capacity.[62]

La littérature, considérée de près, n'a jamais reconnu le Peuple et, quoiqu'on dise, elle l'ignore encore aujourd'hui. On dirait qu'il y a, au moins jusqu'à présent, incompatibilité entre les professions libérales d'une part et, de l'autre, le rude et vigoureux génie des démocraties....Je ne sais rien de plus rare, même dans ce pays, qu'une estimation exacte et une appréciation respectueuse du Peuple, de son inépuisable richesse de puissance et de capacité cachées.[63]

---

62 op. cit.
63 op. cit.

Part II

Translations from English: The Master Translator

Chapter 4

Butler: Introduction

We now arrive at the translation of five important works by Samuel Butler. These may be considered the centrepiece of Larbaud's entire career as a translator. Although encouraged by André Gide, who clearly saw important parallels between Butler's social critique and his own, and also by Arnold Bennett, who, as we have seen, was a close friend, it appears that he did not immediately appreciate Butler's importance when he first read *The Way of All Flesh* in 1912.[1] However, he did soon come to realize that Butler was the creator of a highly original humanism deriving from such sources as his own well developed evolution theory and, in another department, his admiration for the life of rural Piedmont, where he had sojourned almost every year, as well as from his preoccupation with challenges in the works of Homer and Shakespeare.

In fact, the more Larbaud explored Butler's work, the more enthusiastic he became, leading him to the realization that a major English writer, Shaw's master, in many respects comparable not only to Goethe but also to Montaigne and Pascal, had not yet been translated into French. He then made a thorough study of all of Butler's works to the extent that they were available before the publication of the definitive Shrewsbury Edition in the early 1920s, and became totally captivated, convinced, in fact, that he had found *une âme soeur*, the expression with which Baudelaire had characterized his own identification with the work of Edgar Allan Poe.

There had been mentions of Butler in France in the context of evolution theory since 1885,[2] and Jean Blum had published a glowing account in *Le Mercure de France*[3] in which he preferred Butler's orderly "eighteenth-century" prose to the alleged "vagaries" of Dickens and Thackeray. He compared *The Way of All Flesh* with Goethe's *Wilhelm Meister* and translated a short

---

1 Cf. G. Jean-Aubry, op. cit., p. 193.
2 For example, in Vianna de Lima, *Exposé Sommaire des théories transformistes de Lamarck, Darwin et Haekel* (Paris: Delagrave, 1885).
3 16 juillet 1910.

passage from *Erewhon Revisited* in which Higgs, the protagonist, abjures the relics of the "Sunchild" cult (having been deified as the "Sunchild" after his first departure from Erewhon in a balloon in the *dénouement* of *Erewhon*) suggesting, in the manner of Voltaire, that these relics be turned to dust to pave the roads of Erewhon. This fragment may be taken as the first translation of Butler into French.

Larbaud's diaries show that he became more and more impressed with Butler's achievement the more he explored it and it is clear that it was his conviction of the intrinsic integrity of Butler's work and Butler's undeniable stature as a major writer in several genres, in fact as a latter-day man of the Enlightenment, in many respects comparable to the French *philosophes* of the eighteenth century, that won him over to it.

Larbaud's sympathy for the satirist in Butler (as in the latter's satires of Victorian English society) might at first seem surprising, but he had himself written satires in his youth including *Les Archontes ou la Liberté religieuse*, "a comedy translated from the Greek" (1900) which was anti-republican. Another, *Gaston d'Ercoule*, (1906) is about a snobbish young man in a small provincial city (a transparent thrust at Vichy, where one of Larbaud's family homes was located) a large fragment of which was discovered by Robert Mallet of the Gallimard firm and has since been published in the *Pléiade* edition of Larbaud's works. There is also the caricature of the myths surrounding the very rich in the New World, taking the form of Barnabooth's fictitious *Biographie* in the first edition of the latter's poems.[4]

The circumstances under which Larbaud carried out his Butler translations were certainly singular enough to warrant special mention. During the first year of the First World War, and for several more months, Larbaud worked conscientiously in a military hospital in Vichy, until the effects of this work proved a serious threat to his own health. There were furloughs from time to time[5] during which he was able to pursue various literary projects. One was the abortive translation of Meredith's *Lord Ormont and his Amynta* which had been suggested by André Gide. However, he wrote to Gide explaining that he would prefer not to continue with the project and asked him if he might have another suggestion.[6] It was then that Gide, in January 1915,[7] suggested that he might consider translating some of Samuel Butler's works. Jean-Aubry affirms that it was during a short leave of approximately a week, in May 1915, which

---

4 Cf. *Poèmes par un riche amateur*, 1908 (cf. Pléiade, pp. 1135–1155).
5 Cf. Jean-Aubry, op. cit., pp. 244–245.
6 Ibid.
7 Ibid.

Larbaud spent in Sens on the river Yonne (to the south-east of Fontainebleau) where he stayed at the "Hôtel de Paris," that he first read Butler's *Erewhon* carefully and soon began translating it, leading to a preoccupation with Butler translations which would last for several years.

It was quite characteristic of Larbaud to isolate himself from the world by setting himself up in a provincial town or small city and studying its history while he was there, seeing such places as having a special interest and becoming a *connaisseur* of parts of France, and indeed Europe, that might seem off the beaten path.

He left his work at the military hospital in early November, 1915,[8] having thus devoted himself to assisting the wounded for well over a year. He was then free to pursue, in a much more thorough manner, his translations of *Erewhon* and *Erewhon Revisited*, often at the family's country home, Valbois, near St. Pourçain-sur-Sioule in Bourbonnais.[9] Jean-Aubry indicates that he had finished the first draft of his translation of *Erewhon* and a considerable part of that of *Erewhon Revisited*, by early December 1915.[10]

On January 2, 1916 he left for Spain on a diplomatic passport and went to Seville via Barcelona and Valencia, going partly by sea via Malaga and Cadiz, and expecting at first to work on behalf of the London periodical *The New Weekly*, to which he had been contributing articles on contemporary French literature. Instead he found himself reporting for the Parisian newspaper *Le Figaro*.[11] In a letter to Gide of January 22, 1916, he is expressing ever more interest in Butler despite having met an English gentleman in Seville who "detested" Butler's work. This negative reaction to Butler and refusal to recognize his undeniable merit, on the part of some people in the English speaking world, is thus a phenomenon that Larbaud discovered at an early stage during his years as Butler's French translator. Such critics seemed to discern a note of "one-up-manship" in Butler's love of paradox and in his various demonstrations of views which they apparently took as merely "clever." Others obviously experienced Butler as exposing uncomfortable truths about Victorian society which they may have found threatening.

Larbaud remained in Seville for two and a half months, and compared it to Montpellier, his favourite city in southern France. In January 1916 he sent Gide a sample of his translations which the latter found "excellent."[12]

---

8 Jean-Aubry, p. 248.
9 Ibid.
10 Ibid.
11 Ibid., p. 249.
12 Ibid.

From April to July 1916 Larbaud sojourned in Barcelona and on June 5, 1916 mentions in another letter to Gide that he has finished his translations of "les deux *Erewhon* ".[13] In the same letter he writes: "Je suis en train de me ceindre les reins pour *The Way of All Flesh*; c'est très dur mais j'arriverai."

Note-Books, on the other hand, were at first the object of considerable hesitation.

> "Pour les *Note-Books*, j'éprouve de grands scrupules de conscience à cause de l'irreligiosité imbécile de certaines pages. Pour traduire ces pages-là je serai obligé de me raccrocher fortement à la grande sympathie que m'inspire S. Butler personnellement, comme homme socialement taré, comme artiste méconnu, et comme âme pleine d'amour et de foi...."[14]

At this point two important changes in his life had come into play. The first was that after carefully exploring the Mediterranean coast of Spain, he made a firm decision to settle down near the attractive small coastal city of Alicante, whose palm esplanades, botanic garden and *tours de porcelaine*, not to mention its very salubrious winter climate, proved irresistible. (He sometimes spells its name "Alakant" when writing in English, an eighteenth-century variation he had found in his studies of Beckford.)

The other change was that he began, from February 17, 1917, to keep a very detailed diary in which he recorded in English the inward and outward experiences of his daily life. As a result we have, from this point, a thorough documentation of his work on the Butler translations and also of the various ways in which this work related to his daily life in Alicante.

On Saturday March 3, 1917 he notes in his diary that he has "got to page 284 of *The Way of All Flesh*, and has immediately begun the translation of the *Note-Books*, just as I began translating *The Way* last year on the very night when I finished translating *Erewhon Revisited*... and for the same reasons."[15] Although he does not explain these reasons, it is clear that this practice of translating or revising the translations of two works during the same period is part of an effort to maintain the appropriate tone for each, quite apart from the circumstance, on this occasion, that he had just run out of the English foolscap he called *vélin*[16] on which he was copying his first French version of *The Way of All Flesh*.

---

13   Ibid., p. 251.
14   Ibid., pp. 251–252.
15   Ibid., p. 205.
16   Ibid., p. 256.

This is, therefore, an important statement for the understanding of his methodology as a translator, besides indicating that he had become reconciled to the importance of *Note-Books* which he very soon realized were comparable in part to Pascal's famous *Pensées*, despite anticlerical or anti-religious expression in them.

The question of the quality of the paper on which he would write his translation of *Note-Books* seems to assume an even greater importance than that of the *vélin* of *The Way of All Flesh*, and provides the reader with a particularly intimate view of the translator at work, as in the entry in his *Journal* for March 5, 1917:

> Out at 8:30 and to the *Explanada*, where I idled among the palm-trees and along the harbour, so empty and silent....Then I went to the *papelaria* in front of St. Nicholas' and resolved the problem of the *falta de papel*....I bought 250 sheets of the best Spanish foolscap to be had. It is *papel de barba*...just hard enough, just smooth enough, with a look of something old, which makes me imagine that it was first manufactured in the admirable times of Isabel II....I have transcribed all I wrote on Saturday night, using the old blue-black American ink.[17]

Since Isabel II of Spain is sometimes referred to as "the Spanish Victoria," this fine paper becomes doubly significant as the appropriate kind for a Butler translation. On Tuesday July 10, 1917, at 6:00 AM, he notes in his *Journal*: "I have just put the last full stop to my translation of *The Way of All Flesh*, *alabado sea Dios*....just as the sun began to throw a first ray over the garden wall and the first birds began to sing."[18]

A year later, on August 1, 1918, he is nearing completion of the translation of Butler's *Note-Books* (*Carnets*)[19] and also translating a generous selection of Ramon Gomez de la Serna's *Gregarias* from Spanish into French. He would also soon be preparing for his translation of Butler's major scientific work, *Life and Habit* which was completed on March 25, 1919[20] after a detailed study of the entire field of evolution (*le transformisme*), in virtually all of the works on the subject available at the time in French, English, German and Italian.

---

17   *Journal*, p. 206.
18   Ibid., p. 244.
19   Ibid., p. 451.
20   Ibid., p. 489.

Back in Paris on Tuesday September 23, 1919, Larbaud presented a typed copy of the French *Erewhon* to Gaston Gallimard in person and prepared to leave for London the same day, having arranged a meeting with Butler's alter ego, Henry Festing Jones, whose publishers had just produced his major two-volume literary biography of Butler, which remains a primary source for research on the work of Butler.[21]

The first meeting with Jones took place on Friday, September 26. Among the many matters that came up was the question of whether the name Towneley in *The Way of All Flesh* might have been inspired by the Towneley who, in 1757, had translated into French the popular anti-republican satire *Hudibras* which had been the work of the first literary Samuel Butler (1612–1680). Jones expressed the view that Butler had probably never heard of this Towneley, but had probably just wanted to give the Towneley in *The Way of All Flesh* a name that suggested the idea of "a man about town."[22] Larbaud's *Journal* shows that Jones and Larbaud quickly became good friends. Jones was clearly impressed with Larbaud's detailed knowledge of Butler's work and the many signs of his commitment to it. On September 30 they went together to the Library of the British Museum (now the British Library) and saw Butler's famous seat there in Row B. Larbaud ordered one of Maupertuis's works with the purpose of explaining to Jones why he felt that Maupertuis, in the eighteenth century, had developed an evolution theory that seemed to foretell Butler's. After lunch they even went to see Butler's apartment at Clifford's Inn, although the tenant at the time at first showed absolutely no understanding of their reasons for wanting to see it.[23]

Larbaud was soon invited to the home of Jones and his sister[24] and found Miss Jones very well versed in French literature. He thought she might like to read Proust, whose work was then only beginning to become known in Britain. Thus Larbaud participates significantly in Butler's "vicarious life" (an expression that had interested Butler who had given much thought to its significance) by becoming an important member of Butler's extended family.

Before returning to France, Larbaud made a trip to Cambridge where he met another dedicated Butlerian, A.T. Bartholomew, who showed him the remarkable Butler Collection at St. John's College containing many of Butler's paintings, including a landscape he had painted in Italy in 1854. Thus his intimate identification with Butler becomes a veritable cult,

---

21 Henry Festing Jones, *Samuel Butler Author of Erewhon (1835–1902)* (London: MacMillan and Co. Ltd., 1919).
22 *Journal*, pp. 526–527.
23 Ibid., p. 531.
24 Cf. *Journal*, p. 536; October 4, 1919.

destined to survive the future demands of Larbaud's many other literary interests, even the very considerable demands that would later be made upon him by his supervision of the first French translation of James Joyce's *Ulysses* into French. In May 1934, Larbaud and his spouse "Mariuccia" will make a pilgrimage to Butler's birthplace, Langar Rectory, and compare the neighbouring villages to the villages surrounding their own country home in Bourbonnais (Valbois).[25]

After his return to Paris, Larbaud continued his promotion of Butler's work in France and eventually published five presentations of Butler in various literary journals, as it had soon become clear that Butler required such a promotional campaign before the significance of his work could be properly appreciated by a French public. The first and most important of these appeared in *La Nouvelle Revue Française* for January 1920, and also served as the introduction to the French translation of *Erewhon*. Then in April 1920 an article entitled *L'Enfance et la Jeunesse de Samuel Butler* appeared in *Les Ecrits Nouveaux*. Another article designed for a broader public appearing in August 1923 was entitled *L'Avènement d'un grand écrivain anglais: Samuel Butler*. (This article later became the introduction to the translation of *Erewhon Revisited: Nouveaux Voyages en Erewhon*.) The *Avant-propos* to the *Note-Books (Carnets)*, also first appeared as an article in *La Nouvelle Revue Française* for June 1st, 1935.

The French *Erewhon* appeared in 1920 (July 2), *Ainsi va toute chair* in 1921 (March 16), *La Vie et l'habitude* in 1922 (July 3), *Nouveaux Voyages en Erewhon* in 1924 (May 22), and *Carnets* in 1936 (January).

---

25 *Journal*, p. 1166; May 16, 1934.

Chapter 5

Butler: Erewhon

Erewhon, which Butler had published anonymously in 1872, belongs in the lineage of satire now known as the *satirical dystopia*, which had been revived from classical models during the Renaissance. Like Voltaire's *Candide*, it is actually a "dystopia" only partially, in other parts showing elements of a true utopia, setting forth Butler's vision of the ideal society. Inevitably, *Erewhon* reminds readers of Swift's *Gulliver's Travels*, and Butler is known to have made a careful study of this famous antecedent in preparation for *Erewhon*, resulting in occasional echoes of Swift's prose and situations in his own work.

In creating a "French Butler," Larbaud had no difficulty in locating a satirical French source that had been assimilated by Swift: Cyrano de Bergerac's remarkable and already very Voltairean *L'Autre Monde ou les Etats et empires de la lune et du soleil* (1656).[1] He also reread Voltaire's *Candide* as well as works of a number of other eighteenth-century French satirists, including Chamfort, Senancour, and Maupertuis, in preparation for his translation.

Gulliver's Travels had been translated into French in the eighteenth century by L'Abbé Desfontaine, whose views on translation had been creative to an extreme: not only did he use the censor's scissors at times, but, as he wrote in a letter to Swift, he added certain elements "selon que votre génie échauffait la mienne."[2] Larbaud found this comment significant in terms of the evolution of translation theory, which had only begun to express a need for more scrupulous precision at a later period in the eighteenth century, as set forth in English particularly in A. Fraser Tytler's *Essay on the Principles of Translation* (1781) which Larbaud saw as a particularly important turning point.[3]

The narrator of *Erewhon*, having "crossed the range," awakens, like Gulliver, from a deep sleep, to the sound of tinkling bells, and then sees two beautiful girls who scurry away. This is clearly an allusion not only to Gulliver but

---

1 Cf. Butler, *Erewhon* "Avertissement" (Paris: Gallimard, 1920, p. xxi).
2 Butler, *Nouveaux Voyages en Erewhon* (Paris: Gallimard, 1924, Préface du Traducteur, p. xxiv).
3 Cf. Larbaud, *De la Traduction* A. Fraser Tytler, In: *Sous L'invocation de St. Jérome* (*Oeuvres Complètes*, 8, p. 117).

also to the Nausicaa episode in *The Odyssey*. The *Odyssey* is thus present as an undercurrent in this passage rather as it is (almost ubiquitously) in Joyce's *Ulysses*. The episode might likewise be interpreted as an augury of Butler's later theory of Nausicaa as the authoress of *The Odyssey* and of his own future translations of Homer in the 1890s.[4]

Turning to the text of the translation one could stop at Chapter XV ("Les Banques Musicales") where Butler's satire is aimed directly at the Anglican Church, as it is again, more forcefully still, in Chapter 17 ("Ydgrun et les Ydgrunistes"). As we have seen, Larbaud had expressed reservations about Butler's anticlericalism and anti-church stance in general, but nevertheless manages to incorporate them into the tradition of French satire, especially as it had evolved in the eighteenth century. In this passage the narrator is observing life in one of the "musical banks":

> "A sinister-looking person in a black gown came and made unpleasant gestures at me for peeking."[5]
>
> "Un homme en robe noir, l'air sombre et méchant, s'approcha et me fit des gestes menaçants parce que je regardais."[6]

The tone and manner of Voltaire in *Candide* are evident here. Larbaud clearly thought of Butler as to some extent a Victorian Voltaire before Wilde and Shaw took up the role. *Erewhon Revisited* (1901) was later to give Butler the opportunity of introducing accents that seem even more Voltairean, especially with respect to the relics of the Sunchild cult, reaching a crescendo at the height of the drama when Higgs, visiting Erewhon twenty years after his original discovery of the country, is exposed as the "Sunchild" and might at any moment be condemned as an impostor.

Butler's efforts to show up, and possibly correct, what he considered misguided tendencies in Victorian society, may also be understood as being universally valid and thus equally relevant at the time Larbaud's translation was published in France, although some French critics challenged that point. Thus in *Erewhon*, regarding the education of students destined for the priesthood, which the narrator sees as an indoctrination, we find this comment:

> They had had the misfortune to have been betrayed into *a false position* at an age for the most part when their judgment was

---

4 Cf. George Steiner (Ed.), *Homer in English* (London: Penguin, 1996), p. 210.
5 Butler, *Erewhon* (Signet Classic, The New American Library, 1872/1960), p. 210.
6 transl., p. 101.

not matured, and after having been kept in studied ignorance of the real difficulties of the system.⁷

Ils avaient eu le malheur d'avoir été placés malgré eux dans *une situation fausse* à un âge où la plupart d'entre eux n'avaient pas encore de maturité de jugement, et après avoir été habilement tenus dans l'ignorance des vraies difficultés de l'organisation.⁸

When "false position" becomes *une situation fausse* it is apparent that Larbaud is situating Butler in the movement toward a reinvention of ethics that was to become an important intellectual climate in France from the early twentieth century, soon leading to *la littérature engagée*, which Larbaud was to oppose when it took the form of explicit advocacy. (He later also opposed the use of literature for the purposes of the social sciences.) However, there is, occasionally, in the work of Larbaud, an implicit *engagement profond*.⁹ The expression "*une situation fausse*" also occurs in *Ainsi va toute chair*, Larbaud's translation of *The Way of All Flesh*. The theme would eventually become an obsessive one (*un thème obsédant*) in the works of Gide and Sartre. Thus, in retrospect, it becomes evident that Larbaud managed to integrate his translations of Butler into an important aspect of the intellectual movements of France in his time. In making this possible he was clearly indebted to the encouragement of André Gide.

At the time, Butler's works were undergoing a period of "apotheosis" in Britain and Larbaud was clearly concerned to extend this in some measure to France, possibly in the hope of achieving a degree of justification for his Herculean task as translator.

In Chapter 17, "Ydgrun and the Ydgrundites," Larbaud does explain to his readers the history of "Mrs. Grundy," the traditional incarnation in Britain of the village gossip. When the narrator quotes the opponents of a sect that believes in immortality, one finds a manifesto of positive humanistic values whose advocacy is thus twice removed from Butler, although this well-worn satirical technique can disguise neither the depth of Butler's revolt nor his specific attack on fundamentalism. This is how these "good" Erewhonians develop their critique of the immortality doctrine:

---

7 p. 121.
8 transl., p. 106.
9 The words *une situation fausse* occur in Gide's *Les Faux-Monnayeurs*, with respect to Bernard's mother when he discovers that her husband is not his real father. Cf. André Gide, *Les Faux-Monnayeurs* (Paris: Gallimard, 1926/1955), p. 25.

> It would lead people to cheapen this present life, making it appear to be an affair of only secondary importance....The doctrine tended to encourage the poor in their improvidence, and in a debasing acquiescence in ills which they might well remedy.[10]

These words seem clearer and hence more radical in Larbaud's French, and in general the translation is an improvement on the English original:

> Ils seraient amenés à faire trop peu de cas de la vie présente, que cette doctrine représentait comme une chose d'importance secondaire....Cette doctrine tendait à encourager les pauvres dans leur imprévoyance, et dans leur avilissante tolérance à l'égard de maux dont ils étaient très capables de s'affranchir.[11]

These very humanistic Erewhonians continue:

> The rewards were illusory and the result, after all, of luck, whose empire should be bounded by the grave;...its terrors were enervating and unjust; and...even the most blessed rising would be but the disturbing of a still more blessed slumber.[12]

> Que les récompenses n'étaient qu'illusoires et ne seraient, après tout, que le résultat de la chance, dont l'empire devrait s'arrêter aux portes du tombeau. Que les tourments qu'elle prévisait étaient angoissants et injustes; et que même la résurrection la plus heureuse ne ferait que mettre fin à un sommeil encore plus heureux.[13]

Phrases like "debasing acquiescence" (*avilissante tolérance*) do, however, convey the critique of "superstition" which various socialist movements of the nineteenth century had been putting forth. Devastating though this understanding of Victorian Anglicanism is, the narrator also finds very admirable traits among other Erewhonians he has met and in particular the "High Ydgrunites."[14]

However, it is clear that we have here a revelation of the narrator's own duplicity, as astutely crafted in the following sentence:

---

10 Butler, p. 136.
11 transl., pp. 120–121.
12 Ibid., p. 136.
13 Ibid., p. 121.
14 Larbaud translates: "les Hauts Ydgrunistes."

I have always liked and admired these men, and although I could not help regretting their ultimate perdition (for they had no sense of a hereafter, and *their only religion was that of self-respect and consideration for other people*). I never dared to take so great a liberty with them as to put them in possession of my own religious convictions, in spite of my knowing that they were the only ones which could make them really good and happy, either here or *hereafter*.[15]

Je ne me laissais pas d'admirer et d'aimer ces hommes: et tout en ne pouvant m'empêcher de déplorer leur perdition finale certaine (car ils n'avaient aucune idée de l'au-delà, et *leur seule religion consistait dans leur respect de soi-même et leur considération pour les autres*) je ne me risquai jamais de prendre la liberté grande de les mettre en possession de mes convictions religieuses; et pourtant je savais que ces convictions étaient les seules qui pussent les rendre vraiment bons et heureux, soit ici-bas, soit *là-haut*.[16]

Here Larbaud manages the irony in a manner that is no doubt milder than Voltaire's but hardly less effective, showing his ability to craft a polemical prose that is indeed worthy of that of the *philosophes* of the eighteenth century, especially in this expression of the positive values in the parenthesis, defining with the dignity of simplicity the "religion" of these virtuous citizens while reducing to the absurd and to hypocrisy any missionary zeal that might try to replace such values with the narrator's own "religious convictions." (At the level of words it is amusing to find Larbaud translating the notion of the "hereafter" with the colloquial *là-haut*: up there.)

As we have seen, Larbaud's translation theory consists essentially in his adherence to the De Sanctis principle, but to the extent that translation is a craft before it can become an art, he was also concerned with a number of practical matters. Thus he returns to the allegory of the translator weighing his words on a pair of scales, "*les balances du traducteur*," long since imagined by Cicero and St. Jerome and familiar to all translators.

The English words in both the noun "a balance" and the verb "to balance" also become very relevant in any discussion of translation theory but it must be noted that they are of course not to be confused with the French term *les balances* (the scales). In Anna-Marie Aldaz's excellent thesis, *Valery Larbaud*

---

15 Butler, p. 134.
16 transl., 128.

as *Translator of Samuel Butler*,[17] this traditional notion of a "balance" (in the English meaning of the word) is extended further to include the related notion of "compensation." Since a translation can clearly not be merely a matter of *mot à mot* without consideration of its effect, we may have to take a liberty in one place and compensate for it in another in order to ensure that the content of a particular passage is precisely rendered. To make this possible Larbaud reaffirms the translator's "rights" to suppression and substitution, although, as Aldaz points out, he seldom resorts to these rights himself.

An excellent example of Larbaud's skill in "balancing" is to be found in the translation of *The Book of the Machines* in *Erewhon*. Here the narrator discovers in a museum a very old document in which certain Erewhonian philosophers, hundreds of years before his arrival, had proposed the abolition of all machines because they were convinced that the idolatry of machines was threatening to turn Erewhon into a nation of slaves, victims of the very machines whose evolution they had so "cunningly" pursued for centuries.

Machines, then, are seen as a particular, and disturbingly rapid, manifestation of evolution. The philosophers had come to the conclusion that machines represented evolution in an ultimately disastrous direction and that they might blind people to this danger through the power of ingrained habit. The abolition of machines had eventually been accomplished by decree during Erewhon's revolution and was followed by a time of civil strife between the defenders and opponents of this decree.

A key sentence in the defenders' exhortation to their fellow citizens is:

> "Our bondage will *steal upon* us noiselessly and by imperceptible *approaches*."[18]
>
> "Notre esclavage *s'approchera* de nous sans bruit et à *pas* imperceptibles."[19]

The concepts "stealth" and "approaches" are interchanged and the cognate adjective "imperceptible" moved from one to the other, the noun "approaches" suggesting the French verb "*s'approcher*" and "steal upon" suggesting the French noun *pas*, which might evoke the movement of a predator. The balancing of the original sentence with its translation is thus achieved by means of the linguistic resources of the original sentence itself, in such a way that its content (*le contenu*) is translated precisely.

---

17 University of Oregon, 1969.
18 Butler, pp. 194–195.
19 transl., p. 181.

Thus we have here an example of the "art" of Larbaud's translation as opposed to the "craft," a distinction expressed in the title of the second part of *Sous l'invocation de St. Jérôme*: "L'Art et le Métier."

The philosophers' justification for the abolition of machines is founded on the reasoning that machines had evolved very rapidly over the previous few centuries by comparison with the infinitely slower evolution of the natural world, and that if their evolution were allowed to continue at the same pace then there would be a serious possibility that a mechanical consciousness could become a formidable threat to the animal and vegetable kingdoms.

There seemed no certain proof that this might not happen. "Is it not safer to nip the mischief in the bud and to forbid them further progress?"[20]

> But who can say that the vapour engine has not a kind of consciousness? Where does consciousness begin and where end? Who can draw the line? Is not everything interwoven with everything? Is not machinery *linked* with animal life in an infinite variety of ways?[21]

> Mais qui peut affirmer que la machine à vapeur n'a pas une espèce de conscience? Ou' la conscience commence-t-elle? ou' finit-elle? Qui peut fixer la limite? Toute chose n'est-elle pas solidaire de toute chose? Est-ce que les machines *ne se rattachent pas* de mille manières à la vie animale?[22]

The philosophers also provide an example of the propensity of the mechanical in nature to have a role in organic evolution which might someday have disastrous consequences:

> The shell of a hen's egg is made of a delicate white ware and is a machine as much as an egg cup is: the shell is a device for holding the egg, as much as the egg cup for holding the shell: both are phases of the same function; the hen makes the shell in her inside, but it is pure pottery. She makes her nest outside of herself for convenience' sake, but the nest is not more of a machine than the egg shell is. A machine is only a "*device*."[23]

---

20 Butler, p. 173.
21 Ibid.
22 transl., p. 158.
23 pp. 173–174.

> La coquille d'un oeuf est faite d'une matière blanche et délicate et c'est une machine au même titre que le coquetier qui est fait pour le recevoir: l'une et l'autre sont deux modes de la même fonction. Sans doute la poule fait la coquille à l'intérieur de son corps, mais cela n'empêche pas que ce soit tout simplement de la poterie. Elle fait son nid en dehors de son corps parce que cela lui est plus commode, mais le nid est une machine ni plus ni moins que la coquille de l'oeuf. Ce qu'on nomme "machine" n'est qu'un *"expédient."*[24]

Here we have the principle that the living and non-living can be combined in what is now called a symbiotic relationship, so that machines could assume more and more importance in living processes, possibly to the point at which they might be in a position to have a determining role in certain designs of humanity, since humanity has placed them in that position.

Then, returning to the phenomenon of consciousness and endeavouring to detect its earliest manifestations, the writer continues:

> There is a kind of plant that eats organic food with its flowers: when a fly settles upon the blossom the petals close upon it and hold it fast till the plant has absorbed the insect into its system; but they will close on nothing but what is good to eat; of a drop of rain or a piece of stick they take no notice.
>
> Curious! that so unconscious a thing should have such a keen eye to its own interest. If this is unconsciousness then where is the use of consciousness?[25]
>
> Il y a une espèce de plante qui mange des matières organiques avec ses fleurs: quand une mouche se pose sur la fleur, les pétales se referment sur elle, et la tiennent solidement jusqu'à ce que la fleur se soit assimilé l'insecte; mais les pétales ne se referment que sur ce qui peut servir de nourriture. Ils ne feraient nul cas d'une brindille de bois ou d'une goutte de pluie. C'est bien étrange qu'une chose si inconsciente sache si bien veiller à ses intérêts. Si c'est là de l'inconscience, à quoi servira la conscience?[26]

---

24 transl., pp. 158–159.
25 Butler, p. 174.
26 transl., p. 159.

Here Butler is showing his preoccupation with biological phenomena in these years that found him grappling with Darwin's *Origin of Species*. The whole notion that the very rapid development of machines in the nineteenth century is something to be concerned about in view of the possibility that humanity might ultimately not be able to control them, makes the conclusions of Butler's fictitious "*philosophes*" universally relevant. There is a demonstration of something fatal in human nature which remains as disturbing as ever, given that the sages' decree banishing all machines is, of course, as unlikely to come about in the "real world" as the weeping of Montesquieu's king in the *Troglodyte* episode of *Les Lettres Persanes*, while he is being crowned, weeping, that is, at the thought of the arbitrary power he will have. Thus Butler is using a famous technique of the Enlightenment by demonstrating the limits of human aspirations. This technique is also reminiscent of Swift's use of the relativity theme in *Gulliver's Travels* and Voltaire's in *Candide* (in which the Lisbon earthquake answers Pangloss's "optimism") for the purpose of exposing fatal flaws in human nature.

One may speculate on whether Butler might have been aware of the banning of the gun in Japan for a period of more than three centuries (1543–1879).[27]

Certainly Butler's *Erewhon* was far from being the only literary expression of concern about applied technology in the nineteenth century. It has been pointed out that in Dickens's *Sketches by Boz* the narrator attends a (very Butlerian) balloon ascent In Vauxhaull Gardens and hears someone comment: "I don't know where this here science is to stop, mind you; that's what bothers me."[28] There had also been Thoreau's famous pun in *Walden* on the word "sleeper," as railroad ties were called in his time, suggesting that we are the real "sleepers" over whom the train is passing.

The question of whether Butler's fiction could eventually influence policy making in "the real world" in its English form and in its translations arose shortly after the use of the atomic bomb at the end of World War II in Lewis Mumford's *Program for Survival*. (1945)[29] In this exposé, Mumford makes a significant reference to Butler's "Book of the Machines" in *Erewhon*:

> If science today were the main obstacle to mankind's continued existence, reasonable men, fully awakened to the danger, would demolish science as readily as they would demolish a Congo

---

27 Cf. Noel Perrin, *Giving Up the Gun* (Boston: David R. Godine Publisher Inc., 1979).
28 Cf. *The Times Literary Supplement* (June 21, 2013, p. 23).
29 Cf. Lewis Mumford, *Values for Survival* (New York: Harcourt Brace & Co., 1946).

fetish. They would know that if intellectual progress had caused mankind to reach the edge of the abyss, it is better to recoil than to take the last step that will send us hurtling downward. If that were the price of survival, we would have to pay it, as cheerfully as the Erewhonians did when they made the invention of the machine a criminal offence.[30]

Mumford regards his view as a particular manifestation in a lineage of thought possibly originating with Leonardo's refusal to invent a proposed submarine "because man was too 'devilish' to be entrusted with such an invention."[31]

Thus we have here evidence that Mumford was well aware of Butler's eloquent warning, veiled in fiction. Importantly, Mumford also wrote the introduction to the 1927 Modern Library edition of *Erewhon*, that is, during the period when Butler, in his "vicarious life," was achieving recognition on both sides of the Altlantic, a recognition to which Larbaud's translation (1920) had clearly contributed.

In fact Mumford develops this theme in terms that seem almost a quotation from Butler's "Book of the Machines" in *Erewhon*:

> If we cannot control ourselves sufficiently to create a harmonious world order, then *we shall have to destroy our machines* as the only other means of guaranteeing our survival.[32]

Having long since absorbed Butler's fictitious scenario he was able to refer to it at a crucial moment in human history, so that it may be assumed to have played a role in the debates that followed Hiroshima and Nagasaki. Hence we do indeed have a curious actualization of Wilde's famous paradox that "life imitates art more than art imitates life."

Larbaud's translation of *Erewhon* created the possibility of familiarization with this scenario in the francophone world. This gives the translation an important role, considering that the French tradition of skepticism, as incarnate in the work of Voltaire and other *philosophes*, seemed not to be effective in the matter of machine "evolution," which has always been one of great pride in its French versions. Butler could not easily be reconciled with pride in France's

---

30 Mumford, reprinted in *The Human Prospect* (Boston: Beacon Press 1955, p. 229). Cf. pp. 227-260.
31 op. cit., p. 332.
32 op. cit., p. 230.

nuclear capability, for example. But importantly, as a result of the translation, this uncomfortable scenario of the abolition of machines is nonetheless there and its "being there" cannot be ignored.

The final revisions and typing of the French *Erewhon* in August and September 1919 were accompanied by further readings of eighteenth-century French prose when it is "*engagée*":

"Began reading pages and pages of Chamfort in order to get "du français dans l'oreille."[33] At this point Larbaud gives us another picture of himself at work on the revisions of the French *Erewhon*:

> I work very hard at it and "con animo." It is *comimg out* as a drawing when the artist thickens with his pencil the more important lines...in doing this I find new things in it, deeper meanings etc. Of course the fact that I have, (since 1915), read nine or ten books of Butler....helps me to understand better many intentions and allusions in *Erewhon*. These I am bringing out in my translation.[34]

Larbaud's typist in Paris lived in a small flat on the seventh floor of a building near the famous markets (Les Halles) and Larbaud, who had put on weight at the time, had to climb the stairs. He described the flat as "looking like the berths on board of a third class emigrants' ship."[35] The many typing errors had to be corrected: "Worked at the correction of Miss X's typing, which is, in fact, another revision of *Erewhon*." Not the least memorable of his many comments in English on her might be: "Hope she'll have as much of orthography as she has of legs."[36]

It is not surprising to find examples in *Erewhon* of quotations which had already been translated into French. Thus two separate lines from Shakespeare's *Hamlet* are quoted as a couplet (in Chapter 16, *Arowhena*) when the narrator is introduced to the king of Erewhon and makes an amusing *faux pas* by reciting them to the king:

> There's such divinity doth hedge a king,
> Rough hew him how we may.

---

33 *Journal*, p. 511 (August 25, 1919).
34 Ibid.
35 *Journal*, p. 517 (September 12, 1919).
36 *Journal*, p. 514 (September 6, 1919).

These lines each occur in a separate act but are here combined as in the game of misquotations in which Butler and his friend Miss Savage indulged. The second line is from the original couplet, well known to anglophones:

> There's a divinity that shapes our ends,
> Rough-hew them how we will.[37]

Larbaud provides his own translation and then, in his *Notes du Traducteur*, gives Pierre Letourneur's eighteenth-century version. (It was Letourneur who had translated Shakespeare's entire work into French for the first time in translations which continue to be admired.)

> Letourneur: Il est une force divine qui environne et défend la majesté des rois; quelqu'informe qu'en soit le plan ébauché par l'homme.[38]
>
> Larbaud: Quelque chose de divin protège encore les rois, Si informes que soient les blocs que nous en ayons faits.[39]

In the second line Larbaud follows Letourneur in using the adjective *informe* but improves on him with *les blocs*, corresponding to the verb "hew" in the text, as well as inventing a syntactic scheme whose rhythm is poetic.

Thus, as Anna-Marie Aldaz has pointed out in her thesis (*Valery Larbaud as Translator of Samuel Butler*), there are occasions when Larbaud manages to make use of the greater regularity of French to achieve an improvement over the original:

"Surely to be *responsible* means to be liable to have to give an *answer* should it be demanded."[40]

"Assurément être *responsable* signifie être soumis à l'obligation de donner une *réponse* si on vous la demande."[41]

Here Larbaud improves upon the original by formulating an appropriate play on words to bring out the etymological relationship between *réponse* and *responsable*.[42]

---

37 *Hamlet*, V.ii.10.
38 *Notes*, p. 223.
39 *Notes*, p. 110.
40 *Erewhon*, Ch. 12 (Signet p. 96).
41 *Erewhon* transl., Ch. 12, p. 81.
42 Aldaz, op. cit., p. 153.

Since Butler used his Note-Books as a reservoir of observations about human nature and life in general, one occasionally finds the same comment both there and in one of the creative works. Aldaz points this out with reference to "virtue": "The most that can be said for virtue is that there is a considerable balance in its favour...but it lets people in very badly sometimes.[43]

In *Erewhon* we have almost the same words but with the notion of "pseudo-virtue" inserted.[44] In Larbaud's translation we find a clarification: "Tout ce qu'on peut dire avec raison en faveur de la vertu, c'est qu'elle a un gros compte créditeur en banque... mais (la fausse vertu) peut fort bien vous duper."[45]

As noted, the translations of *Erewhon* and *Erewhon Revisited* were the first Butler translations Larbaud undertook and he later expressed a certain dissatisfaction with the parts of *Erewhon* he had translated in France before going to Spain, having found "a few interpretations that will do better,"[46] and even considering rewriting these two translations. He felt he had "worked hastily and among uncongenial surroundings," and that "Butler's style was not so familiar...as it is now."[47] This concern demonstrates how very conscientious he was in his role as translator, as reaffirmed two years later when he expresses indignation at what he considers an imperfect translation into French, by another translator, of Hardy's *A Pair of Blue Eyes*. Then, referring to his translation of *Erewhon*, he is prompted to assert:

> Not only have I not left one word untranslated, but there is not a shade of meaning that I have not at least attempted to give in the French....All this means hours and hours in La Thébaide, turning over the leaves of the big dictionaries, English, French, Latin, Greek, and of many works of reference on special subjects...even the *French Criminal Code!*[48]

This passage provides a particularly intimate view of Larbaud at work on his translations. The mention of "La Thébaide" (which he occasionally expresses in Italian as *La Tebaide*) evokes one of the more colourful aspects of his "legend," which intrigued Fargue shortly after they first met in 1909.

---

43 Butler, *Note-Books*, p. 25.
44 op. cit. (Signet), p. 88.
45 *Erewhon* transl., p. 72. Cf. Aldaz, p. 159.
46 *Journal*, p. 210 (March 19, 1917).
47 Ibid.
48 *Journal*, pp. 511–512 (September 25, 1919).

It is the name Larbaud gave to a small building in the grounds of the family home in Vichy where he could pursue his work in peace for reasons that Fargue suggested "se rient du commentaire."[49] It was in "La Thébaide" that Larbaud kept his library at the time the earlier work on the Butler translations was being carried out.

---

49 Léon-Paul Fargue, *Portraits de Famille* (Paris: Janin, 1947, p. 79).

Chapter 6

Butler: The Way of All Flesh

Butler's satirical *Bildungsroman The Way of All Flesh (Ainsi va toute chair)* was to become a much greater success in its French translation than *Erewhon*, possibly because of the universal qualities which Larbaud, among many others, had recognized in it. It also corresponds to a particular type of novel which the Hungarian critic Georges Lukacs had studied and to which Lucien Goldmann drew attention in France: the novel that depicts a "degraded" society through the eyes of a protagonist who is its victim and therefore also, at first, "degraded," but who is ultimately capable of achieving a new equilibrium in his own life on a foundation of new values.[1]

In the perceptive study of Butler that was published as a preface to the French *Erewhon* in 1920, Larbaud had remarked that in many respects Butler was still contemporary. As we have seen (with regard to *Erewhon*), Europe was considered by a number of observers to be undergoing *une crise de valeurs* at the time, a crisis which was to be reflected six years later in Gide's *Les Faux-Monnayeurs* (1926) and in a number of other works. A number of Gide's earlier works, and in particular *Les Caves du Vatican* (1914), had already expressed this crisis. In fact Gide, as we have seen, showed a particularly keen interest in the Butler translations, reading the proofs as they became available. Larbaud expressed his appreciation for this support in a letter to Gide of June 5, 1916: "Je vous remercie de l'intérêt que vous prenez aux traductions de Butler."

It is quite conceivable that the counterfeiter allegory, in the first named novel, may have been suggested to Gide in part by Butler's *The Way of All Flesh*. In this respect one could refer to Chapter 57. Ernest, the antihero, who is now an ordained Anglican priest, has come under the influence of a wayward brother:

---

1   Lucien Goldmann, *Pour une Sociologie du Roman* (Paris: Gallimard [Bibliothèque des Idées], 1964), p. 18.

> He had fallen, as I have shown, among a gang of spiritual thieves or coiners, who passed the basest metal upon him without his finding it out.[2]

> Ainsi que je l'ai fait voir, il était tombé au milieu d'une bande de voleurs ou de faux-monnayeurs de la vie intellectuelle, qui lui passaient toute espèce de pièces fausses sans qu'il s'en rendît compte.[3]

From our perspective, it is by translating "coiners" as *faux-monnayeurs* and "spiritual" as *la vie intellectuelle*, that Larbaud manages to place Butler in the intellectual context of the 1920s, as he had already done with the translation of *Erewhon*. However, he is taking a considerable liberty in this rendering of the English word "spiritual," (a notorious *faux ami*) because of the two distinct denotations of the French *spirituel*. (Assuming that he would of course have been well aware of the usual meaning of *spiritual*.)[4] This boldness in exercising the translator's right to substitution appears, in this instance, to be another reflection of his desire to promote the translation, the same concern that is also expressed in the articles he published on Butler's work.

In this story of Ernest Pontifex, the young man who imagines he wants to be a priest, there is also another allusion to some of Hamlet's famous words, on this occasion from the well-known suicide soliloquy, which Butler parodies.[5] Only certain phrases of the original remain. Larbaud appears not to have used an existing French translation of *Hamlet*: "The world was *out of joint*, and instead of feeling that it was *a cursed spite* that he was *born to set it right*, he thought he was just the kind of person that was wanted for the job."[6]

> Le monde *allait tout de travers*, et au lieu de sentir que c'était *une vraie malédiction* pour lui *que d'être né avec la mission de le remettre sur la bonne voie*, il pensait qu'il était exactement l'espèce d'homme à qui cette tâche convenait.[7]

---

2 Butler, *The Way of All Flesh* (1903) (New York: Signet Classic, 1960), p. 233.
3 Butler, *Ainsi va toute chair* (Paris: Gallimard [1921], 1936), p. 259.
4 Cf. Ibid., p. 44.
5 In Chapter 55: I.v.189–190.
6 op. cit., p. 228.
7 op. cit. transl., pp. 252–253.

These allusions are rendered in the same unassuming and very proper prose style that we find throughout the translated narrative. Consequently there is a problem in translation here. Could most francophone readers recognize their source? This important matter is unfortunately not addressed, as no *Notes du Traducteur* are attached to *Ainsi va toute chair*. The satirical comparison between Ernest and Hamlet, an important element in the narrator's subtle mockery of his "antihero," may therefore perhaps not be experienced by the francophone viewer or reader, unless she/he happens to be very well versed in Shakespeare. Once again we find that allusions to Shakespeare are often a major hurdle in Larbaud's translations. (Larbaud was himself an avid Shakespearian, later taking part in the famous debate over the authorship of Shakespeare's work.)

The young Ernest, then, in this *fausse situation* in which he is training to be a priest (a projection of the young Butler) is constantly observed by Overton, the narrator, (a projection of the mature Butler) who, at one point, learns about Ernest's life in a somewhat seedy boarding house.

When Ernest decides it is time to convert some of the other tenants, beginning with a wife beater who lives directly above him, Butler the humourist (much admired by Shaw) presents another challenge to his translator:

> If the man were to be violent what should he do? Paul had fought with wild beasts at Ephesus…but perhaps they were not very wild wild beasts; a rabbit and a canary are wild beasts; but formidable or not as wild beasts go, they would, nevertheless, stand no chance against St. Paul.[8]
>
> [Si] cet homme s'emportait que ferait Ernest? Saint Paul avait lutté contre des animaux sauvages à Ephèse…mais peut-être que ce n'était (sic) pas des animaux sauvages très sauvages; un lapin et un canari sont des animaux sauvages; mais féroces ou non, ces animaux sauvages n'avaient aucune chance de vaincre Saint Paul.[9]

The mere fact that St. Paul is portrayed in the midst of such "casuistry" could easily seem irreverent although we cannot be sure that this is intentional, even when Butler continues:

---

8 op. cit., p. 237.
9 op. cit. transl., p. 263.

> The miracle would have been if the wild beasts escaped, not that St. Paul should have done so.[10]

> Le miracle eût été que les animaux sauvages en réchappassent et non que St. Paul les vainquît.[11]

By belabouring this point Butler seems to imply that things could perhaps have been the other way around but it is more difficult to see this "insinuendo" in the French translation. (Butler had invented this portmanteau word (*mot valise*) for the purposes of his campaign against what he interpreted as the frequent duplicity of the language of Victorian society.) In this context it is the narrator who is making an "insinuendo" with respect to Ernest's wavering doubts as expressed in this interior monologue. The translation could be read at the literal level just as the original could; Larbaud leaves any interpretation to the reader rather than attempting to suggest a possible ironic meaning, thus maintaining the placid surface of Butler's own ambivalence. It is also impossible to determine whether Larbaud might be deliberately attempting to conceal the implications of Butler's satire here.

There are other passages that seem much more to Larbaud's taste, bringing out the very genuine affinity between the two humanists. Their styles of travel through continental Europe, for example, are often expressed in similar terms. Larbaud may well have identified with this evocation of a stop in Marseilles when Ernest and Overton are on their way to Italy. Ernest is here recovering from the nervous breakdown resulting from the disturbing events of the novel's central crisis:

> I remember being ill once in a foreign hotel myself and how much I enjoyed it. To lie there careless of everything, quiet and warm, and with no weight upon the mind, to hear the clinking of the plates in the far-off kitchen as the scullion rinsed them and put them by; to watch the soft shadows come and go upon the ceiling as the sun came out or went behind a cloud; to listen to the pleasant murmuring of the fountain in the court below, and the shaking of the bells on the horses' collars…not only to be a lotus-eater but to know that it was *one's duty* to be a lotus-eater.[12]

---

10 op. cit., p. 237.
11 op. cit., p. 363.
12 op. cit., p. 327.

> Je me souviens d'avoir été malade, une fois, dans un hôtel, à l'étranger, et je me rappelle combien cela était agréable. J'étais couché, bien tranquille, au chaud, sans aucune espèce de souci...j'entendais le bruit lointain des assiettes qu'un marmiton lavait et posait l'une sur l'autre, là-bas dans les cuisines; je suivais des yeux les ombres atténuées qui paraissaient et disparaissaient sur le plafond selon le mouvement des nuages sur le soleil; j'écoutais le joli murmure de la fontaine, en bas, dans la cour, et le tintement des clochettes sur les colliers des chevaux.... Non seulement j'étais un mangeur de lotus mais je savais que *mon devoir* était d'en être un.[13]

The passage provides insight into the epicurean balance between work and leisure to which both of these two model writers aspired; when Larbaud, in his various studies of Butler, sees an epicurean in him, as conveyed in the slightly paradoxical use of the word "duty" here, he is at the same time quite clearly indicating an important aspect of his own philosophical ideal.

Butler's admiration for Italy and his ability to identify with everyday Italian life, is another aspect of Butler which seems particularly meaningful to Larbaud. In their mutual love of Italy they quite literally crossed paths, Larbaud pointing out the exact hotel in Turin where Butler had stayed. And as we have seen, Larbaud and Henry Festing Jones, Butler's "Boswell" and companion on many a trip to Italy and Sicily, were to become very good friends. In his "Lettre d'Italie"[14] Larbaud relates a visit to the hill top Republic of San Marino with Jones.

Jones had been there with Butler more than twenty years before. As they bravely descend in a somewhat dilapidated Ford from the citadel to the plain near Rimini, Jones performs a parody on the style of W.H. Hudson which Larbaud greatly enjoys. However, the symbolic meaning of this episode may perhaps have escaped Larbaud's readers when "Lettre d'Italie" was first published.[15] Jones is now accompanied by Butler's French translator who replaces Butler in the car just as his translations replace Butler's originals. Thus it is not only five of Butler's works that are "translated": it is now Butler the man if we may be permitted to return to the latin roots of the word.

---

13 op. cit. transl., p. 360.
14 *Jaune Bleu Blanc* (cf. Pléiade, p. 809).
15 In *Commerce* 3 (Hiver 1924), pp. 233–285.

In another major essay, "Le Vain Travail de voir divers pays," also first published in *Commerce*,[16] Larbaud observes that Butler was an important participant in a debate in the world of art history in his (Victorian) time. There had been an attempt to redefine the Renaissance, in part as a reaction against the Pre-Raphaelite movement in England. It was within the context of this debate that Butler attempted to rehabilitate such worthy sixteenth-century artists of north-western Piedmont as Gaudenzio Ferrari, Giovanni d' Enrico and Tabachetti, whose paintings and sculptures (and combinations of these in scenarios) he saw as representing an important manifestation of the work of the original Pre-Raphaelites, in spirit, if not always chronologically.

In *Alps and Sanctuaries* and *Ex Voto*, which Larbaud read carefully but chose not to translate, towns and villages in which Butler sojourned, such as Varallo and Varese, also inspired Butler's work as an artist, yielding sketches, paintings, and photographs. This aspect of Butler's work is studied in detail by Elinor Shaffer in the handsomely produced *Erewhons of the Eye*.[17]

Life in Piedmont, to which Butler had returned almost every summer in his mature years, did clearly inspire him as a corrective to a number of the imbalances and societal neuroses which he had experienced in his own family life in England before breaking away from it. In *The Way of All Flesh* we find a brilliant analysis, expressed through particular episodes, of this "sick society" he had left behind. One such example, projected into the novel, concerns the Victorian attitude toward children. The narrator illustrates this through comments on the Anglican Catechism:

> That work was written too exclusively from the parental point of view; the person who composed it did not get a few children to come in and help him; he was clearly not young himself, nor should I say it was the work of one who liked children.... The general impression it leaves upon the young is that their wickedness at birth was but very imperfectly wiped out at baptism, and that the mere fact of being young at all has something with it that savours more or less distinctly of the nature of sin.[18]
>
> Cet ouvrage a été trop écrit du point de vue des parents. Celui qui l'a composé n'a évidemment pas réuni autour de lui quelques enfants qui l'auraient aidé. On voit bien qu'il n'était

---

16 6, Hiver 1925, pp. 27–79.
17 op. cit. (London: Reaktion, 1988).
18 op. cit., p. 32.

> pas jeune et je ne crois pas, à lire son ouvrage, qu'il aimât les enfamts....L'impression générale que ce livre laisse dans l'esprit des enfants est que le péché originel chez eux n'a été que très imparfaitement effacé par le baptême et que le seul fait d'être jeune a en soi quelque chose qui participe plus ou moins de l'essence du péché.[19]

When Butler suggests here that children must be allowed to participate in this educational process, there is a reminder of Larbaud's own original pedagogy in one of his most remarkable short stories about children, *Devoirs de Vacances*, which appeared in the collection entitled *Enfantines* and which may be considered one of his major creations, in fact sometimes seen as his masterpiece. (He was working on the final revision of *Enfantines* in 1917–18 during his prolonged sojourn in Alicante, while pursuing the Butler translations.) In this particular story the protagonist, who is not named, is thirteen years old, almost fourteen, and because of the details suggesting that the setting is mainly Valbois, Larbaud's family home in the Bourbonnais countryside, near St. Pourc,ain-sur-Sioule, there would be little risk in assuming that he is a projection of Larbaud himself at the same age. Finding himself liberated from the lycée's program because the holidays have begun, he freely sets about inventing his own program of summer studies for the sheer joy of it. This of course implies a critique of the official one, to which he has been subjected during his last term at the *lycée*.

He dreams of being invited to participate in the elaboration of a scholarly work such as a "Lexique de la langue de Racan par MM. les Elèves de Quatrième du Collège X de Paris."[20] His criticism of the system is that students are always doing exercises but never really working on a serious project: *"Toujours s'exercer et ne jamais rien faire."*[21]

It thus becomes clear that Larbaud and Butler are in agreement on this particular point of pedagogy, confirming Larbaud's growing conviction that there were large ideological aspects of Butler's work with which he could identify.

The boarding house in which Ernest lives in *The Way of All Flesh*, as he begins his work as a missionary, is run by Mrs. Jupp, who becomes a considerable *personnage* in the novel. Her boarding house provides this critical part of the novel with a certain unity of place, and in fact much more: it soon becomes

---

19   op. cit. transl., pp. 36–37.
20   Pléiade, p. 494.
21   Pléiade, p. 493.

a highly dramatized microcosm and may possibly have been inspired by Madame Vaucquer's Parisian boarding house in Balzac's *Le Père Goriot*. As Larbaud points out in the preface to the French *Erewhon*, Butler's friend Miss Savage had attempted to interest Butler in the works of Balzac, Taine, Flaubert and Renan, with varying success.[22]

Mrs. Jupp's colourful language might pose a problem for a translator here, for example when, in Chapter 61, as the drama moves toward its climax, she protests against being considered old: "and beyond a haricot vein in one of my legs I'm as young as ever I was."[23]

Larbaud maintains the word *haricot* in French. In the next sentence she utters the malapropism "*insinuendo*" combining the words *insinuation* and *innuendo*. This word may be considered a very appropriate *mot valise* (Larbaud uses the term *pataquès*) for some of the novel's other dialogues, for example in characterizing the language of Ernest's parents.

However, its translation posed a problem for the printers and Larbaud relates in some detail the story of his struggle to convince them that his solution, *insuination*, was well founded, as it combined the suggestive French verb *suinter* (ooze) with the cognate *insinuation*. Despite his note explaining why this version of the word must be maintained, it was "corrected" during proof reading, much to his dismay.[24]

It was at Mrs. Jupp's boarding house that Butler set the stage for the traumatic event that triggers the central crisis of the novel and allows him to dramatize his ideas about unconscious repression as a significant Victorian problem at both the individual and societal levels. Although the theories of Freud on this subject would become known in the English speaking world among some of his colleagues in both Britain and the United States before the First World War, shortly after the time when *The Way of All Flesh* was first published (1903) and became a major literary event in Britain, Freud was not a literary influence until the 1920s. Larbaud's French translation of *The Way of All Flesh* (*Ainsi va toute chair*) now appears to have accompanied (if it did not immediately precede) the early impact of Freud in France.

Ernest, maintaining his blundering image as the "antihero," makes the mistake of accosting an innocent young lady who is another of Mrs. Jupp's tenants. He soon finds himself in court at a hearing before a magistrate, after which he is condemned to a prison sentence, providing Butler with an opportunity to satirize the judiciary of the time in a caricature implying that

---

22 op. cit., p. ix.
23 op. cit., p. 249.
24 *Sous L'invocation de St. Jérôme* (O.C., 8). Troisième Partie: "Technique," p. 360.

the universities, as well as society at large, had become virtual police states, as shown in the presiding judge's summation:

> At Cambridge you were shielded from impurity by every obstacle which virtuous and vigilant authorities could devise.... At night proctors patrolled the streets and dogged your steps if you tried to go into any haunt where the presence of vice was suspected. By day the females who were admitted within the college walls were selected mainly on the score of age and ugliness.[25]

The French translation of this caricature underscores its absurdity, lending a farcical and entertaining note to an excellent example of Butlerian wit. It is of course this amused observation of human folly from the point of view of the mature narrator, Overton, that gives the novel its particular appeal. Larbaud rises to the occasion:

> A Cambridge toutes les barrières qu'une vertueuse et vigilante autorité a pu imaginer ont été dressées en vue de vous protéger contre l'impureté....La nuit, les censeurs parcouraient les rues et épiaient vos pas si vous essayiez d'aller dans quelque lieu ou on soupçonnait la présence du vice. Le jour les femmes qu'on laissait entrer dans l'enceinte du collège étaient choisies en raison de leur âge et de leur laideur.[26]

The language of "officialese" is somewhat exaggerated here, creating a mockery that is in keeping with certain modes of popular French humour, and giving the impression that Ernest's seeming *naiveté* is part of his offence, thus placing Victorian moralizing and hypocrisy above the law. This inference does not escape Larbaud: "Vous n'avez même pas eu le bon sens de distinguer une fille honnête d'une prostituée."[27]

As we can see in the rendering of this episode, one of several ways in which *The Way of All Flesh* pointed in the direction of the twentieth century novel on both sides of the Channel and of the Atlantic, was in its expression of the notion of the "unconscious mind" both incidentally and in the development of the plot. This is clearly related to the notion of repression. In Chapter 29,

---

25 *Way of all Flesh*, p. 251.
26 transl., p. 278.
27 Ibid.

when Ernest is left by his parents in Dr. Skinner's boarding school he finds himself alone for a time:

> Here Ernest's unconscious self took the matter up and made a resistance to which his conscious self was unequal, by tumbling himself off his chair in a fit of fainting.[28]

> Mais ici *le moi inconscient* d'Ernest se chargea de l'affaire et fit une résistance dont son moi conscient était incapable: il le fit tomber de sa chaise par terre, sans connaissance.[29]

Thus the expression *le moi inconscient* had already demonstrated that the language of psychiatry, already well established, was no hurdle for Larbaud. In Butler's time, however, psychiatry was only beginning to be developed in London and Paris as a branch of medicine and after Ernest's major "nervous breakdown" (described as "nervous prostration")[30] when his marriage ends in disaster, Overton takes him to see "one of the most eminent doctors in London" who practises his own version of "psychiatry," although the term was not yet used.

The doctor's prescription consists of a visit to Westminster Abbey to hear the *Te Deum* played on the organ and secondly a visit to the London Zoo, where the value of observing, for a half hour or so, the large mammals, and particularly the hippopotamus, the rhinoceros and the elephants, is stressed.

Larbaud, while translating this passage, may have experienced an amusing reference to a play on the word *hippopotame* that was very familiar to him, given that in some of the letters exchanged with his friend the poet Léon-Paul Fargue, we find Fargue addressing Larbaud as: "Vieux Papotame" or" Vieux Dépotame"[31] and further examples of Larbaud signing himself "Dépothèse"[32] and again "Hippotade."[33]

This is clearly a private joke which expressed Fargue's allegedly "*gaulois*" personality well. Larbaud and Fargue played important roles in one another's lives, Larbaud finding a publisher for Fargue, whom he (like St.John Perse) considered one of the major French poets of the time. It was also Fargue who discovered the secluded courtyard in the Latin Quarter in Paris, off the rue

---

28 *Way of all Flesh*, p. 171.
29 transl., pp. 189–190.
30 *Way of All Flesh*, p. 324.
31 Cf. Léon-Paul Fargue–Valery Larbaud *Correspondance* (Paris: Gallimard, 1971), p. 266.
32 Ibid., p. 148.
33 Ibid., p. 266.

du Cardinal Lemoine, in which Larbaud's Paris apartment, from the early 1920s until 1935, was situated.

It seems that this private joke may have begun with a comment on the part of Fargue on a well-known photo of Larbaud wearing a panama hat, which Fargue seems to have interpreted as "hippopotamic." Later, while visiting the Lisbon zoo, Larbaud made a point of tossing a treat to the hippopotamus and in his diary we also find references to his visits to the hippo which, at that time, resided in the zoo of the Jardin des Plantes, not at all far from Larbaud's apartment.

Although the psychiatrical understanding of terms such as "unconscious mind" and "the subconscious" clearly leads to Freud and his disciples, and to the development of psychoanalysis, in his work on evolution Butler had been theorizing on another kind of unconsciousness: that which may be deduced in animal and human instincts inherited from the past. He considered these to be vital factors in evolution.

One example of this kind of unconsciousness is incarnate in the character of the admirable Towneley in *The Way of All Flesh*, in the form of what was, at the time portrayed in the novel, called "good breeding," applying the concept of natural selection to humans. Towneley represents a character who in literary terms might have descended from the traditional heroes of early romantic novels. Butler, creating a structural reversal, makes this paragon of civilized virtues, (who might indeed have been the novel's "hero") into a minor character, but nonetheless with an important role.

It is as if unconscious "good breeding," a natural product of human evolution over many generations, had resulted in a being who is well balanced, at ease in the world, talented and happy. Ernest and Towneley had been fellow students at Cambridge. Butler brings them together unexpectedly, some time after Ernest's ordination as a priest, creating a vivid contrast which gives full expression to Towneley's "good breeding":

> One evening, however, about this time, whom should he see coming along a small street not far from his own but, of all persons in the world, Towneley, looking as full of life and good spirits as ever....Much as Ernest liked him he found himself shrinking from speaking to him, and was endeavouring to pass him without doing so when Towneley saw him and stopped him at once, being pleased to see an old Cambridge face. He seemed for a moment a little *confused* at being seen in such a neighbourhood, but recovered himself so soon that

Ernest hardly noticed it, and then plunged into a few kindly remarks about old times. *Ernest felt that he quailed as he saw Towneley's eye wander to his white necktie* and saw that he was being reckoned up and rather disapprovingly, reckoned up as a parson. It was the merest passing shade upon Towneley's face, but Ernest had felt it.[34]

Mais voici qu'un soir de l'époque dont nous parlons, Ernest vit venir, du bout d'une petite rue pas très éloignée de la sienne, la personne du monde qu'il s'attendait le moins à rencontrer: Towneley lui-même, aussi plein de vie et d'entrain qu'autrefois.... Malgré toute la sympathie qu'il avait pour lui, Ernest se sentit gêné à l'idée d'avoir à lui parler et il essayait de passer près de lui sans paraître le reconnaître, lorsque Towneley l'aperçut et l'arrêta net, tout heureux de voir une figure de Cambridge. Il parut d'abord un peu *confus* d'être rencontré dans un pareil quartier, mais il se remit si vite que ce fut à peine si Ernest s'en aperçut, et tout de suite il parla aimablement de leurs souvenirs communs. *Ernest se sentit frémir lorsqu'il vit le regard de Towneley se poser un instant sur sa cravate blanche*, et qu'il se dit que l'autre découvrait, et découvrait avec désapprobation, qu'il était curé. Ce n'avait été qu'une ombre qui avait passé sur la figure de Towneley, mais Ernest l'avait sentie.[35]

(Regarding a detail of this translation, Larbaud evidently considers the adjective *confus* (suggesting embarrassment) as an appropriate translation for the English *confused* since they are etymologically related even though not quite cognate.)

This trauma ends when Ernest makes an inconsequential remark and Towneley replies with a "No, no, no," and goes away, forcing Ernest to face up to the realities of his life and leading him to the realization that he has been little more than a "fraud." Ernest must remake himself and become "*un nouvel être*" to use Gide's excellent expression in his early novel *L'Immoraliste*, and one can appreciate Gide's admiration for Butler's humanism. The process whereby Ernest will attain his eventual self-realization has now been set in motion.

Larbaud translates the traumatic word *eye* here as *le regard* (de Towneley) when the latter disapproves of Ernest's priesthood, reminding present

---

34 op. cit. ch. 57, p. 234.
35 op. cit., transl., ch. 57, p. 259.

day readers of one of Sartre's expressions in his exposition of his form of "existentialism" which later came to be known with the publication of *La Nausée* in 1938 and especially with *L'Existentialisme est un humanisme* (1946). We see this, for example, in the importance Sartre attached to "*le regard de l'autre*" in the acknowledgement of another's being. Certainly Ernest's self identification as a priest has been suddenly shattered and he is confronted with what might now be called the necessity of an existential choice. This of course implies that everything Ernest does and says until he has made that choice will have the hollow, dishonest ring, deriving from not courageously facing up to his real situation, a symptom of what Sartre was later to term *la mauvaise foi*.

Indeed, Butler uses expressions in various parts of *The Way of All Flesh* which seem, in Larbaud's translation, to anticipate expressions and notions that will later become familiar in Sartre's epistemology. In the early chapters, for example, Butler traces the careers of Ernest's grandfather (George Pontifex) and father (Theobald). We learn that Theobald had had no genuine desire to be ordained a priest but had been pressured by his father. Thus his priesthood puts him in a false position which is further intensified when Theobald, a generation later, attempts to induce his own son Ernest into adopting the same vocation. Butler's narrator observes:

> I have heard it said sometimes that such and such a person's life was a lie.[36]
>
> J'entends dire quelquefois que la vie d'Un Tel ou d'Une Telle n'est faite que de mensonges.[37]

This notion that a life can be a living lie is not as satisfactorily expressed in French as might be desired, in this respect, since Butler, foretelling Sartre, is suggesting that the very "essence" of a life can amount to a lie.

However, Larbaud's translation of *lie* in the plural (*mensonges*) doesn't quite convey this concept. Since we have here one of the important themes of the novel, at both explicit and implicit levels, it is to be expected that Larbaud will have to face this challenge in other places. For example, at the beginning of Chapter 4 of *Erewhon Revisited* we find that Professor Panky is characterized explicitly as having "thrown himself so earnestly into his work that he had become a living lie."[38]

---

36 *The Way of All Flesh*, ch. 19, p. 78.
37 Transl., ch. 19, p. 87.
38 op. cit., Everyman edition, ch. 4, p. 218.

This time Larbaud translates: "Il avait pris sa fonction tellement au sérieux qu'il était devenu un mensonge incarné."[39] Thus Butler is putting forth a critique of Ernest's family that now seems to exemplify Sartre's interpretation of *la mauvaise foi*, as, for example, when Sartre (in *L'Existentialisme est un humanisme*) says: "tout homme qui invente un déterminisme est un homme de mauvaise foi."[40]

Some French novels published in the late nineteenth century, before the appearance of *The Way of All Flesh*, had protagonists who had yielded to the determinism of either exterior or psychological forces which become "excuses" for a stance that could be seen as irresponsible, as for example the conditioning of the murder in Barrès' *Les Déracinés* (1897) or the disastrous consequences of the teaching of Adrien Sixte in Bourget's *Le Disciple* (1889) and again in Zola's *Rougon-Macquart* series in which Taine's notion that we are all "products" of *"race, milieu, moment"* is presupposed. Sartre, in fact, does refer to one novel in this series, *La Terre*, as an example.

Butler seems to create another very Sartrean "situation" when, in Chapter 83, some time after Ernest has been metamorphosed into his *vita nuova*, he revisits his family home and finds that the decorative scheme has not changed at all since he had last been there a very long time before. Sartre's use of Second Empire furniture in his drama *Huis Clos* in order to convey the notion of the *en soi*, as opposed to the *pour soi*, that is the reduction of the human to the status of "things," comes to mind:

> The furniture and the ornaments on the chimney piece were just as they had been....In the drawing room and on either side of the fireplace there hung the Carlo Dolci and the Sassoferato as in old times; there was the watercolour of a scene on the Lago Maggiore....The paper on the walls was unchanged; the roses were still waiting for the bees.[41]

> Le mobilier et les ornements qui décoraient la cheminée étaient exactement tels qu'il les avait toujours vus....Au mur du salon de chaque côté de la cheminée, il y avait, comme autrefois, le Carlo Dolciet le Sassoferato; il y avait l'aquarelle, représentant une scène qui se passait sur le lac Majeur....Le papier des murs était le même; les roses attendaient encore les abeilles.[42]

---

39 op. cit., p. 62.
40 op. cit. (Paris: Nagel, 1964), p. 81.
41 op. cit., p. 278.
42 op. cit.transl., ch. 83, p. 379.

The reference here to Lago Maggiore, quite apart from its significance in expressing the notion that Ernest had by this time evolved into a new being (a "*pour soi*") before returning to his family home, and could therefore experience the latter as an "*en soi*," no doubt held another very different significance for Larbaud as it was one of the locations in Italy, as was also the Lago di Orta, where his paths literally crossed those of Butler. He explains this in *Le Vain Travail de voir divers pays*.[43] Varallo, a particularly significant Butlerian site, as Butler's *Alps and Sanctuaries* demonstrate, is also not far to the west of Lago Maggiore.

This scene in *The Way of All Flesh*, by confronting Ernest, now a "*nouvel être*," with the family setting he had long left behind, expresses, then, in dramatic terms, the metamorphosis that has taken place in his very definition of himself. Thus Butler's novel demonstrates a refusal of determinism in Ernest's life, meaning that the publication of the French translation of the novel would inevitably place it among the French novels of the period, which, as we have seen, were reacting against the dogmas of the school of "*naturalisme*" as illustrated especially by Zola, and doing so by refusing determinism and replacing it more optimistically with the Gidean notion of "becoming." Hence the translation of *The Way of All Flesh (Ainsi va toute chair)* corresponded well to the revitalized humanism that was then being cultivated by *La Nouvelle Revue Française* (both as a publishing firm and a periodical).

However, this perspective does not seem to have been recognized at the time of the publication of Larbaud's transltion, at least not developed in critical articles or studies, and *Ainsi va toute chair* had, at first, only a "lukewarm" reception. Shortly after its appearance Emile Henriot, one of the more prominent critics of the period, expressed reservations about Butler's "démonstrations sociologiques et moralisantes."[44] Gilbert de Voisins, seemingly offended by Butler's irony (although it might have been compared with Stendhal's) also expressed a very conservative reaction to Butler.[45] *Ainsi va toute chair* was preferred, nonetheless, to the French *Erewhon* and was eventually published in Gallimard's *Livre de Poche* series where it has since remained in print.

Thus Ernest, in *The Way of All Flesh*, does achieve liberation from various forms of potential determinism and Larbaud's translation would, in fact, place *The Way of All Flesh* among the more recent, deliberately anti-deterministic French novels of the time, published before and just after the First World

---

43 Larbaud, *Oeuvres* (Pléiade), p. 853.
44 E. Henriot, "La Découverte de Samuel Butler." *L'Europe Nouvelle* (1921), p. 1597.
45 In "Notes," *La Nouvelle Revue Française*, 1 juillet 1921.

War, which were reacting against the "naturalistic" novel. Some of these do so by exploring the theme of the gratuitous act and "gratuitous life" as a means of achieving a total liberation from any form of determinism. This highly experimental phenomenon is illustrated in several important novels of the time: Larbaud's own *A.O. Barnabooth*, (1913) in which a multi-millionaire suffers from the temptations of kleptomania, Gide's *Les Caves du Vatican* (1914) in which the murder is meant to be seen as "gratuitous" and later *Les Faux-Monnayeurs* (1926) in which one of the principal protagonists, Bernard, after he has discovered that he is "illegitimate," has to invent a new identity. In the meantime his very life has become "disinterested."

Another example occurs in Alain-Fournier's novel *Le Grand Meaulnes* (1913). One of the three male protagonists, Frantz de Galais, whose bride has not shown up on their wedding day, attempts to shoot himself but fails and then lives "only for the game" with gypsies. In Jules Romains' *Les Copains* (1913) an alliance of close friends decides, "just for fun," to awaken a sleepy town in a remote part of central France. In these novels it is, then, the notion of the "gratuitous" that provides a potent symbolic means of refusing the threat of forces that might otherwise have been capable of predetermining the actions of the protagonists. The mature Ernest, in the *dénouement* of *The Way of All Flesh*, has been liberated from outside forces through good fortune and finds himself confronted with many choices. These now classical novels of the time do therefore provide a context for Larbaud's translations.

The choices Ernest says he would now like to make for his destiny have a resemblance with those that Samuel Butler actually did make: those of a traveller and a writer, and the sort of writing Ernest proposes to do appears to belong to the same *genres* as Butler's.[46] Significantly, Ernest's destiny is in no way "congealed": we are left with the assurance that he is *disponible*, in a state of readiness to assume new forms.[47] The splendid title that Julien Green much later borrowed from Racine's tragedy *Phèdre* comes to mind: "Mille Chemins ouverts" (*A Thousand Open Roads*).

---

46 Butler, *The Way of All Flesh* (1903), Ch. 84, Signet ed., p. 356.
47 Ibid., pp. 356–357.

Chapter 7

Butler: Life and Habit

Undoubtedly the most ambitious and challenging of the Butler translations was *La Vie et l'habitude*, Larbaud's translation of *Life and Habit*, the first of the four book-length treatises in which Butler developed the "neo-Lamarckian" theory of evolution which also permeates much of his other work.

This translation could indeed be understood as the most significant achievement of them all: just as the "Butlers" represent the centrepiece of all Larbaud's translations, *La Vie et l'habitude* could be seen as the centrepiece of the "Butlers."

Larbaud was genuinely impressed with *Life and Habit*, to the point of considering it to have been "la vraie *Evolution Créatrice*" referring, in a letter to Gide, to Bergson's famous treatise, *Creative Evolution*.[1] In the first part of this work Butler is not yet opposed to Darwin but saw his (Butler's) demonstrations of unconscious habits becoming "second nature" as merely an "extended footnote" to *The Origin of Species*.

His intention was merely to modify Darwin somewhat by working in the lineage of Lamarck and the earlier *transformistes*. Darwin, after all, had shown awareness of the importance of unconscious habits in his own evolution theory. Larbaud familiarized himself thoroughly with this entire field before beginning his translation.

When Butler had come upon St. George Jackson Mivart's work, *The Genesis of Species* (1871), while finishing *Life and Habit* (1877) it opened his eyes to the need for something to account for variations, and that led him in turn toward a more skeptical view of Darwin's theory. The earlier chapters of *Life and Habit* were then incorporated as support for his new position. The development of this new anti-Darwinism is admirably explained by Basil Willey in *Darwin and Butler: Two Versions of Evolution*.[2]

During his New Zealand years (early 1860s) on his isolated sheep ranch, Butler had become fascinated with Darwin's *Origin of Species*, which had only

---

1 Larbaud, *Lettres à André Gide* (Stols: La Haye, Paris, 1948), p. 121.
2 op. cit. (London: Chatto and Windus, 1960) p. 72.

recently appeared in 1859. Nevertheless, his readings in earlier evolution theory and his own observations, led him gradually to believe that Darwin had been too "mechanistic" in his premise that evolution combined the principle of natural selection (that is pure chance, including possibilities of variation) with the principle of the survival of the fittest. He came to think that Darwin had dismissed the work of the earlier *transformistes* too arbitrarily, including that of his own grandfather Erasmus Darwin, and especially Lamarck's, whose theory that acquired characteristics could be transmitted to later generations he thought required a more cautious and respectful examination.

Darwin does sometimes make statements in *The Origin of Species* that sound Lamarckian. For example, in Chapter 8 ("Instinct") we read: "No complex instinct can possibly be produced through natural selection, except by slow and gradual accumulation of numerous slight yet profitable variations."[3] However, in such passages Darwin is not necessarily suggesting that variations are caused by small acts of will power or "design" as Lamarck had done and as Butler was in effect to do.

Darwin and Butler were clearly participating in one of the major debates of the nineteenth and twentieth centuries. Much of this debate had been published in French, so that Larbaud, in his translation of *Life and Habit*, would have little difficulty in placing Butler in a French language context. Among the many French works on the subject of *transformisme* which Larbaud read, he found the most relevant for his purposes to be:

> A. Armand Bréau de Quatrefages: *Charles Darwin et ses précurseurs Français* (Paris: Baillère, 1870) and *Emules de Darwin.*
>
> B. Edmond Perrier: *La Philosophie zoologique avant Darwin.*[4]
>
> C. Félix Le Dantec: *Néo-Lamarckiens et néo-Darwiniens,*[5] *La Crise du Transformisme*[6] and *Théorie Nouvelle de la vie.*[7] The latter work gives a complete exposé of his doctrine.

Larbaud also consulted *Evolution individuelle et l'hérédité.*[8]

---

3 Charles Darwin, *The Origin of Species* (1859; New York: Modern Library Paperbacks, 1998), p. 320.
4 Paris, 1884.
5 Larbaud, *Journal*, op. cit., p. 320.
6 Ibid., pp. 608–609.
7 Ibid., p. 348
8 op. cit., p. 355.

Larbaud considered Quatrefages "the best critic on these questions."[9] He also preferred Le Dantec to Perrier.[10] He attached particular significance to an eighteenth-century work: Pierre L.M. de Maupertuis, *Le Système de la Nature*.[11] Maupertuis is familiar to students of Voltaire, who targeted Maupertuis in his *conte philosophique* "*Micromégas.*"

Larbaud consulted many other works, in particular: Yves Delage (1854–1920): *Théorie des causes actuelles*, *Les Faits*, and *L'Hérédité et les grands problèmes de la biologie générale*.[12] Works by Geoffroy St. Hilaire (1772–1844) were also consulted, as well as Vianna de Lima, *Exposé sommaire des théories transformistes de Lamarck, Darwin et Haeckel*.[13] Butler's *Life and Habit* is mentioned in the latter work.

A remarkable feature of the evolution debate in the nineteenth century is that it depended entirely on observation, deduction, and hypothesis, given that the work of Gregor Mendel on the genetics of peas, leading to his discovery of chromosomes and genes—that is, of the actual biology of hereditary transmission—was unknown to both Darwin and Butler because of the long delay in its diffusion. (It is well known that Mendel sent Darwin a copy of one of his articles on his discovery, but that it was found unopened in Darwin's mail by his estate following his death.)

In *Life and Habit* Butler also quotes liberally from another French source, Théodule Ribot: *L'Hérédité, étude psychologique sur ses phénomènes, ses lois, ses causes, ses conséquences*.[14] In this work he found an excellent synthesis of the subject.

Modifying Lamarck's hypothesis on the transmission of acquired characteristics, Butler set out, in *Life and Habit*, to show that life, over a great number of generations, does make innumerable small choices such as those that might result from a need to adapt to new environmental conditions. These choices, he believed, may be described as demonstrating a rudimentary form of purposefulness or striving. They could be understood as minimal acts of will. Butler was particularly concerned with the ways in which certain acquired skills, once they are assimilated, are performed without conscious effort as "second nature." He used the example of the piano virtuoso among others, and believed that once skills and habits

---

9 Cf. *Journal*, p. 234, June 17, 1917.
10 Ibid., p. 257, August 16, 1917.
11 In *Les Oeuvres de Monsieur de Maupertuis* (Lyon: Bruyset, 1756), pp. 139–168.
12 Paris, 1903.
13 Paris: Delagrave, 1885.
14 Paris, 1873.

among sentient beings had become unconscious, they (or a predisposition to redevelop them) could then be transmitted to later generations. His thesis was that evolution must be understood as more than an effect of mere "luck," as the Darwinians thought.

As is well known, Butler's theory was once considered erroneous by a majority of scientists. For example, Garrett Hardin, in *Nature and Man's Fate*[15] was incensed by Butler's challenge. Niels Bohr was among the first to defend this "neo-Lamarckian" proposition in recent times, bringing "purposiveness" back into the picture in *Physical Science snd the Problem of Life*.[16]

More recently still, a major work by two eminent scientists in this field has not only defended Butler but gives the theory great prominence in its final chapter: Lynn Margulis & Dorion Sagan, *What is Life?*[17] This remarkable work revives Butler's notion of the unconscious as a factor that must not be neglected. In fact we have here a virtual rehabilitation of Butler the evolutionist. Margulis and Sagan point out that we humans like to imagine that we are in part responsible for our own evolution but refuse irrationally to grant this ability to the rest of life. Butler's thesis is that all living matter is "mnemic," i.e., "it remembers and embodies its own past."[18]

Thus there may be said to be "purposefulness" in all life. Life is "teleological." Darwin, according to Butler, excluded divine purpose but in doing so neglected to address the question of whether there might not be living purpose.

An important theme, developed from the first chapter of *Life and Habit*, is that actions often repeated become instinctive, or, as is said of humans, "second nature." All living matter can "memorize" its behaviour, as in the phenomenon of instinct, which is clearly congenital.

Butler also famously put forward the notion that the "evolution" of machines may be seen as a development that is parallel to biological evolution but occurs at an infinitely faster pace, even to the point at which it could become a threat to life. Since Margulis and Sagan have not only vindicated the significance of Butler's position, but have also made their own excellent *résumé* of it, one could scarcely do better than to follow their own words:

> One Butlerian theme stands out: living mater is mnemic, it remembers and embodies its own past....Life is endowed with consciousness, memory, direction, goal-setting. In Butler's view

---

15 New York: Mentor, 1959.
16 New York: Wiley, 1958, p. 100.
17 New York: Simon and Schuster, 1995.
18 op. cit., p. 183.

> all life, not just human life, is teleological, that is, it strives. Butler claimed that Darwinians missed the teleology, the goal-directedness of life acting for itself.[19]
>
> We agree with Butler that life is matter that chooses. Each living being, Samuel Butler argued, responds sentiently to a changing environment and tries during its life to alter itself....Gradually, in tiny increments, living systems with non-negotiable needs for food, water, and energy, transformed themselves in wily and persistent ways.[20]
>
> Butler believed minute changes effected by organisms and their environment begin as conscious pursuits, but end as unconscious practice. For Butler amoebas too have their little wants, their little spheres of influence, their little "tool boxes" with which they materially change their environment, pursue their little goals.[21]

They also quote an article of Butler's in which he sums up a part of his thinking on evolution, explaining why he defended the pre-Darwinian evolutionists, that is, because "living beings themselves were involved in natural selection.....The development of the steam engine and the microscope is due to intelligence and design, which did indeed utilize chance suggestions, but which improved on these, and directed each step of their accumulation, though never foreseeing more than a step or two ahead."[22]

Butler had first developed his thesis in *Darwin among the Machines* and *Lucubratio Ebria*.[23] These are highly significant reprints of two letters (long thought to be lost) to the editor of the Christchurch, New Zealand, *Press*, originally published on June 13, 1863 and July 29, 1865 respectively. In a much more recent work, Lynn Margulis describes an experiment by Sonneborn and Jannine Beisson on a cell, some of whose cilia constituents were turned around 180 degrees and then replaced.[24] It was found that these appeared in offspring cells... in this reversed position....for at least two hundred generations."[25]

---

19 Ibid.
20 op. cit., p. 185.
21 Ibid.
22 Butler, Samuel. "The Deadlock in Darwinism," in *The Humour of Homer and Other Essays* (Freeport, NY: Books for Libraries Press, pp. 253–254).
23 Cf. Samuel Butler, *The Note-Books of Samuel Butler* (London: Fifield, 1912) pp. 42–53.
24 Lynn Margulis, *Symbiotic Planet* (Amherst, MA: Science Writers, 1998).
25 op. cit., p. 27.

As the results of this experiment demonstrated the inheritance of acquired characteristics, they could be described as "Lamarckian." Margulis, then, far from dismissing the Lamarckian hypothesis, finds evidence that the Lamarckian and Butlerian views must no longer be considered unorthodox.

Although he was writing before genes were understood, it was important to Butler to demonstrate that organic life must, of necessity, be a continuum from one generation to the next through the transmission of unconscious memory. There is an intuitive understanding here of a process that is analogous to that of the functioning of the genes which he describes as "a continuation of the personality of every ovum in the chain of ancestry."[26] Larbaud's comments in English on *Life and Habit*, in his *Journal* for 1917, express his understanding of the book's importance not only in the context of the evolution debate but among all the great books of the nineteenth century:

> *Life and Habit* is much more than a theory....*Life and Habit* is one of the grandest books of the XIXth Century, and, indeed, of the last three hundred years. It covers an immense area of life, thought and experience. Indeed it seems as if Lamarck, Darwin and all the Evolution writers had been sent only to prepare the way for *Life and Habit*, to announce it and to make it possible.[27]

The translation of *Life and Habit* into French therefore becomes a significant commitment, and Larbaud prepares himself for the task in a thoroughly professional manner. In the *Journal* entry for April 11, 1917, he says he is rereading Darwin's *Origin of Species* for a comparison with Moulinié's French translation, and he notes his intention to make a list "of all the technical terms used by both Darwin and Butler." He says he will then compare these with terms used by Quatrefages and Perrier.[28] "I mean that I wish to choose (only) those renderings which are commonly used by the greatest French authorities on Evolution."[29]

In his translation Larbaud constantly clarifies Butler's text by improving his style, which is sometimes weak in logical connections and at other times doesn't seem to emphasize important points effectively. So again the French version becomes a considerable improvement of the original. One example might be:

---

26 Cf. Butler, *Life and Habit* (1877), Shrewsbury ed., vol. 4, p. 70.
27 Larbaud, *Journal* (December 30, 1917), pp. 281–282.
28 op. cit., p. 214.
29 Ibid.

> The weak point in Mr. Darwin's theory *would be a deficiency, so to speak, of motive power* to originate and direct the variations which time is to accumulate.[30]

> Le point faible de la théorie de Mr. Darwin, *c'est qu'on n'y trouve pas ce qu'on pourrait appeler la puissance motrice* qui produit et dirige les variations que le temps se charge d'accumuler.[31]

Here Larbaud replaces a somewhat imprecise expression in the original with a much bolder, unhesitant phrasing that reinforces Butler's argument.

The phenomenon of mimicry is introduced by Butler to establish his position:

> [Some] creatures have conceived the idea of *making themselves* like other creatures or objects which it was to their advantage or pleasure to *resemble*.[32]

> Il y a des êtres qui ont conçu l'idée de *s'efforcer* de se rendre semblables à d'autres êtres ou à des objets qu'ils avaient avantage ou plaisir à *copier*.[33]

Thus Larbaud translates *making themselves* with *s'efforcer* and *resemble* with *copier*. These terms reinforce Butler's neo-Lamarckian argument by being more explicit and "outspoken." This view has, of course, remained controversial, but the opposing view, to the effect that these results, like all other forms of *transformisme*, could be obtained only by natural selection over time, has itself been opposed by the observation that the realization of the precise and necessary markings (on insects' wings for example) that would be required, would take far too long a time to occur by a fortunate accident.

On Saturday May 19, 1917, Larbaud makes a comment that relates Butler's conceptions to the French tradition of evolution:

> I see from what Quatrefages says that, as I suspected, many of S.B.'s ideas are not new. They have much in common with those of De Maillet, Robinet, and other French *philosophes* and "rêveurs" of the XVIIIth Century. However, he gives them a much more serious basis, and all the clearness and strength of his style.[34]

---

30 Butler, *Life and Habit*, ch. 13 (Champaign, IL: Book Jungle Reprint), p. 174.
31 Butler, op. cit., transl. (Paris: Gallimard, 1922), p. 241.
32 Butler, op. cit. Book Jungle Reprint: ch. 11, p. 138.
33 Butler, op. cit., transl., op. cit. ch. 11, p. 191.
34 op. cit., p. 223.

In his entry for May 31, 1917, Larbaud expresses strong reservations about Darwin's *The Descent of Man* which he calls "a really bad book."[35] He then praises Butler: "Un-scientific as he is, Butler is by far the greater man of the two, and Darwin looks sadly '*officiel*' when compared with S.B."[36]

On June 11, 1917, Larbaud finished reading Butler's *Evolution Old and New* and writes very enthusiastically about it to the point of feeling an urge to translate it along with the five volumes to whose translation be is already committed. However, he soon comes to the realization that such an additional translation might lead to *el cuento de no acabar*. (The story of the work that is forever unfinished.)[37]

Larbaud's reaction to *Evolution Old and New* amounts to a final conversion to almost all that Butler stands for. Having just read the last pages of the section entitled *Rome and Pantheism* he writes:

> Indeed I have become much attached to S.B. That man whom I knew only vaguely before 1915, appears to me, now, as 'une âme soeur' almost. Well, he feels like me on: (a) The relations between parents and children; (b) Money and rich people; (c) Europe "une et indivisible"; (d) Rome and the Church; (e) His love for London and Italy; (f) His taste for French literature.

Besides, there is his way of putting things, which pleases me more than I am able to express it in my translation.[38]

The expression "*une âme soeur*" is a quotation of the phrase Baudelaire had used to express his commitment to the work of Edgar Allan Poe, whose *Tales* he famously translated into French.

The effort to place Butler precisely in the evolution of evolution theory led Larbaud to see him as an "outsider scientifically." "But from a literary point of view he is not. Indeed he belongs to the highest and best tradition and I think we cannot ask for (anything) more than this."[39]

As spring merges into summer Larbaud's Journal also reports on how his work merges into other pleasures:

---

35 op. cit., p. 227.
36 Ibid., p. 228 (May 31, 1917).
37 Ibid., p. 232.
38 Ibid.
39 Ibid., June 17, 1917, p. 234.

> I woke up at 5½ a. m., made coffee, washed, dressed, breakfasted, and then began to work, *sin parar*, up to dinner-time. I spent two hours on my *gandulona* chair, then worked again. Then we went to Don José's where we played tennis for an hour. Then, as there was *tertulia* in front of the house, we joined the ladies. Kiddie was not there. When we came home we found *tertulia* at our own house (Pepita S., Maria A. etc.). I am reading Quatrefages' *Emules* and have just finished the long chapter on A.R. Wallace.[40]

Somewhat later he writes one of his more memorable comments on Alicante: "When I am well enough to work Alicante is not a provincial town without life....Alicante is a town where something important is taking place: the translating of Samuel Butler's books into French."[41]

When certain parts of Larbaud's *Journal* were published for the first time in October 1954, passages concerning his life in Alicante are known to have "raised eyebrows," given that the First World War was raging at the time. However, since Larbaud implicitly considered himself a citizen of Europe, able to see the world from the viewpoint of several of Europe's nations and speaking and writing in their various languages, his situation in Alicante provides a very good example of this all encompassing view. At no point in his *Journal* does he attempt to analyse, justify, or defend Europeanism as understood in this way, but he is nonetheless living out his commitment to it.

His study of evolution theory meant a search for expressions of it in various cultures at various periods. In his diary entry for October 28, 1917,[42] he believes he has found a relationship between the evolution movement and the Romantic movement in literature:

> The origin of both movements can be traced back to the XVIIIth century *philosophes*; later on, the literature of Evolution gets more and more scientific just as Romantic poetry and literature get more and more "egocentric."...Le Dantec is just a neo-romantic.[43]

---

40 Ibid. pp. 235–236.
41 Ibid., p. 277.
42 *Journal*, p. 266
43 Ibid.

In pursuing this interest Larbaud noted that the eighteenth-century *philosophe* Maupertuis had already developed a theory of transmissible unconscious memory and he discussed this at some length with Henry Festing Jones when the two met in London in September 1919. The question of the neglect of Maupertuis in the great debate intrigued Larbaud. He comments:

> Strange that neither Charles Darwin nor Butler nor Francis Darwin ever said anything about Maupertuis...that so many scholars, writers etc. should have passed by such a great precursor....Both Edmond Perrier and Yves Delage seem to believe they are discovering him.[44]

The particular significance of Maupertuis as an eighteenth-century predecessor of Butler is that Maupertuis appeared to have been the first to have proposed the inheritance of unconscious memory. Larbaud also points out that Edmond Perrier develops this notion in detail in the first chapters of his *La Philosophie Zoologigue avant Darwin*.[45] Referring to Butler's German correspondent Professor Ewald Hering, Larbaud suggests that this theory ought to be called: " The Maupertuis and Yves Delage-Hering-Butler theory."[46]

Maupertuis had arrived at a deistic interpretation of evolution to the effect that there must be "something more" to it than a mere matter of chance and environment, and in *Le Système de la Nature* he brings in the influence of the "Supreme Being."[47] He concludes: "Les éléments, eux-mêmes doués d'intelligence, s'arrangent et s'unissent pour remplir le vues du Créateur."[48]

This notion of "something more" might be interpreted as pointing toward what Bergson was later to call *l'élan vital*, this also being an excellent expression of Butler's view. The "something more" was becoming a central concept in the evolution debate as it developed through Lamarck and Darwin to Butler and on to Margulis, in their various interpretations of exactly what it was.

Another of Larbaud's comparisons between the work of Butler and works in other languages, on this occasion the Spanish language, concerned a study by the sixteenth-century writer Juan Huarte (c. 1530–1592) entitled *Examen de Ingenios* (1575). Larbaud comments with respect to Huarte: "It gives us an

---

44 op. cit., pp. 275–276, December 6, 1917.
45 Larbaud, *Journal*, p. 342 (31 juillet, 1917).
46 Ibid., p. 279.
47 In *Les Oeuvres de Monsieur de Maupertuis* 2 (Lyon: Bruyset, 1756), pp. 139–168.
48 op. cit., p. 167.

idea of how *Life and Habit* will look two hundred years hence....A beautiful mind, a sympathetic, noble and brave man. Such will appear Samuel Butler, I think, to his readers of the twenty-second century."[49]

Regarding prose in classical French works that might serve as a model for his translation of *Life and Habit*, Larbaud refers to the polemical prose of Pascal in *Les Provinciales* (1657) published during the ongoing debates of the Counter Reformation concerning the subject of divine grace.

Thus on January 8, 1919, he writes:

> After dinner the reading of *Les Provinciales* preparatory to the translation work. A short *paseo*....I dare say it would be possible to translate the whole of *Life and Habit* (except what there is of "Evolution" expressions and technicalities) without using any word or *giro* (turn of phrase) that were not to be found in *Les Provinciales*.[50]

Ten days later he makes a comment on his work which expresses a deeply felt sense of identity with both Butler and Pascal: "More work in the afternoon (SB) translating *(Life and Habit) con gusto* and sometimes with the idea that I am translating it in order that Pascal (might) read it and not be shocked by the language."[51] Paule Moron, the editor of the complete (2009) edition of Larbaud's *Journal*, suggests that it is particularly the tone of "refutation" in Pascal's *Lettres Provinciales* that Larbaud found helpful to have in mind while translating *Life and Habit*.[52]

The next day, reading Lamarck, Larbaud finds "curious coincidences in the expressions used, between Lamarck and Samuel Butler."[53]

Larbaud was very pleased with his translation of *Life and Habit*. It could be noted in passing that he also held a very high opinion of Butler's French:

> [Butler] knew French very well. I have already remarked how well he has translated pages and pages of Lamarck in *Evolution Old and New*, and how almost always he has known the exact value of the French words or phrases which he has thrown in here and there in his books, especially in *The Way*, where I have

---

49 Ibid., p. 407, January 11, 1918.
50]]Larbaud, *Journal*, pp. 471–472.
51 Ibid., p. 474, January 23, 1919.
52 op. cit., p. 804, note 156.
53 Ibid., p. 475.

let them stand (except in two or three instances) just as they were in the English text.⁵⁴

Larbaud considers Butler's translations of Lamarck "good but very freely done."⁵⁵

Before looking at examples of Larbaud's translation of *Life and Habit*, we might well refer to examples already selected by Anna-Marie Aldaz in the dissertation to which we have already referred: *Valery Larbaud as Translator of Samuel Butler*.⁵⁶ She points out, for example, that Larbaud is somewhat perplexed about the appropriate French translation of the English biological term "sport" (which Butler also used as a verb) for an "abrupt variation." Larbaud notes that the word in this sense had previously been translated by Barbier as *variations brusques* and by Naudin as *variation désordonnée*.⁵⁷

> Which of the two must I use? I suppose I must reject "variation désordonnée" on the same principle that made me reject "transformisme"—that is, as *continental* expressions. The English School (at least in the days of S.B.) used "Evolution" and "Evolutionism" and not "Transformism"; it used "sports" and not *variation désordonnée*....Still I am sorry to have to give up *variation désordonnée*.⁵⁸

Larbaud goes further and creates the verb "sporter" in French, (following Butler) as he points out in an article in *La Nouvelle Revue Française* for September 1, 1920: "La Question des anglicismes." He describes this in the article as "un anglicisme dont je prends l'entière responsabilité."⁵⁹

Aldaz also comments on some of Larbaud's solutions to stylistic hurdles in *Life and Habit*, given that Butler's sentences are often long, and often contain parentheses. One means by which she believes Larbaud achieves greater clarity is by resorting to a milder kind of parenthesis which he considered to have a greater degree of subordination to the main clause, rendered in French by what is known as "la virgule-tiret," that is, a comma followed by a dash.⁶⁰ Larbaud

---

54 *Journal*, p. 253, July 22, 1917.
55 *Journal*, p. 461, Dec. 8, 1918.
56 University of Oregon, 1969.
57 op. cit., p. 227, May 31, 1917.
58 Ibid.
59 op. cit., p. 480. Cf. Aldaz, op. cit., p. 140. Ch. 5, "Foreign Expressions in the Original and in the Translation" (pp. 138–140).
60 Cf. Larbaud, "Technique" in *Oeuvres Complètes* 8, p. 281.

believed that *la virgule-tiret* had first been introduced to French from English by Balzac, in view of its frequent use in Balzac's early novels.

Aldaz provides an example from Chapter 8:

> But as regards the actual memory of such identity (unconscious memory, but still clearly memory), we observe…[61]

> Mais ce qui est de la mémoire réelle de cette identité,—mémoire inconsciente mais évidemment mémoire,—nous remarquons…[62]

As we have seen, Larbaud was very scrupulous about the need to express all of Butler's meaning and equally so about avoiding any additional meaning. However, Aldaz does discover a passage in which Larbaud developed the meaning in his own way. Pursuing his concept of unconscious "grace" Butler writes (in figurative language) referring to St.Paul:

> The true grace he drove out into the wilderness…into Piora, and into such-like places."[63]

Larbaud, for the sake of euphony, adds a few words:

> À Piora et dans ces coins obscurs de l'Italie et de Sicile."[64]

As Aldaz points out, Larbaud excuses himself in his *Notes* at the end of the translation, remarking that this is the only place where he had been knowingly unfaithful to the text. [65] He adds that in his conversations with H. Festing Jones, the latter observed that Butler had not yet been to Sicily at the time *Life and Habit* was published. Butler did visit Piedmont almost every year for many years, however, and there were still harvest festivities at Piora which reflected an originally pagan tradition.[66]

---

61 op. cit., p. 101.
62 op. cit. transl., p. 141. Cf. Aldaz, op. cit., p. 164.
63 op. cit., ch. 2, p. 35.
64 op. cit., transl., p. 50.
65 Ibid., p. 288.
66 Ibid.

Chapter 8

Butler: Life and Habit—Further Considerations

One: On Certain Acquired Habits (De Certaines Habitudes acquises)
Possibly one of Butler's most famous demonstrations, in *Life and Habit*, concerning the manner in which frequently repeated acts may eventually be possessed to such a degree that they tend to become instinctive, occurs early in Chapter 1. It is fundamental to his argument:

> Taking then, the art of playing the piano as an example of *the kind of action we are in search of*, we observe that a practised player will perform very difficult pieces apparently without effort, often, indeed, while thinking and talking of something quite other than his music; yet he will play accurately and, possibly, with much expression.[1]
>
> Si donc nous prenons l'art du pianiste comme exemple de *ces actions quasi-inconscientes dont nous parlions*, nous remarquerons qu'un bon pianiste peut jouer des morceaux très difficiles sans effort apparent, et même qu'il est capable de les jouer tout en occupant sa pensée _ et en parlant _ de choses complètemnt étrangères à sa musique. Et cependant il jouera sans se tromper, et peut-être même d'une manière expressive.[2]

Here Larbaud makes a "mild" parenthesis using dashes as well as changing Butler's short clause in the last line to a sentence, this latter solution being characteristic of the translation of all five of Larbaud's "Butlers." It could also be noted that in this passage, he changes Butler's vague expression: "the kind of action we are in search of," to the specific "actions quasi-inconscientes dont nous parlions."[3]

---

1   op. cit., Book Jungle Reprint, p. 12.
2   Butler, *La Vie et l'habitude* (Paris: Editions de la Nouvelle Revue Française, 1922), p. 18.
3   Ibid.

On the same page Butler makes a remarkable deduction about the attention capacity of the piano virtuoso which is central to his argument:

> It may not be too much to say that the attention of a first rate player may have been exercised to an infinitesimally small extent but still truly exercised on as many as ten thousand occasions within within the space of five minutes, for no note can be struck nor point attended to without a certain amount of attention, no matter how rapidly or unconsciously given.[4]

> En sorte qu'il n'y a pas d'exagération à dire que, dans un espace de cinq minutes, l'attention d'un pianiste de première force a pu s'exercer dans une mesure infinitésime sans doute, mais enfin s'exercer effectivement en pas moins de dix mille rencontres: car il est impossible de produire une note ou de tenir compte d'un signe sans faire un certain effort d'attention, si court et si inconscient qu'il soit.[5]

In passing, it could be noted that instead of translating the key word "occasions" by "occasions" in French (since they are in fact cognate) Larbaud prefers the term *rencontres*.

Butler then points out that once a skill has become unconscious, it becomes very difficult to return it to consciousness:

> We shall observe that he finds it hardly less difficult to *compass a voluntary consciousness* of what he has once learned so thoroughly that it has passed, so to speak, into *the domain of unconsciousness*, than he found it to learn the note or passage in the first instance. The effort after a second consciousness of detail baffles him, compels him to turn to his music or play slowly. In fact it seems as though he knew the piece too well to be able to know that he knows it, and is only conscious of knowing those passages which he does not know so thoroughly.[6]

Here the expression of Butler's conception is a little challenging to the reader because of such turns of phrase as "compass a voluntary consciousness."

---

4 op. cit., p. 12.
5 op. cit., transl., pp. 18–19.
6 op. cit. Ch. 1, pp. 12–13.

The use of the first term, ("compass") in that sense, seems reminiscent of the prose of such Victorian *prosateurs* as Newman or Arnold. Larbaud's French style, on the other hand, exemplifies Voltaire's famous dictum: "Tout ce qui n'est pas clair n'est pas français":

> Nous constaterons en effet qu'il éprouve presque autant de difficulté pour *se rendre volontairement conscient* d'une note ou d'un passage musical appris et retenu par lui au point d'avoir, peut-on dire, *passé dans le domaine de l'inconscient*, qu'il en a éprouvé jadis pour apprendre cette note ou ce passage. L'effort qu'il fait pour redevenir conscient du détail le déroute, et l'oblige à consulter sa musique ou à jouer lentement. En vérité on dirait qu'il sait ce morceau trop bien pour savoir qu'il le sait, et que les seuls passages qu'il a conscience de savoir sont ceux qu'il ne sait pas aussi bien.[7]

This example of the pianist leads into similar conclusions concerning writing, reading, walking and talking. Butler sums these up:

> We may observe therefore in this ascending scale, imperfect as it is, that the older the habit the longer the practice, the longer the practice, the more knowledge or, the less uncertainty; *the less uncertainty the less power of conscious self-analysis and control.*[8]

We are clearly invited to take this summary as a key statement of the argument. Larbaud translates:

> Nous pouvons donc remarquer, d'après cette gradation ascendante (toute imparfaite qu'elle est) d'abord, que plus ancienne est l'habitude et plus longue a été la pratique; ensuite, que plus longue a été la pratique et plus grand est le savoir, ou moins grande est l'incertitude; et qu'enfin, *moins grande est l'incertitude et moins grand est le pouvoir d'analyser consciemment et de dominer l'action.*[9]

---

7 op. cit., transl., p. 19.
8 op. cit. 1, pp. 18–19.
9 op. cit., transl., 1, p. 27.

Certainly one of Larbaud's most frequent means of achieving clarity (often greater clarity than is achieved in Butler's original), is by breaking up long sentences into shorter ones or creating clauses. Thus at the end of Chapter 1 a sentence takes up an entire short paragraph. To quote the last part of it:

> Unconscious knowledge and unconscious volition are never acquired otherwise than as the result of experience, familiarity, or habit; so that whenever we observe a person able to do any complicated action unconsciously, *we may assume both* that he must have done it very often before he could acquire so great proficiency, and also that there must have been a time when he did not know how to do it at all.[10]

> Que le savoir et le vouloir inconscients ne s'acqièrent jamais autrement que comme le résultat de l'expérience, de la familiarité ou de l'habitude. En sorte que chaque fois que nous voyons qu'une personne est capable d'accomplir inconsciemment une action compliquée, *nous pouvons* être *aussi certains de deux choses*: d'abord que cette personne a dû accomplir très souvent cette action avant d'arriver à un tel degré d'habileté, et ensuite qu'il y eut forcément un temps ou elle ne savait pas du tout l'accomplir.[11]

On this occasion, while creating once again a new sentence where a subordinate clause begins in the original, Larbaud, seemingly with the greatest of ease, brings to bear the mark of his own original style. Since French has no direct equivalent in one word for "both" he makes explicit the two propositions in question by separating them. (The "he" of the English becomes "elle" in French only because its reference is to "cette personne.")

Chapter 1 concludes with the invention of an aphorism whose French translation is in the manner of Chamfort: "One can neither learn nor unlearn without pains or pain."[12] "Pains" here clearly means "taking pains" so Larbaud clarifies its meaning: "On ne peut ni apprendre, ni désapprendre, sans prendre, ou sans éprouver de la peine."[13]

---

10   op. cit. 1, p. 22.
11   op. cit., transl., 1, p. 32.
12   op. cit., p. 22
13   op. cit., transl., p. 32.

Two: "Conscious and Unconscious Knowers—The Law and Grace" (Savants conscients et savants inconscients—La loi et la grâce)

This chapter further develops the theme of knowledge and experience, as well as habits, becoming unconscious. By "grace" Butler refers to the condition in which knowledge (for example, of a skill) is held to such perfection that it is no longer conscious. *The Way of All Flesh* probably presents this important concept in Butler's "world view" more clearly than any dissertation on the subject could possibly do. Thus Ernest, in his awkward apprenticeship to the profession of living (as in Goethe's image) and in his struggle to achieve even the most basic enlightenment, is constantly taking wrong turns and getting hurt. He is learning "the law" but has not yet achieved genuine enlightenment of the kind Butler calls "grace." In *The Way of All Flesh* grace is incarnated specifically in the personality of Towneley.

Butler develops this obsessive theme in considerable detail in Chapter 2 and its essence is often expressed in very familiar language: "As the fish in the sea, or the bird in the air, *so unreasoningly and inarticulately* safe must a man feel before he can be said to know."[14] Here Larbaud turns the sentence around and develops the concepts "unreasoningly" and "inarticulately": "Pour qu'on puisse dire qu'un homme *sait*, il faut qu'il soit aussi sûr de soi, *sans faire appel à sa raison ni discourir sur ses motifs*, que le poisson dans la mer ou l'oiseau dans l'air."[15]

Since a like conception of "grace" is implicit in much of Larbaud's creative work, his translations of Butler's disquisitions and examples of it are of particular interest:

> Knowledge is in an inchoate state as long as it is capable of logical treatment; it must be transmuted into that sense or instinct which rises altogether above the sphere in which words can have being at all, otherwise it is not yet vital.[16]

> Tant qu'il reste susceptible d'être traité logiquement, notre savoir en est encore à ses débuts. Pour qu'il soit vraiment vital, il faut qu'il soit transmué en ce sens ou instinct qui dépasse complètement la sphère ou' les mots peuvent exister.[17]

---

14 op. cit. 2, p. 28.
15 op. cit., transl., II p. 40.
16 op. cit., p. 29.
17 op. cit., transl., p. 41.

This thought is expressed more clearly in the translation when the words: "otherwise it is not yet vital" become *"pour qu'il soit vraiment vital,"* having been moved to the head of a newly created sentence, a transposition that has become characteristic of Larbaud's manner:

> As long as a demonstration is still felt necessary, and therefore kept ready at hand, the subject of such demonstration is not securely known. *Qui s'excuse s'accuse*; and unless a matter can hold its own without a brag and self-assertion of continual demonstration, it is still more or less of a parvenu.[18]
>
> Tant qu'on juge qu'une demonstration est encore nécessaire, et par suite tant qu'on la tient toujours en état de servir, la chose démontrée n'est pas encore sue d'une façon définitive et complète. *Qui s'excuse s'accuse* et si une idée a besoin pour s'affirmer, d'avoir recours à la vantardise et à la jactance de la démonstraton continuelle, c'est qu'elle n'est encore qu'une epèce de parvenue.[19]

This demonstration occurs in the midst of a very long paragraph and it is characteristic of Larbaud that he breaks it into two shorter ones, as he frequently does with Butler's sentences, always to good effect.

The distinction between "the law" and "grace" could also be applied to the art of translation itself as Larbaud understands it. Butler's original text, in its concern to express certain novel points of view on evolution, makes demands on the reader. She must go slowly and often read some clauses and sentences a second or third time. Thus Butler's style may be said to be often lacking in the very sort of innate "grace" he is discussing: one cannot always read "smoothly," even with some previous knowledge of the subject. The text does nonetheless follow the "law" of the language.

However, it is Larbaud's translation that exemplifies true grace as Butler understands it. Larbaud may now be considered one of the model stylists of what appears to have been a generation of remarkable literary integrity, that of the early period of *La Nouvelle Revue Française*. The reader of *La Vie et l'habitude*, unlike the reader of *Life and Habit*, is a "gourmet," rhythmically turning its pages.

---

18 op. cit. 2, pp. 29–30.
19 op. cit., transl., p. 42.

Butler pursues the theme of knowledge in the same paragraph:

> It is perhaps fortunate for our comfort that we can none of us be cultivated upon very many subjects, so that considerable scope for assurance will still remain to us; but however this may be we certainly observe it as a fact that the greatest men are they who are most uncertain in spite of their certainty, and at the same time most certain in spite of their uncertainty, and who are thus best able to feel that *there is nothing in such complete harmony with itself as a flat contradiction in terms.*[20]

> Il est peut-être heureux pour notre bien-être que personne d'entre nous ne puisse posséder une culture très profonde sur un grand nombre de sujets: de cette façon il nous reste encore un vaste champ de certitude. Quoiqu'il en soit, c'est un fait que nous constatons tous, que les plus grands hommes sont ceux qui doutent le plus en dépit de leur certitiude, et qui en même temps sont les plus certains en dépit de leur doute, étant ainsi les plus capables de sentir qu'*il n'y a rien qui soit plus d'accord avec soi-même qu'une absolue contradiction dans les termes.*[21]

The challenge in this *pensée* is, of course, that it runs the risk of seeming to state a principle that is deliberately illogical, or at the very least paradoxical, so that Larbaud has to find a way of making it acceptable to the presumably rationalist francophone reader. The expression "rien qui soit plus d'accord avec soi-même" may have a suggestion of reassurance to some readers that the irrational is voiced in terms of the rational. At the very least it is the expression of a Butlerian paradox which need not be held to negate the rational but rather be seen as a special aspect of it.

However, Butler is preparing the ground here for a much more explicit development on his special understanding of "grace." His division of "scientific people" (using the word "scientist" in its broad, original, connotation) into "two distinct classes" is a case in point:[22]

> The one class is deeply versed in those sciences which have already become the common property of mankind; enjoying, enforcing, perpetuating and engraving still more deeply onto

---

20 op. cit. pp. 28–29.
21 op. cit., transl., p. 40.
22 op. cit., p. 30.

the mind of man acquisitions already approved by common experience, but somewhat careless about *extension of empire*, or at any rate disinclined, for the most part, to active effort on their own part for the sake of such extension.[23]

Larbaud's translation of this sentence also illustrates his constant effort to clarify Butler's style when it tends toward outdated mannerisms, as in the instance of the word *empire* becoming *le domaine*:

> Les gens qui composent la première de ces classes sont profondément versés dans les sciences qui sont devenues déjà la propriété du genre humain tout entier. Ils possèdent, confirment et perpétuent, en les faisant pénétrer plus profondément dans l'esprit des hommes, des acquisitions déjà approuvées par le consentement universel, mais ils sont peu préoccupés d'étendre le champ de ces acquisitions, ou du moins ils sont, pour la plupart, peu enclins à faire, eux personnellement, les efforts nécessaires pour accroître *le domaine de leurs connaissances*.[24]

> The other class is chiefly intent upon pushing forward the boundaries of science, and is comparatively indifferent to what is known already save in so far as is necessary for purposes of *extension*. These last are called "pioneers" of science, and to them alone is the title "scientific" commonly accorded; but pioneers, as important to an army as they are,[25] are still not the army itself, which can get on better without the pioneers than the pioneers without the army. Surely the class which knows thoroughly well what it knows and which adjudicates upon the value of the discoveries made by the pioneers, surely this class has as good a right or better to be called scientific than the pioneers themselves.[26]

> Les gens de l'autre classe, au contraire, ont pour préoccupation dominante l'extension des frontières de la science, et sont relativement indifférents à l'égard de tout ce qui est déjà su, sauf dans la mesure ou les acquisitions passées peuvent ouvrir

---

23   Ibid.
24   op. cit., transl., pp. 42–43.
25   op. cit., transl., p. 40.
26   op. cit., p. 30.

la voie aux *acquisitions futures*. Ce sont les pionniers de la science, et c'est à ceux-là seulement que le public accorde le titre de "savants." Mais les pionniers, si importants qu'ils soient dans une armée, ne sont pas l'armée elle-même: l'armée peut se passer plus facilement de ses pionniers que les pionniers ne peuvent se passer de l'armée. Et certes la classe qui sait parfaitement bien ce qu'elle sait, et qui juge de la valeur des découvertes faites par les pionniers,—certes, cette classe-là mérite aussi bien, sinon mieux que les pionniers eux-mêmes, qu'on lui applique l'épithète de "scientifique."[27]

Here the English "extension" becomes *acquisitions futures*.

It could be noted in passing that this concept of the two "classes" of the enlightened who each possess a different kind of acquired knowledge is one of the Butlerian concepts that place Butler among aspects of Enlightenment thinking and relate him to the French *philosophes* of the seventeenth and eighteenth centuries, which is, as we have seen, the context in which Larbaud frequently places him, for example when Larbaud sees Butler as belonging to the lineage of Maupertuis or of earlier Enlightenment figures such as Cyrano de Bergerac.

Certainly the final pages of Chapter 2 do resonate with points of view that seem to confirm this. The agnostic Butler's development of the notion of "grace" as an unconscious inheritance of the experience of many previous generations, finds one of its expressions in the faith of the Church of the Middle Ages as opposed to the analytical defences of Christianity in the "introspection" of his time:

> Do what we may we are still drawn to the unspoken teaching of her less introspective ages with a force which no falsehood could command. Her buildings, her music, her architecture, touch us as none other on the whole, can do; when she speaks there are many of us who think that she denies the deeper truths of her own profounder mind and unfortunately her tendency is now towards more rather than less introspection.... But still her ideal is in *grace*.[28]

Nous avons beau faire, l'enseignement muet des époques les moins introspectives de l'histoire de l'Eglise nous attire encore

---

27 op. cit., transl., p. 43.
28 op. cit., p. 36.

> avec une puissance qu'aucun mensonge ne pourrait s'arroger. Ses monuments, sa musique, son architecture, éveillent en nous des émotions que l'art d'aucune époque, pris dans son ensemble, ne peut nous donner; et lorsqu'elle parle, beaucoup d'entre nous pensent qu'elle dément les vérités plus profondes qu'elle possède dans l'intimité de sa pensée; et malheureusement, aujourd'hui sa tendance la porte vers plus que vers moins d'introspection. Mais, malgré tout, son Idéal est la *grâce*.[29]

Thus we find here a mind of the Enlightenment able to apply the tools of rationalism to matters of faith not only in order to oppose them, but to defend them when they are authentic. Butler might thus be better understood as an English Pascal than an English Voltaire. Larbaud clearly appreciated this and reread Pascal's *Lettres Provinciales* among the many works which he consulted while working on his translations, in order to establish an appropriate tone.

Three: Application of the Foregoing Chapters to Certain Habits Acquired after Birth which are Commonly Considered Instinctive (Application de ce qui a été dit dans les précédents chapitres à certaines habitudes acquises après la naissance et qui sont d'ordinaire considérées comme instictives)

This chapter begins the demonstration of the biological transmission of unconscious memory. Curiously, Butler plunges *in media rei* into his biological examples of this phenomenon before actually labelling his principle with the words *unconscious memory*, the phenomenon he is concerned to demonstrate, as is normally done in expository prose in French, the examples being brought forward to buttress the argument. The translator, being obliged to follow the text, can do little to overcome this problem, but he can make the argumentation easier to follow by creating a sense of its "flow" which also makes the reading more pleasurable. In this respect, Larbaud is particularly competent.

Hence Butler's observations concerning the new born baby and its early acquisition of such basic skills as eating and drinking and even more of swallowing, which he suggests is "the earlier habit":

> The ease and unconsciousness with which we eat and drink is clearly attributable to practice; but a very little practice seems to go a long way—a *suspiciously* small amount of practice—as though somewhere or at some other time there must have been more practice than we can account for.[30]

---

29 op. cit., transl., p. 51.
30 op. cit., p. 39.

> La facilité et l'inconscience avec lesquelles nous mangeons et buvons sont évidemment attribuables à la pratique, mais c'est une pratique bien courte pour faire tant de chemin *en si peu de temps*, une somme d'experience d'une petitesse *qui éveille nos soupçons*, et nous fait nous demander si nous n'aurions pas eu, quelque part ailleurs, ou dans un autre temps, plus de pratique qu'il nous est possible d'en constater.[31]

The "suspicions" here are clearly significant, deducing that there must be a memory of earlier existence or chain of existences which, if proven, would place the baby's existence in a lineage of life that must be very ancient. Butler leaves this inference to the reader and possibly does so in order to avoid sounding pedantic or giving the impression that he fancies himself saying it for the first time.

Unfortunately, it is known that he did give that impression to some readers, which might be assumed to account in part for the "conspiracy of silence" to which he was said to have been subjected at times. In Larbaud's French translation, however, such an inference is no way implied. The hypothesis in question is expressed in the sort of normal expository prose that does indeed remind the reader of the style of the eighteenth-century *philosophes* but is not intentionally provocative.

In this chapter, Butler provides variations on his main theme, leading to the virtually irrefutable conclusion (which takes up a paragraph) and which Larbaud, contrary to his usual practice, expresses in a single sentence:

> Shall we say that a baby can do all these things at once, doing them so well and so regularly, without being even able to direct its attention to them, and without mistake, and at the same time not know how to do them, and never to have done them before?[32]

> Dirons-nous que le nouveau-né, qui est capable de faire toutes ces choses à la fois, et de les faire si bien et si régulièrement, sans même pouvoir y applquer son attention et sans se tromper, ne sait pas les faire, et ne les a jamais faites auparavant?[33]

---

31 op. cit., transl., p. 55.
32 op. cit., p. 45.
33 op. cit., transl., p. 63.

Finally, Butler, like Rousseau in his *Discours sur L'Inégalité*, Voltaire in the Eldorado episode of *Candide* and Montesquieu in the Troglodyte episode of *Les Lettres Persanes*, concludes that he can best formulate his point by imagining a hypothetical humanity. It is one which is imagined as once having been far more advanced than the society to which he now belonged but which had been almost completely destroyed by a planetary cataclysm. A remnant, however, is imagined to have survived and struggled with basic tasks while still being able to read, write and add, skills which they can learn as easily "as we now learn to talk." Hence, as we might say today, the propensity to acquire such skills has become genetically "programmed."[34]

> Et pourtant ils savent lire, écrire et compter, car en ce temps-là ces connaissances seront devenues universelles, et s'acquerront aussi facilement qu'à présent nous apprenons à parler, mais ils le font tout naturellement et sans en avoir conscience.[35]

Four: Application of the Foregoing Principles to Actions and Habits Acquired before Birth (Application des principes énoncés à des actions et à des habitudes acquises avant la naissance)

Our attention is first drawn to the phenomenon of the hen's egg in such statements as: "There is no man in the whole world who knows consciously and articulately as much as a half hatched hen's egg knows unconsciously."[36]

Curiously, Larbaud translates "half hatched" by "au dixième jour de couvaison,"[37] possibly demonstrating his own (or his family's) observations in this regard on his estate at Valbois in the Bourbonnais countryside near St. Poucain-sur-Sioule. Butler then draws attention to the specially reinforced bill which the chick develops within the egg in order to break its way out, and sees the temporary growth at the end of the bill as a "tool" resulting from many generations of chicks "knowing" that they would need it. There then follows a particularly significant sentence which expresses the essence of his thought:

> It seems impossible to refrain from thinking that there must be a closer continuity of identity, life, and memory, between successive generations, than we generally imagine.[38]

---

34 op. cit., p. 47.
35 op. cit., transl., p. 66.
36 op. cit., p. 49.
37 op. cit., p. 48, transl., p. 68.
38 op. cit., p. 49.

> Il paraît impossible de douter qu'il y ait, entre les générations successives, une continuité d'identité, de vie et de mémoire beaucoup plus étroite que nous le supposons d'ordinaire.[39]

It might be observed in passing that this example of Larbaud's translation skills is particularly relevant, since a roundabout expression is collapsed into one word and the edge of doubt in "must be" finds a convenient solution in the subjunctive form of *il y a*: *il y ait*.

There then follows a series of reflections on the theme that instinct is a form of knowledge perfected by long practice, and Butler defends the view that it ought to be recognized as such, referring to the work of Dr. W.B. Carpenter, the author of *The Microscope and its Revelations* (1856) and *Principles of Mental Physiology*. The construction capabilities of the "microscopic" amoeba and the terebella are compared with those of human masons.

A key sentence in the argumentation is a challenge to translation into French because of its paradoxical hypothesis:

> Dr. Carpenter evidently feels…that there is no sufficient reason for supposing that these little specks of jelly, without brain or eyes or stomach, or hands, or feet, but the very lowest form of animal life, are not imbued with consciousness of their needs, and the reasoning faculties which shall enable them to gratify those needs in a manner, all things considered, equalling the highest flights of the ingenuity of the highest animal, man.[40]

Larbaud translates:

> Il est évident que le Dr. Carpenter sent bien…qu'il n'y a pas de raison suffisante pour supposer que ces petites parcelles de gelée, dépourvues de cerveau, d'yeux, d'estomac, de mains et de pieds, mais qui sont les formes les plus basses qu'on connaisse de la vie animale, ne soient pas remplies de la conscience de leurs besoins, et qu'elles ne possèdent pas les facultés raisonnantes qui leur permettent de satisfaire ces besoins d'une manière qui, tout bien considéré, égale les plus hauts efforts de l'ingéniosité de l'animal le plus élevé: l'homme.[41]

---

39 op. cit., transl., p. 69.
40 op. cit., p. 55.
41 op. cit., transl., p. 76.

Thus Butler manages, in only one sentence, to make his argument sound "reasonable" by founding it on Dr. Carpenter's authority, which, at the time, was clearly considerable. However, a skeptical French reading public would require more solid proof here. Larbaud is therefore in a somewhat difficult position although there is no evidence in the *Notes* to *La Vie et l'habitude* that he commented on this. Clearly, his own faith in Butler's authority and Dr. Carpenter's seemed support enough since a translator has no means of buttressing an argument he may be translating, other than total fidelity to the original.

A further important example of Larbaud's efforts to make Butler's hypotheses acceptable is seen in the exposition concerning the perpetual replication of the chicken's egg:

> The fact that the embryo chick makes itself always as nearly as may be in the same way, would lead us to suppose that it would be unconscious of much of its own action, *provided it were always the same chicken which makes itself over and over again*. So far as we can see, it always is unconscious of the greater part of its own wonderful performance. Surely then we have *a presumption that it is the same chicken which makes itself over and over again*; for such unconsciousness is not won, so far as our experience goes, by any other means than by frequent repetition of the same act on the part of one and the same individual.[42]

> Le fait que le poussin embryonnaire se fait lui-même toujours aussi exactement que possible de la même manière, nous amène à supposer qu'il serait inconscient de la plus grande partie de son travail à condition que ce fût toujours le même poussin qui se fît lui-même et se refît un nombre illimité de fois. Or tout ce que nous voyons nous autorise à affirmer qu'il est en effet toujours inconscient de la plus grande partie du merveilleux travail qu'il execute. Et par conséquent nous avons là une présomption en faveur de l'hypothèse *que c'est bien le même poussin qui se refait lui-même un nombre illimité de fois*. Car, d'après le témoignage de notre propre expérience, une telle inconscience ne s'acquiert que par un seul moyen, qui est: la répétition fréquente du même acte par un même individu.[43]

---

42 op. cit., p. 57.
43 op. cit., transl., p 79.

There is, possibly, a slight problem in the use of the verb "see" in the second sentence ("so far as we can see") as it is interpreted in the sense of "as far as we can tell." Of course both English and French use "see" ("voir") figuratively in the sense of "comprehend" or "understand." ("Je vois ce que vous voulez dire" etc.) However, by translating as "tout ce que nous voyons" Larbaud extends its figurative use in a way that may risk making it also sound literal (i.e. actually "seeing."). Hence there may be slight ambiguity as to whether the "seeing" is literal or figurative or even intended to be both at the same time. However, the translation ("tout ce que nous voyons") still conveys the meaning since the possible interpretation of literally seeing still expresses the image.

Five: Personal Identity (L'Identité Personnelle)

Butler now addresses the very tenuous matter of personal identity, as experienced both by the person in question and by other people. Here Butler's English text requires careful attention. Indeed a second, slower reading might often be required of the reader. Larbaud's French translation, however, flows at its normal pace. Translation becomes *explication*. Thus, in the following passage, although the argumentation seems expressed in unduly intricate terms, the French translation makes it clear:

> A famished man eats food; after a short time his whole personality is so palpably affected that we know the food to have entered into him and to have taken, as it were, possession of him.... Thus we find that we are rooted into outside things and melt away into them, nor can any man say he consists absolutely in this or that, nor define himself so certainly as to include neither more nor less than himself; many undoubted parts of his personality being more separable from it and changing it less when so separated, both to his own senses and those of other people, than other parts which are strictly speaking no parts at all.[44]

(These last remarks are further developed in the next paragraph through a consideration of the effects of a person's clothes and "gain or loss of money" on both the self and others.)

> Un homme affamé mange; et, au bout d'un court espace de temps toute sa personnalité s'en trouve si évidemment influencée

---

44 op. cit., p. 61.

> que nous connaissons que la nourriture a pénétré en lui et a pris, peut-on dire, possession de lui. On voit donc que nous plongeons nos racines dans les choses extérieures et que nous nous fondons en elles, et que nul homme ne peut dire qu'il consiste absolument en ceci ou cela, ni se définir avec assez de certitude pour ne pas comprendre dans sa définition de lui-même plus, ou moins, d'éléments qu'il n'en contient. Car bien des choses qui font indubitablement partie de sa personnalité en sont plus aisément séparables et, en s'en détachant, le modifient moins à l'égard de ses propres sens et de ceux d'autrui, que d'autres choses qui, strictement parlant, n'en font aucunement partie.[45]

Larbaud stops the involved second sentence at Butler's semi-colon in order to create a new explanatory sentence, beginning with "car," but the concept remains very abstract until we finally reach the example of "clothes…that lie on a chair at night."[46]

To the extent that Butler, in this chapter, keeps referring to the degree to which personal identity is dependent on other people who witness one's life, he is again a precursor of Sartre and his famous "regard de l'autre" as a determinant.

Larbaud doesn't actually assimilate Butler's views on expressions of personal identity into his own creative work but he may nonetheless be thinking of Butler at times. For example, in the full-length *nouvelle* entitled *Le Vaisseau de Thésée*, which relates the interior monologues of a genuinely good-hearted businessman, we find that the latter, reviewing his past life, arrives at a very positive sense of his own identity, in which he may take well-earned pride. Thus the notion that personal identity, through whatever attempts may be made to experience it, is something very uncertain, is not a theme that we find in this example of Larbaud's own creative work. To the contrary, the symbolic legend of Theseus' ship, preserved for centuries in the port of Athens until every plank had been replaced many times but its "being" preserved intact, expresses in very positive terms the notion of the preservation of integrity, not only during life but far beyond.[47]

Language itself, according to Butler in this chapter, is almost always inadequate. On this theme Butler quotes a letter from a friend:

---

45 op. cit., transl., p. 85.
46 op. cit., p. 61.
47 Cf. "Le Vaisseau de Thésée." *Oeuvres* (Pléiade), pp. 1079–1105.

> Until you think of things as they are, and not of the words that misrepresent them, you cannot think rightly. Words produce the appearance of *hard and fast lines where there are none*.... To think of a thing they must be got rid of: they are the clothes that thoughts wear—only the clothes.[48]

Larbaud translates this passage as follows:

> On ne peut penser juste et bien que lorsqu'on arrive à penser aux choses telles qu'elles sont et non plus aux mots, qui les représentent mal. Les mots donnent l'apparence de *lignes droites et dures là ou il n'y a que des courbes*....Pour penser à un objet il est nécessaire de s'affranchir des mots: ils sont les vêtements que portent les pensées—les vêtements et rien de plus.[49]

Butler again seems to be foreseeing certain issues here that were later to be raised by Saussure along with the whole question of the possibility of linguistics being considered a science, just as he had seemed to foresee Freud in *The Way of All Flesh*.

However, the essential point in this chapter is that the impregnate ovum should be considered as being "a continuation of the personality of every ovum in the chain of its ancestry."[50]

> This process cannot stop short of the primordial cell, which again will probably turn out to be but a brief resting place. We therefore prove *each one of us* to *be actually* the primordial cell which never died nor dies, but has differentiated itself into *the life of the world*, all living beings whatever being one with it and members one of another.[51]

> Cette marche ascendante ne peut pas ne pas remonter jusqu'à la cellule primordiale, laquelle ne sera probablement qu'une courte halte *avant de remonter plus loin encore*. Par suite il est clair que nous sommes *tous véritablement* la cellule primordiale qui n'est jamais morte et qui ne meurt jamais; mais qui s'est différenciée à l'infini jusqu'à constituer *toute la vie du monde,*—

---

48 op. cit., p. 63.
49 op. cit., transl., p. 88.
50 op. cit. pp. 64–65.
51 Ibid.

tout être vivant, quel qu'il soit, étant un avec elle, et membre de tous les autres.⁵²

The first phrase in italics: *avant de remonter plus loin encore* was inserted to complete the meaning, which is merely inferred in Butler's English. Such clarifications do occur in the translation, resulting in an argumentation that is, once again, easier to follow in Larbaud's French than in the original. (It might be supposed that Larbaud found Butler too elliptical in this passage as in many others.)

The translator also provides an example here of an addition of just one word that succeeds in clarifying the meaning in an important way: the "primordial cell" which has "differentiated itself into the life of the world" is too vague an expression since the concept is felt to be "into *all* the life of the whole world." Larbaud translates it as: "*toute* la vie du monde."

As the hypothesis expressed here might seem somewhat daring to many readers Butler clinches it by imagining the situation that would obtain if the primordial cell had been killed, resulting in its not having any descendants at all. This shows, he implies, that if it lived, there could, to the contrary, be a long line of descendants which could survive and reproduce. He calls such a proposition a "bayonet" of logic that would tend to prove "an identity between any creature and all others that are descended from it."⁵³

The question of whether personal identity is modified as life progresses is also raised by Butler and he refers to Bishop Butler (Dr. Samuel Butler 1774–1839) his grandfather, who had previously wrestled with it. Bishop Butler had refuted the notion that one is constantly becoming another person by reducing it to the absurd. (Curiously, the question of responsibility is not brought into the discussion but only the probability that, in an extreme case, a person who constantly became "somebody else" would lose interest in her (his) life of the previous day or the potentialities of the next day.)⁵⁴

The implications of the notion of "becoming," from a moral viewpoint, had developed into a matter of considerable concern to André Gide, as illustrated by his concept of *le nouvel être* in his early novel *L'Immoraliste* (1902) because this concept might be said to refute determinism. This may also possibly represent a context within which Gide had become aware of Butler's significance, resulting in his suggestion to Larbaud that he might consider translating Butler's work.

---

52 op. cit., transl., p. 90.
53 op. cit., p. 65.
54 Ibid.

Six: Personal Identity—Continued

In this chapter we continue to be concerned with the phenomenon of the continuity of life, from one generation to the next, and life's replication down the generations. The importance of unconscious memory in creating an ongoing link between generations is stressed. (We cannot remember consciously having been one year old but unconsciously we can.) There are several examples designed as support for this proposition. One of them brings in the moth:

> A moth becomes each egg that she lays, and that she does so, she will in good time show by doing, now that she has got a fresh start, as near as may be what she did when first she was an egg, and then a moth, before; and this, I take it, so far as I can gather from looking at life and things generally, she would not be able to do if she had not travelled the same road often enough already, to be able to know it in her sleep and blindfold, that is to say to remember it without any conscious act of memory.[55]

Larbaud prefers to change the moth to a butterfly. However, his French flows without the least sign of occasional Butlerian awkwardness, especially when a thought is a little paradoxical:

> Le papillon devient chacun des oeufs qu'il pond, et la meilleure preuve qu'il le devient, il la donnera au moment voulu, en refaisant, à présent qu'il a pris un nouvel élan, aussi exactement que possible tout ce qu'il a fait auparavant lorsqu'il était oeuf d'abord, et ensuite lorsqu'il était papillon. Et, autant que j'en peux juger d'après tout ce que l'observation de la vie et des êtres m'apprend, c'est là une chose qu'il ne pourrait certainement pas faire s'il n'avait déjà parcouru la même route assez souvent pour la pouvoir reconnaître même dans son sommeil, et les yeux bandés; autrement dit pour se la rappeler sans aucun acte conscient de sa mémoire.[56]

Butler refers to cases of asexual generation in plants through bulbs, offsets, cuttings, etc., as particularly good examples of natural mechanisms that tend to guarantee plant life's continuity of identity, before approaching the question of

---

55 op. cit., p. 73.
56 op. cit., transl., p. 102.

continuity through normal reproduction in animals. Here too Larbaud solves the problems of translating a somewhat specialized argumentation, seemingly with the greatest of ease:

> Not much difficulty will be felt about supposing the offset of a plant to be *imbued* with the memory of the past history of the plant of which it is an offset. It is part of the plant itself; and will know whatever the plant knows. Why, then, should there be more difficulty in supposing the offspring of the highest mammals to remember in a profound but *unselfconscious way*, the anterior history of the creatures of which they too have been *part and parcel*?[57]

Larbaud translates:

> On n'a pas beaucoup de peine à supposer que le rejeton d'une plante est *imprégné* du souvenir de l'histoire antérieure de la plante dont il provient. Il fait partie de cette plante, et par conséquent il sait tout ce qu'elle sait. Eh bien, pourquoi nous serait-il plus difficile de supposer que les descendants des mammifères les plus élevés se souviennent, profondément mais *d'une manière inconsciente*, de l'histoire antérieure des créatures dont ils ont été, eux aussi, *partie intégrante*?[58]

In using the word *unselfconscious*, Butler is again emphasizing the notion that this process is unconscious by resorting to colloquial rather than strictly scientific language. Regarding its French translation, Larbaud seems to infer that this emphasis is already sufficient in *d'une manière inconsciente*. Thus Butler's emphasis on the concept of an unconscious memory that undergoes genetic transmission from one generation to the next is fully expressed in the translation.

Seven: Our Subordinate Personalities (Nos Personnalités subalternes)

In this chapter, Butler boldly wrestles with the problem of individual identity and the difficulty of defining it. He points out that "every individual person is a compound creature"[59] ("chaque individu est un être composé").[60]

---

57 op. cit., p. 75.
58 op. cit., transl., p. 195.
59 op. cit., p. 76.
60 op. cit., transl., p. 106.

Butler develops and illustrates this conception by drawing attention to well-known situations in which we are not our true selves, such as those brought about by the effects of social conventions, or illness (and by inference inebriation) or the influence of parasites that may not be beneficial. He also dwells at some length on a phenomenon of abnormal psychology, the symbiotic relationship, that comes into being when one partner in that relationship is dominated by the overbearing personality of the other and subordinates his or her will to that of the dominant person (to whatever degree).[61]

The essential theme, then, is that of the instability of the self (*le moi*) and that we are not "one" (although we may presume to be) but "many." Novelists, soldiers, actors and ballet dancers among many others, demonstrate this principle since they must make use of it, to one extent or another, in their professional roles, as Butler himself may be presumed to have done as a novelist and as Nijinski and T.E. Lawrence, among many others, were later to do to great effect on the stage of the twentieth century.

In expressing this notion of the multiplicity of the self, Butler produces another challenging sentence:

> It would appear, then, as though "we," "our souls," or "selves," or "personalities," or by whatever name we may prefer to be called, are but the *consensus* and full flowing stream of countless sensations and impulses on the part of our tributary souls or "selves," who probably know no more that we exist, and that they exist as part of us...until some misconduct on our part, or some confusion of ideas on theirs, has driven them into insurrection, than we do of the *habits and feelings of some class widely separated from our own*.[62]

Here Larbaud's rearrangement of this sentence consists partly in changing the order of the last two clauses, which is done to good effect:

> Il semblerait donc que "nous" nos "âmes" ou nos "moi" ou nos "personnalités"—ou de quelque nom qu'il nous plaise de les nommer,—ne sont que le *consensus* et l'ensemble du courant en marche formé par d'innombrables sensations et impulsions provenant de nos âmes tributaires, ou de nos "moi." Lesquels, probablement, ne savent pas... que nous existons ou qu'ils

---

61 op. cit., p. 77.
62 op. cit., p. 79.

> font partie de nous....tandis que, de notre côté nous ne les connaissons pas plus que nous ne connaissons *les habitudes et les sentiments des animaux d'une classe très éloignée de celle à laquelle nous appartenons*—jusqu' au moment ou quelque faute commise par nous, ou quelque trouble dans leurs idées, les oblige à s'insurger.[63]

Larbaud appears to have based his understanding of the word "class" here on the biological usage of the word, given the biological context of the whole work, and then to have clarified this by extending the word to a phrase: *les animaux d'une classe*. This is certainly a plausible understanding. Nonetheless it is also possible that Butler intended the notion of "social class" or at least the suggestion that social classes in the England of his day might be understood as analogous to biological classes, a notion also found in the works of other satirists of his time.

The word *personality*, in this chapter, is used in the strict sense given by the Oxford Dictionary and the theme is of course that the limits of the personality are difficult to define. (The term *the person* might be preferred today in order to avoid ambiguity.) To support his view Butler again brings in Dr. Carpenter, this time concerning his experiments with frogs, which appear to have been well publicized.

Thus in a series of experiments which might seem repellent to readers today, Dr. Carpenter, in one variation, cut off a frog's head and applied acid to one of its hind legs. It was observed that the other hind leg then attempted to remove the acid. This phenomenon was interpreted as meaning that the frog had centres of command other than its head, creating a difficulty in defining its "personality." Butler upholds the view that a piece of the frog might, for a short time, be considered sentient. Hence his view of the problem of defining the limits of personal identity is founded on a physiological phenomenon, as was the academic fashion at the time.

Butler concludes:

> Each individual may be manifold in the sense of being compounded of a vast number of subordinate individualities which have their separate lives within him, with their hopes and fears and intrigues, being born and dying within us.[64]

Larbaud translates in a rhythmic prose quite equal to Butler's:

---

63 op. cit., transl., pp 110–111.
64 op. cit., p. 88.

> Chaque individu peut être multiple en ce sens qu'il est composé d'un nombre immense d'individualités subalternes qui vivent en lui d'une vie séparée, avec leurs espoirs, leurs craintes, et leurs intrigues; et dont *de nombreuses générations* naissent et meurent en nous pendant l'espace d'une seule de nos vies.[65]

Larbaud invents the phrase *de nombreuses générations* for the sake of clarity here. Butler then quotes Darwin who, on this occasion, seems to support him, with the words:

> An organic being is a microcosm, a little universe, formed of a host of self propagating organisms, inconceivably minute, and numerous as the stars in heaven.[66]
>
> Un être organique est un micrcosme, un petit univers, composé d'une multitude d'organismes se reproduisant eux-mêmes, inconcevablement petits, et aussi nombreux que les étoiles du ciel.[67]

Eight: Application of the Foregoing Chapters—The Assimilation of Outside Matter (Application des précédents chapîtres: Assimilation de la matière extérieure)

Butler now challenges his readers on the question of identity in its continuity over great periods of time and returns again to the famous example of the chicken and egg. The following passage, in its French translation, is a remarkably clear rendition of the essence of Butler's thought in this arena of the evolution debate. No longer does the reader have the feeling that Butler might well have revised his text further before considering it ready for publication. Larbaud once again performs this task for him by creating a French version which is much more finished than the original English:

> So far then, as regards actual identity of personality; which, we find, will allow us to say that *eggs* are part of the present phase of a certain past identity, whether of other eggs, or of fowls, or chickens, and in the like manner that chickens are part of the present phase of certain other chickens, or eggs, or fowls; in fact that *anything* is part of the present phase of any past identity

---

65 op. cit., transl., p. 123.
66 op. cit., p. 88.
67 op. cit., transl., p. 123.

in the line of its ancestry. But as regards the actual memory of such identity (unconscious memory, but still clearly memory) we observe that the egg, as long as it is an egg, appears to have a very distinct recollection of having been an egg before, and the fowl of having been a fowl before, but that neither egg nor fowl appear to have any recollection of any other stage of their past existences than the one corresponding to that in which they are themselves at the moment existing.[68]

Voilà donc pour l'identité personnelle réelle; laquelle, nous le voyons, nous permet de dire que *des oeufs* font partie de la phase actuelle d'une certaine identité passée, que ce soit l'identité d'autres oeufs, ou de poulets ou de poussins; et, de même, que des poussins font partie de la phase actuelle de certains autres poussins, oeufs ou poulets; et bref, que *tout être vivant* fait partie de la phase actuelle de n'mporte quelle identité passée comprise dans sa chaîne ancestrale. Mais pour ce qui est de la mémoire réelle de cette identité,—mémoire inconsciente, mais évidemment mémoire,—nous remarquons que 1'oeuf, aussi longtemps qu'il est oeuf, paraît avoir le souvenir très net d'avoir déjà été oeuf, et le poulet d'avoir déjà été poulet; mais que ni l'oeuf ni le poulet ne semblent avoir le moindre souvenir d'aucune autre phase de leurs existences passées que celle qui correspond à la phase dans laquelle ils se trouvent actuellement.[69]

However, we do soon discover a problem in this passage: the translation of *eggs* as *des oeufs* (particular eggs) instead of *les oeufs* (eggs in general). This may be a misprint, as the intent is clearly "eggs in general." If it is a misprint, it is unfortunately an example of a seemingly insignificant one that changes the meaning in a significant way. As a proofreader (who often refers to proof reading in his diaries) Larbaud was known to be very meticulous, so that if this is indeed a misprint it is very unlikely that he was responsible for it.

Again, Butler uses very imprecise language here with the word "anything" meaning "any life form" which Larbaud "corrects" by translating biologically as "*tout être vivant.*" One might possibly take this as an example of alleged "hurried editing" on Butler's part, possibly brought about by a desire to participate in a meaningful way in the lively ongoing debates on evolution

---

[68] op. cit., pp. 101–102.
[69] op. cit., transl., p. 141.

in the 1870s and his urgent desire, within that context, to create what he called "a footnote to Darwin" which he said he considered to be his primary motivation in writing *Life and Habit*.

Nine: On the Abeyance of Memory (De la Suspension de la mémoire)

This chapter reflects on the limitations of memory, pointing out that we actually remember in only two ways: first, we remember events which we have experienced as "out of the ordinary," and secondly we remember what has been often repeated. (The seeming inadequacy of this account of memory is corrected by a much more detailed development of the theme later in the chapter.)

The first kind of experience Butler describes metaphorically as "one hard blow"[70] and gives a telling example drawn in all likelihood from a memory of his Atlantic crossing when he was on his way to investigate business he had in Montreal and saw icebergs. It may also reflect a much earlier maritime trauma that occurred while Butler, as a young man, was preparing to leave for New Zealand. He decided not to take the ship he had originally chosen, "The Burmah," which was being refitted, but changed to "The Roman Emperor" instead. The first ship later sailed but was wrecked.[71]

> Thus, if an object or incident be very unfamiliar, as, we shall say, a whale or an iceberg on travelling to America for the first time, it will make a deep impression although not directly affecting our interests; but if we struck against the iceberg and were shipwrecked, or nearly so, it would produce a much deeper impression, we should think much more about icebergs.[72]
>
> Par exemple, si un objet ou un incident est extrêmement nouveau pour nous, comme le serait, pour le voyageur qui en est à sa première traversée de l'Atlantique, la rencontre d'une baleine ou d'un iceberg, l'impression produite sera très profonde, bien qu'elle n'affecte pas directement nos intérêts matériels. Mais si le navire donnait contre l'iceberg et que nous fussions sur le point de faire naufrage, l'impression produite serait beaucoup plus profonde; nous songerions bien davantage aux icebergs.[73]

---

70 op. cit., p. 105.
71 Cf. Henry Festing Jones, *Samuel Butler Author of "Erewhon"* (London: MacMillan & Co. Ltd., 1920), p 71.
72 Ibid.
73 op. cit., transl., p. 147.

Butler does not venture into the arena of "psychic" memory such as direct knowledge of past or contemporaneous events, nor of the experience of a future event in a dream, but it would seem to many contemporary readers that this particular example has something of divination about it since such words as "deeper impression" and "iceberg" immediately evoke the "Titanic" tragedy to readers today. At the very least we become aware of the excellent choice of an example to prove the point, given that the Titanic tragedy, occurring more than thirty years after the publication of *Life and Habit*, was such a traumatic event that it did indeed impress the memory of many millions of people, possibly because the accounts of it amounted to such a powerful allegory of the human condition. (It might be worthy of mention, in this respect, that there had of course already been traumatic losses of "floating palaces" on the Atlantic in Butler's youth, not so long before he sailed for New Zealand, such as that of the *Arctic* (Collins Line) in 1854, which, while retuning to New York collided with another ship off the Grand Banks (resulting in a loss of over 350 passengers and crew) and that of the *Pacific* (Collins Line) in 1856, which simply disappeared.)

Larbaud, although he said he had often given serious thought to the possibility, never did cross the Atlantic. However, the literature on such crossings may nonetheless have a "Larbaldian" ring because of his character Barnabooth, whose origins were South American.

When Butler turns to the question of the human ability to change habits in new environments he uses the example of life on board ship: a passenger may sometimes become a "character in a novel" by adopting new habits:

> It may be that at home they never play whist: on board ship they do nothing else all the evening. At home they never touch sprits; on the voyage they regularly take a glass of something before they go to bed. They do not smoke at home; here they are smoking all day.[74]

> Chez eux, ils ne jouent jamais au whist; à bord ils ne font que cela pendant toute la soirée. Chez eux ils ne touchent jamais à aucune boisson alcoolique; pendant la traversée, ils prennent régulièrement un verre de quelque chose avant de se coucher. Ils ne fument jamais à terre; ici ils fument toute la journée.[75]

---

74 op. cit., p. 112.
75 op. cit., transl., p. 156.

Hence, although *Life and Habit* is a treatise, not intended to be "creative," the reader nonetheless receives impressions of both the author and his translator. At the end of the chapter Butler demonstrates the conditions under which a memory may be "unlocked":

> A smell may remind an old man of eighty of some incident of his childhood, forgotten for nearly as many years as he has lived.[76]

> Une odeur peut rappeler à un vieillard de quatre-vingts ans un incident de son enfance oublié depuis preque autant d'années qu'il en a vécu.[77]

This phenomenon is developed considerably in the final pages of the chapter and since the publication of Marcel Proust's *Du Côté de chez Swann*, the first volume of *A la Recherche du temps perdu*, in 1913, in which it becomes the mechanism of the memory principle which underpins the entire novel, it might now be understood as "Proustian." Thus the publication of *La Vie et l'habitude* in 1922 appears to coincide well with the literary "climate" of the time, a climate of continuing reaction against the tenets of naturalism (as promoted by Taine and Zola in particular) which had seen humankind as merely a "product" determined by *race, milieu, moment*. By 1922 the mood and literary fashion was exactly opposite: it was now the inner world, including, precisely, memory, that took precedence over the outer one.

Ten: What We Should Expect to Find if Differentiations of Structure and Instinct Are Mainly Due to Memory (Ce que nous devons nous attendre à trouver si les différentiations de structure et d'instinct sont dues principalement à la mémoire)

As we have seen, Butler attaches great importance to the role of his particular understanding of memory in the evolution of both animals and plants. Further, for Butler, memory is far more often understood as unconscious than conscious. In either case it is a particularly significant manifestation of the life force and, in effect, in his pre-Mendelian interpretation of the phenomenon, memory is, at the very least, the strong "conditioner" within which the continuity of evolution takes place. Thus memory is formulated in terms that seem a premonition of Proust, as in following passage:

---

76 op. cit., p. 112.
77 op. cit., transl., p. 157.

> A single and apparently not very extraordinary occurrence may sometimes produce a lasting impression, and be able to return with sudden force at some distant time, and then go on returning to us at intervals.[78]

Larbaud translates:

> Un incident unique, mais peu extraordinaire en apparence, peut produire une impression durable, et être sujet à revenir avec une force soudaine longtemps après, et dès lors se représenter de temps à autre.[79]

This theme is of course expressed dramatically in Proust's novel, as in the famous episode of the "*madeleine*" dipped into herbal tea, which, when eaten, opens up the haunting world of Combray, the setting of the first volume, *Du Côté de chez Swann*. Butler, on the other hand is more concerned with unconscious memory and quotes Darwin himself:

> How can we make intelligible, and connect with other facts, this wonderful and common capacity of reversion—this power of calling back to life long lost characters? Surely the answer may be hazarded, that we shall be able to do so when we can make intelligible *the power of calling back to life long lost memories.*[80]

> Comment rendre intelligible et relier à d'autres faits cette faculté à la fois ordinaire et étonnante du retour,—ce pouvoir de rappeler à la vie des caractères depuis longtemps perdus? Certes nous pouvons nous risquer à répondre que nous le ferons lorsque nous pourrons rendre intelligible *la faculté que nous avons de rappeler à la vie des souvenirs depuis longtemps perdus.*[81]

Butler attempts to illustrate the role of memory in evolution, as he understands it, by referring to the sterility of hybrids, and uses the well-known example of the mule. The concept is that the mule's unconscious memory

---

78 op. cit., p. 115.
79 op. cit., transl., p. 160.
80 Darwin, "*Plants and Animals, &c.,*" 2, p. 369 (1875 ed.). In: op. cit., p. 133.
81 op. cit., transl., pp. 185–186.

of previous generations is blocked (or "halved") because it can take him back only as far as its parents' generation, whereas the memory of many ancestors would be required in order to make memory effective as a necessary factor in reproduction. Thus Butler sees the physiological problem as merely an "inhibitor" of memory, memory remaining the significant factor. He explains the mule's predicament in figurative terms:

> For it would appear that this sterility has nothing to do with any supposed immutable or fixed limits of species, but results simply from the same principle which prevents old friends, no matter how intimate in youth, from returning to their old intimacy after a lapse of years, during which they have been subjected to widely different influences, inasmuch as they will each have *contracted new habits, and have got into new ways,* which they do not like now to alter.[82]

> Car [cette hypothèse] démontrerait que cette stérilité n'a rien à voir avec aucune des prétendues limites immuables et infranchissables qui séparent les espèces; mais qu'elle résulte tout simplement du même principe qui fait que de vieux amis, malgré toute l'intimité dans laquelle ils ont pu vivre dans leur jeunesse, ne peuvent pas renouer leurs anciens rapports après qu'ils ont passé, loin l'un de l'autre, un certain nombre d'années durant lesquelles ils ont été soumis à des influences très différentes. Car *ils ont contracté de nouvelles habitudes et ont adopté un autre genre de vie,* qu'ils répugnent à changer désormais.[83]

Hence memory and habits are seen as more important factors in evolution than physiological ones. Butler had already raised the question of conflicting memories and in doing so resorted once again to the analogy of the pianist, who, under certain circumstances, might have received conflicting advice. Such a conflict could sometimes be so severe as to lead to a complete breakdown, which Butler believes can explain "the inability to fuse the experiences into a harmonious whole, or, in other words, to understand the ideas which are prescribed to him."[84]

---

82   op. cit., p. 123.
83   op. cit., transl., p. 171.
84   op. cit., p. 119.

Darwin had expressed his inability to understand why fusion had not occurred on occasions such as these, which had led only to sterility. Butler claims that his explanation of "conflicting ideas" is the answer: "I submit that what I have written above supplies a very fair prima facie explanation."[85]

Such conclusions represent, of course, an aspect of Butler that skeptical readers occasionally found too boastful to be in good taste, especially at a time when Darwin was "the great man" who, even when he expresses modesty, must still be admired. Butler clearly foresaw such reactions on the part of his readers and ends the chapter with a strong and very respectful tribute to Darwin's genius.

Butler had earlier referred to a passage in Darwin's *Origin of Species* concerning the results of an examination of about five hundred eggs produced from various crosses between three species of *Gallus* and their hybrids:

> The majority of these eggs had been fertilized; and in the majority of the fertilized eggs, the embryos had either been partially developed and had then perished, or had become nearly mature, but the young chickens had been unable to break through the shell. Of the chickens which were born more than four fifths died…without any obvious cause, apparently from mere inability to live.[86]

Butler's comment on this expresses his point in terms which state his theory clearly:

> No wonder the poor creatures died, distracted as they were by the *internal* tumult of conflicting memories.[87]

> Il n'est pas surprenant que ces créatures mourussent, tournentées qu'elles étaient par le tumulte *intérieur* des souvenirs contradictoires.[88]

Butler's word "internal" translated by Larbaud as "intérieur" becomes a key to the argumentation here: something "internal" is seen as the determining factor in bringing about an external result.

---

85   Ibid.
86   *Origin* (1876 ed.), p. 249.
87   op. cit., p. 120.
88   op. cit., transl., p. 167.

Eleven: Instinct as Inherited Memory (L'Instinct, Mémoire héréditaire)

This chapter attempts to clarify Butler's position on certain phenomena that could be seen as "Lamarckian," such as the "equilibrium" he observes in bee and ant societies, and which he says raises the question whether evolution leads to a kind of perfection when "equilibrium" is attained "leaving upon the whole and under ordinary circumstances little further to be desired, and hence that it should have varied little during many generations."[89] On the other hand matters appear to Butler to be very different with respect to many human civilizations and machines. As in *Erewhon*, Butler attaches great importance to (and implicitly expresses great concern over) the rapidly "evolving" machinery of his time:

> Every instinct must have passed through the laboriously intelligent stages through which human civilizations and *mechancal inventions* are now passing; and *he who would study the originality of an instinct* with its development, partial transmission, further growth, further transmission...*and, finally, its perfection as an unerring and unerringly transmitted instinct, must look to laws, customs and machinery as his best instructors.*[90]

> Tout instinct doit forcément avoir passé par les phases laborieusemnt conscientes par lesquelles passent actuellement les civilisations et *les inventions mécaniques* de l'homme; *et quiconque voudrait étudier l'origine d'un instinct,* son développement, sa transmission partielle d'abord, son accroissement; sa transmission plus complète...*et enfin sa perfection vers un instinct infaillible infailliblement transmis, doit prendre pour points de comparaison et pour guides: les lois, les coutumes et les progrès des inventions mécaniques.*[91]

Larbaud adds an unusually long phrase of his own here in order to achieve the necessary clarification, namely, *"pour points de comparaison et pour guides,"* in keeping with his understanding of "translators' rights."

These ideas, as in *Erewhon* in the matter of the machines, might be seen as somewhat obsessive in Butler as he looks at situations in which the amelioration of life's conditions can be understood as relatively rapid, as in the social and economic "climbing" of Victorian times, which he notes depends

---

89 op. cit., p. 135.
90 op. cit., ch. 11, p. 136.
91 op. cit., transl.,pp. 188–189.

on the will power of the creature or person "climbing," but occurs nonetheless within limits.

At this point he invents one of his more characteristic aphorisms:

> Every man and every race is capable of education up to a certain point, but not to the extent of being made from a sow's ear into a silk purse.[92]

> Tout homme et toute race sont capables d'être éduqués jusqu'à un certain point; mais toute l'éducation du monde ne fera pas, comme on dit, d'un goujat un grand seigneur.[93]

These words are very much in the manner of Chamfort into whose *Maximes et Pensées* Larbaud regularly dipped while translating Butler, as his *Journal* frequently shows.[94]

Butler gives the example of the "plough boy" ("garçon de ferme") who might want to learn or "improve," and stresses the notion that there has to be will power and that if there is, then in time "he becomes very different from what he was originally."[95] Such will power is seen as a human manifestation of a significant driving force in evolution at both the animal and human levels of being, and leads into the question of mimicry as in the example of South American butterflies known (if we are to pursue the "Lamarckian" interpretation) to have "imitated" the markings of another species of butterfly whose strong odour kept away predators. At this stage there is no reference to another form of "Batesian mimicry" concerning Amazonian butterflies which have certain patterns of eye-like spots on their wings so that when their wings are extended they resemble the head of a cat-like creature. Clearly this discovery (on the part of Henry Walter Bates, 1825–1892, who accompanied Wallace in the Amazon) would have provided Butler with grist for his mill, but it would seem that although the "imitation" of the markings of the odoriferous butterfly is mentioned in Mivart's *Genesis of Species* (1871) to which Butler referred, this further example of "Batesian mimicry" may not have been known to Butler before *Life and Habit* was published in December 1877. However, Bates had read his paper, *Insect Fauna of the Amazon Valley*, to the Linnaean Society in 1861.

---

92 Ibid., p. 137.
93 op. cit., transl., p. 190.
94 Cf. Chamfort, *Maximes et Pensées*. Le Monde en 10/18. Présentation par Claude Roy (Paris, 1963), p. 60.
95 op. cit., p. 137.

Nonetheless, Butler clearly attaches great importance to mimicry as an elementary example of will power that could lead to a modification and implicitly a modification that might eventually become part of what is transmissible:

> To mimic, or to wish to mimic, is doubtless often one of the first steps toward varying in any given direction. *Not less, in all probability, than a full twenty per cent of all the courage and good nature now existing in the world, derives its origin, in no very distant date, from a desire to appear courageous and good natured....* Against faith, then, and desire, all the "natural selection" in the world will not stop an amoeba from becoming an elephant if a reasonable time be granted.[96]

Larbaud translates:

> Imiter ou désirer imiter, est certainement souvent un des premiers pas faits vers une variation dans une direction déterminée, quelle qu'elle soit. *Et il est extremenent probable qu'au moins vingt pour cent de la somme totale du courage et de la bonté qui existe actuellement dans le monde tire son origine,— qui ne remonte pas à une date bien éloignée—du désir de paraître courageux et de paraître bon....*Ainsi donc, lorsqu'elle a contre elle la foi et le désir, toute la "sélection naturelle" du monde ne peut pas empêcher une amibe de devenir un éléphant, si on lui accorde pour cela un espace de temps suffisant.[97]

Butler here adopts a firmly Lamarckian position, tending to show that the Darwinian explanation of evolution has to be qualified by the Lamarckian notion of the significance of "will power" rather than rejecting it. In the instance of artificial breeding Butler claims that "the desires of the animal itself"[98] are a factor. He appears to be assuming that this drive is unconscious as in the phenomenon of unconscious memory.

The nature of instinct, the principal subject of this chapter, is developed by Butler through a hypothetical debate with Théodule Ribot:

---

96 op. cit., ch. 11, p. 138.
97 op. cit., transl., pp. 191–192.
98 op. cit., p. 139.

Butler: What is certain is that instinct does not betray signs of self-consciousness as to its own knowledge. It has dismissed reference to first principles, and is no longer under the law, but under *the grace* of settled conviction.[99]

(Ce qu'il y a de certain, c'est que l'instinct ne laisse voir à aucun signe qi'il est conscient de son propre savoir. Il a renoncé absolument à faire appel aux premiers principes, et n'est plus sous la loi, mais sous *la grâce* d'une conviction définitive.)[100]

Ribot: All seems directed by *thought*.[101]

(Tout semble conduit par *une pensée*.)[102]

Butler: Yes, because all *has been* in earlier existences directed by *thought*.[103]

(Oui, parce que, au cours d'existences antérieures, tout *a été* en effet conduit par *une pensée*.)[104]

Ribot: Without ever arriving at *thought*.[105]

(Sans que rien n'arrive à *la pensée*.)[106]

Butler: Because it has *got past thought*, and though directed by thought originally, is now travelling in the exact opposite direction.[107]

(Parce que l'instinct *a dépassé la pensée* et que, encore qu'il ait été primitivement "conduit par la pensée," il avance maintenant dans une direction diamétralement opposée.)[108]

In this dialogue on the question of thought and instinct, the translation of the word "thought" becomes a translator's challenge and Larbaud rises gracefully

---

99 op. cit., p. 140.
100 op. cit., transl., p. 194.
101 op. cit., p. 140.
102 op. cit., p. 194.
103 op. cit., p. 140.
104 op. cit., transl., p. 194.
105 op. cit., p. 140.
106 op. cit., p. 194.
107 op. cit., p. 140.
108 op. cit., p. 194.

to the occasion. In the first two examples concerning thought, "thought" as an abstract concept doesn't fit in French as it alludes to a motive force: it can only be "thought" in the sense of a "particular" thought and is therefore translated as "*une pensée.*" In the last two examples, however, "thought" is indeed an abstraction (the notion of thought in general) and so becomes "*la pensée.*"

Much of this chapter is taken up with a direct development of the theme expressed in its title: the ways in which instinct can be understood as a manifestation of memories of previous lives. Thus the dog's habit of burying bones is given as a well-known example. Butler finds himself in agreement with Ribot on such basic principles as that "all instincts are only hereditary habits,"[109] but he also comes to conclusions concerning hereditary memory that Ribot had not expressed.

One of these is set forth especially well in the last paragraph of the chapter in which Butler gives one of Ribot's examples concerning a new born pup who is presented with an old piece of wolf skin. The pup goes into convulsions, which Ribot explains in a way that disappoints Butler: "We can only explain this alarm by the hereditary transmission of certain sentiments, coupled with a certain perception of the sense of smell."[110] Butler comments:

> I should prefer to say: we can only explain the alarm by supposing that the smell of the wolf's skin—the sense of smell being, as we all know, more powerful to recall the ideas that have been associated with it than any other sense—brought up the ideas with which it had been associated in the dog's mind during many previous existences—he on smelling the wolf's skin remembering all about wolves perfectly well.[111]

Larbaud translates:

> J'aimerais mieux dire: Comment expliquer cette terreur autrement qu'en supposant que l'odeur de la peau de loup—le sens de l'odorat étant, comme chacun sait, celui qui nous rappelle plus intensément qu'aucun autre sens les idées qui ont été associées avec lui,—évoquait les idées avec lesquelles elle avait été associée dans l'esprit du chien pendant un grand nombre d'existences antérieures?—le chien, à sentir la peau de loup, se rappelant parfaitement tout ce qui concerne les loups.[112]

---

109 op. cit., p. 145.
110 Ibid., p. 148.
111 Ibid.
112 op. cit., transl., pp. 204–205.

Twelve: Instincts of Neuter Insects (Les Instincts des insectes neutres)

Butler's continuing preoccupation with the importance of unconscious memory as a driving force in evolution is expressed once again in this chapter, and his book titled *Unconscious Memory* would appear soon after *Life and Habit*, in 1879. He refers, for example, to the consequence of what might today be designated as the "alienation" of a queen bee:

> Thus we see that certain changes in food (and domicile) from those with which its ancestors have been familiar, will disturb the memory of a queen bee's egg, and see it at such disadvantage as to make itself into a neuter bee; *but yet* we find that the larva thus partly aborted may have its memories restored to it, *if not already too much disturbed*, and may thus return to its condition as a queen bee, if it only again be restored to the food and domicile which its past memories can alone remember.[113]

This sentence occurs in a paragraph that is somewhat dense in its argumentation although characteristic of Butler. Larbaud clarifies it in various ways, first by labelling it as referring to bee societies and then changing the (co-ordinate) clause beginning with "but" to a new sentence as well as creating a parenthesis: "if not already too much disturbed." "*But yet*" becomes "mais même dans ce cas":

> C'est ainsi que *chez les abeilles*, une nourriture, et un domicile, différents de ceux qui ont été familiers à ses ancêtres, troublent la mémoire d'un oeuf de reine et lui causent un préjudice si grand qu'ils l'obligent à se faire abeille neutre. Mais *même dans ce cas*, la larve ainsi à demi avortée peut recouvrer ses souvenirs (*à condition qu'elle n'ait pas* été trop troublée) et peut revenir à son état de reine; pour cela il suffit de lui rendre la *seule* nourriture et la *seule* domicile que ses souvenirs lui permettent de reconnaître.[114]

These modifications thus solve a number of problems in Butler's style which create challenges for the translator. Generally speaking, Butler's English in this work often has a density that makes rapid reading a challenge. Larbaud constantly responds to this challenge, so that reading the work in French

---

113 op. cit., p. 150.
114 op. cit., transl., p. 208.

is a pleasure, (in keeping with his principle that reading must always be a pleasure). In the second last line of this passage, for example, the notion that it is a matter of a particular food (and a particular domicile) needs emphasis. Thus Larbaud inserts "seule" (suggested by the English *alone*) in the appropriate places in the French text.

It could be speculated that the reason for this aspect of Butler's challenge might lie in the circumstance that he is engaged here, and in all four of his evolution books (as he had been in his remarkable letters to the editor of the Christchurch, New Zealand, *Press*) in an absorbing debate which demands detailed *exposés* of his position, so that he may be seen to be answering his adversaries effectively. This tone of polemical urgency, giving the impression that these works, including *Life and Habit*, might have ideally required further revision before publication, was undoubtedly very obvious to Larbaud who was clearly not working under any such pressures. Paradoxically it is, therefore, the translation into French that becomes the definitive form of the work, given that the translator has, in the process of translation, also assumed the role of editor.

Butler's mastery of his subject is shown a few pages further on, when he looks at the case of the "aborted" bee and what might have caused the problem, which he sees as one of self-identity:

> We know that the larva which developed into a neuter bee, and that again which in time becomes a queen bee, are the same kind of larva to start with; and that if you give one of the larvae the food and treatment which all its foremothers have been accustomed to, it will turn out with all the structures and instincts of its foremothers—and that it only fails to do this because it has been fed, and otherwise treated, in such a manner as not one of its foremothers was ever yet fed or treated. So far, this is exactly what we should expect, on *the view that structure and instinct are alike mainly due to memory*, or to *medicined* memory. Give the larva a fair chance of *knowing where it is*, and it shows that it *remembers* by doing exactly what it did before. Give it a different kind of food and house, and it cannot be expected to be anything else than *puzzled*. It remembers a great deal. It comes out a bee and nothing but a bee; but it is an aborted bee; it is, in fact, mutilated before birth instead of after—with instinct as well as growth, correlated to its abortion, as we see happens frequently in the case of animals a good deal higher than bees that have been mutilated

at a stage much later than that at which the abortion of neuter bees commences.[115]

> Nous savons que la larve qui en se développant devient une abeille neutre, et celle qui devient, avec le temps, une reine, sont au début des larves de même espèce; et que, si nous donnons à l'une de ces larves la nourriture et le traitement que tous ses ancêtres ont eu l'habitude de recevoir, elle deviendra semblable, de structure et d'instincts, à tous ses ancêtres. Et si elle ne le fait pas, ce sera uniquement parce qu'elle aura été nourrie et traitée comme aucun de ses ancêtres n'a été nourri et traité avant elle. Jusqu'ici, c'est exactement ce à quoi nous devions nous attendre *si nous avons admis que la structure et l'instinct sont principalement dus à la mémoire,*—ou à la mémoire "*droguée.*" Donnez à cette larve une bonne chance de se *reconnaître,* et aussitôt elle montrera, en faisant ce qu'elle a déjà fait jadis, qu'elle *se reconnaît et se souvient.* Donnez-lui une nourriture et un logis différents, et vous devrez vous attendre à ce qu'elle se montre *embarrassée.* Elle se souvient de bien des choses: elle naît abeille, et rien qu'abeille. Mais elle est une abeille avortée. C'est une abeille qui a été mutilée avant sa naissance au lieu de l'être après. Son instinct et sa croissance sont en corrélation avec sa condition abortive, comme cela arrive fréquemment à des animaux bien supérieurs aux abeilles lorsqu'ils ont été mutilés à une phase de leur développement beaucoup plus avancée que celle à laquelle commence l'avortement des abeilles.[116]

This paragraph gets to the heart of the matter of the alleged importance of memory in the realization of identity. In translating the expression "knowing where it is," the French verb *se reconnaître* is used somewhat in the sense of the English verb *reconnoiter* whose origin it is. Larbaud combines it with *se souvient*, a slight rearranging, but balancing the "scales" perfectly. However, it is significant that Butler sees a creature's ability to "know where it is" as an indication of its self identity. (Thus knowing "where it is" also implies knowing "what it is" or "who it is"). This hypothesis, one of Butler's more daring ones in this field, is clearly important within the area of identity.

In stressing particular aspects of his "case against Darwin," Butler often puts them in a very condensed form with multiple implications that might

---

115 op. cit., p. 157.
116 op. cit., transl., pp. 217–218.

be considered to require a more extensive development. The major theme of course, is that there must be a force analogous to will power, a "natural purpose" replacing "divine purpose," in order to make comprehensible the workings of natural selection. One of the expressions of this theme occurs in this chapter:

> One cannot see that the habit of laying this particular kind of egg might not be due to use and memory in previous generations on the part of the fertile parents, "for the numerous slight spontaneous variations," on which "natural selection" is to work, *must have had some cause* than which none more reasonable than *the sense of need and experience* presents itself; and there seems hardly any limit to what long-continued faith and desire, aided by intelligence, may be able to effect. But if sense of need and experience are denied, I see no escape from the view that machines are a new species of life.[117]

> On ne voit pas comment l'habitude de pondre des oeufs de ce genre particulier ne pourrait pas être due, chez les parents féconds, à la coutume et au souvenir des générations antérieures, "car les nombreuses variations légères et spontanées" sur lesquelles doit porter la "sélection naturelle," *ont forcément eu une cause*; et quelle autre cause pouvons-nous avec plus de raison leur assigner, sinon *l'expérience et le sentiment du besoin?* Car il semble à peine y avoir de limite à ce que peuvent réaliser, au cours des siècles, une foi et un désir constants, aidés de l'intelligence. Mais si on refuse d'admettre le sentiment du besoin et de l'expérience, je ne vois pas quelle échappatoire on peut trouver pour ne pas aboutir à la conclusion que les machines sont une nouvelle forme de la vie.[118]

Butler's insistence on the need to find a *cause* for variations is curiously not stressed by the punctuation here. Larbaud, on the other hand, is well aware of the significance of this word for the argumentation and so remoulds the sentence by introducing an important stop after it through the use of a semicolon which provides the necessary strength for Butler's important hypothesis concerning "the sense of need and experience," and to which he then adds "faith and desire aided by intelligence."[119]

---

117 op. cit., ch. 12, p. 162.
118 op. cit., transl., pp. 224–225.
119 Ibid.

Butler's conclusion, namely that if such qualities are not granted, then natural processes are merely mechanistic, leading into the concept that the natural evolution of life could then be seen as directly analogous to that of machines. Butler's ongoing critique of this aspect of Darwin's position becomes somewhat obsessive (as well as being reminiscent of the satirical style of Voltaire).

"The Book of the Machines" in *Erewhon* is usually interpreted as a satirical allegory. As recently clarified admirably by Professor Lynn Margulis, Butler advances the concept of an *élan vital* that is ever present in evolutionary processes and applicable to all life. Regarding this French expression, created by Bergson, it seems impossible to find a more precise one for the essence of Butler's thoughts on the matter, in either English or French. It might be noted that Larbaud, in a letter to Gide, also firmly expressed his preference for Butler's *Life and Habit* to Bergson's *Evolution Créatrice*, which he reduced to "un agréable et *vague* bavardage poétique."[120] Importantly, Butler's pre-Bergsonian notion of the élan vital applies to both evolution and the evolving inventions of humankind.

Thirteen: Lamarck and Mr. Darwin (Lamarck et M. Darwin)

In this chapter, which takes us to the crux of the entire demonstration, Butler brings out emphatically his view of the importance of volition on the part of all beings, including humans, in the evolutionary process. However, he finds that humans are the best example because humans examining this process can communicate with those other humans who, desiring various changes, are "caught in the very act of variation."[121] Thus Butler sees in the development of machines, at the time in which he is writing, an appropriate image with which to argue in favour of a principle of purposeful evolution in nature.

He was impressed (almost "traumatized") by the rapid development in his lifetime of such applications of scientific principles in the interest of the convenience and aspirations of humankind as the realization and rapid improvement of steamships and railways, to mention only those examples which may be taken as particularly emblematic to Butler since they play a particularly important role in the setting of his life. For him, these responses to particular needs become metaphors for the infinitely slower phenomena of alleged applied will power in nature, and which he was convinced were manifested and could be observed at all levels of life.

---

120 Larbaud, *Lettres à André Gide* (Paris-La Haye: Stols, 1948), p. 121.
121 op. cit., p. 171.

Butler: Life and Habit—Further Considerations

It clearly becomes important to examine his precise words:

> Plants and animals under domestication are indeed a suggestive field of study, but machines are the manner in which man is varying at this moment. We know how our own minds work, and how our mechanical organizations…have progressed hand in hand with our desires; *sometimes the power a little ahead, and sometimes the desire*; sometimes both combining to form an organ with almost infinite capacity for variation….Here we are behind the scenes, and can see how the whole thing works. We have man, the very animal which we can best understand, caught in the very act of variation….*I would, therefore, strongly advise the reader to use man, and the present race of man, and the growing inventions and conceptions of man, as his guide, if he would seek to form an independent judgment on the development of organic life*. For all growth is only somebody making something.[122]

Larbaud translates:

> Sans doute, les plantes et les animaux à l'état domestique constituent un champ d'études fécond. Mais les machines sont la façon même dont l'homme varie en ce moment. Nous savons comment fonctionne notre esprit, et comment notre organisation mécanique…a progressé de concert avec nos désirs. *Parfois notre désir prend les devants, et d'autres fois c'est notre pouvoir qui marche en tête.* Quelquefois désir et pouvoir se combinent pour former un organe susceptible de variation presque illimitée….Ici nous sommes dans les coulisses et voyons comment les choses se passent. Ici, nous voyons l'homme, justement l'animal que nos sommes le plus capables de comprendre, nous le surprenons en train de varier….*C'est pourquoi je me permettrai de conseiller vivement à ceux de mes lecteurs qui voudraient se former un jugement indépendant sur le développement de la vie organique, de prendre pour guide l'homme, et les races humaines telles qu'elles existent actuellement, ainsi que les progrès que font sous nos yeux les inventions et les conceptions de l'homme.* Car la croissance n'est que ceci: quelqu'un qui fabrique quelque chose.[123]

---

122 op. cit., p. 171.
123 op. cit., transl., pp. 236–237.

In the first example (concerning "desire" and "power" as factors), it is curious that Butler puts "power" before "desire," which might indeed illustrate the point that the "fortuitous" can always occur, but in the matter of stylistic improvement, Larbaud prefers to mention "desire" before "power," possibly in order to maintain the inherent logic of the language. (The two concepts are, in any case, joined together in the sentence that follows.)

In little modifications of this sort Larbaud again creates improvements, by means of the translation, which constantly tend to make it a more coherent and effective version of the work.

In the second example, "independent judgment" as a desirable aim is mentioned in the French text before its object, presumably as sounding more "elegant" in that order than in the original one, stylistic matters, often very subtle, and taking us to the "music" of the language, being important to Larbaud. This sort of rearranging becomes a more and more familiar "signature" in Larbaud's translation.

Butler was convinced that Darwin's view needed the tonic of Lamarck's sense of purpose and that his deliberate exclusion of Lamarck's sense of "the little purposes" had risked leading Darwin to a misconception, although Butler keeps reminding his readers of Darwin's huge achievement. In fact the crux of the matter is clearly stated:

> The weak point in Mr. Darwin's theory would seem to be a deficiency, so to speak, of *motive power* to originate and direct the variations which time is to accumulate. It deals admirably with the accumulations of variations in creatures already varying, but it does not provide a sufficient number of sufficiently important variations to be accumulated. Given the motive power which Lamarck suggested, and Mr. Darwin's mechanism would appear (with the help of memory, as bearing upon reproduction, of continued personality, and hence of inherited habit, and of the vanishing tendency of consciousness) to work with perfect ease.[124]

Larbaud translates:

> Le point faible de la théorie de M. Darwin, c'est qu'on n'y trouve pas ce qu'on pourrait appeler "*la puissance motrice*" qui produit et dirige les variations que le temps se charge d'accumuler. Elle traite admirablement de l'accumulation de variations

---

124 op. cit., ch. 13, pp. 174–175.

chez les êtres déjà en train de varier, mais elle ne fournit pas un assez grand nombre de variations assez importantes à accumuler. Mais qu'on y introduise *la puissance motrice* indiquée par Lamarck, en y ajoutant les principes suivants: la mémoire agissant sur la reproduction, la continuité de la personnalité, et par suite l'hérédité des habitudes et la tendance qu'a la conscience à s'effacer,—et tout aussitôt le mécanisme de M. Darwin se trouve fonctionner admirablement.[125]

Thus the key words here are *motive power* which imply the notion of a forward progression. They contain what is in effect the essence of the Lamarckian position. In his translation Larbaud "highlights" this expression by making it a quotation (which Butler had not done).

On the same page, Butler sums up the essence of his thoughts on the Lamarckian position:

One wants something that will give a more definite aim to variations, and hence, at times, cause bolder leaps in advance.[126]

Nous sentons la nécessité de quelque chose qui donne aux variations un but plus défini, et qui, par conséquent, provoque de temps à autre des *bonds en avant* plus hardis.[127]

These *bonds en avant* seem reminiscent of Bergson's *élan vital*. Butler politely suggests that Darwin's insistence on a very gradual accumulation of very small variations must be considered inadequate. If there are variations, then given the eventual result, for example an elephant, then there must be a sense of *purpose* to explain why these variations occurred (rather than others) and why they naturally led (after great periods of trial and error) to certain evolved results. Butler then pursues the example of the elephant within this context:

Unless we can explain the origin of variations, we are met by the unexplained *at every step* in the progress of a creature from its original homogeneous condition to its differentiation, we will say, as an elephant; *so to say that an elephant has become an elephant through the accumulation of a vast number of small, fortuitous, but unexplained, variations in some lower creature,*

---

125 op. cit., transl., pp. 241–242.
126 op. cit., p. 175.
127 op. cit., transl., p. 242.

> *is really to say that it has become an elephant owing to a series of causes about which we know nothing whatever*, or, in other words, that one does not know how it came to be an elephant.[128]

Larbaud's French does justice to these significant words:

> Faute d'expliquer l'origine des variations, nous nous sommes trouvés en présence de l'inexpliqué à chaque pas du développement progressif d'un être depuis son état homogène primitif jusqu'à sa différentiation sous la forme, par exemple, d'un éléphant. De sorte que *dire qu'un éléphant est devenu éléphant grâce à l'accumulation d'un nombre immense de petites variations fortuites et inexpliquées survenues chez quelques êtres inférieurs, c'est en réalité dire qu'il est devenu éléphant grâce à une série de causes que nous ignorons complètement*, ou, en d'autres termes, que nous ne savons pas comment il est devenu éléphant.[129]

Regarding the presumed "variations," Larbaud adds the word *survenues* to underline the notion that these variations "occurred" even though their alleged occurrence in the ancestry of the elephant was deemed by Darwin to be haphazard, and could thus have eventually led to the evolution of a very different creature, although neither Darwin nor Butler make such a suggestion.

This passage is also an example of Butler's diplomatic language in expressing an important reservation about Darwin's theory in an effort to make this point of view acceptable to his reader and also, by implication, to Darwin himself. Such gentle diplomacy comes naturally to Larbaud and from that point of view his version could once again be considered an improvement on Butler's original. Variation soon becomes the main topic of this chapter: whether it occurs or not, and since it must (of one kind or another and to one extent or another) whether it is the result of any sort of volition on the part of the plant or animal varying. Before stating his position Butler does agree with Darwin in opposing the notion that plants and animals tend to work toward any predetermined improved state. ("I would admit this as contrary to all experience.")[130]

In order to clarify this last point in favour of Darwin, Larbaud states it much more explicitly: "Je donne raison sur ce point à M. Darwin, car cela est contraire

---

128   op. cit., p. 176.
129   op. cit., transl., p. 244.
130   op. cit., p. 178.

à toute expérience."¹³¹ This sort of clarification, achieved through a few added words, to express what is merely understood in the original, is characteristic of Larbaud and again suggests that the original *Life and Habit* probably could have been further improved by further revision, as well as the possibility that his publisher might have been "overanxious" to publish (as Butler suggests) in view of the continuing intense interest in the evolution debate which prevailed at the time. However that may be, it is clear that the translation became a more perfect expression of Butler's intent than the original.

Butler restates his position succinctly:

> I am inclined...to think that they [plants and animals] have only an *innate power to vary slightly*, in accordance with changed conditions, and an innate capability of being affected both in structure and instinct by causes similar to those which we observe to affect ourselves.[132]

Larbaud translates:

> Je suis disposé...à penser qu'ils n'ont qu'une *faculté innée de varier légèrement*, selon les changements qui surviennent dans leurs conditions d'existence, et qu'une capacité innée d'être affectés dans leur structure et dans leur instinct par des causes semblables à celles qui nous affectent nous-mêmes.[133]

Butler closes this chapter by quoting St. George Jackson Mivart's work *The Genesis of Species* (1871) for support for the notion of purpose and "creativity" in evolution. "Walking stick" insects and "leaf" butterflies are brought into the picture when Darwin's colleague Wallace is quoted referring to the "leaf" butterfly of Borneo which not only imitates a leaf but also certain stages of decay of the leaf, giving the impression that it had been the victim of small fungi. Butler is delighted to have found what he considers convincing evidence of "will power" on the part of that species of butterfly (within the very controversial context of Batesian mimicry) and writes:

> I can no more believe that these artificial fungi in which the moth arrays itself are due to the accumulation of minute, perfectly blind, and unintelligent variations than I can believe

---

131 op. cit., transl., p. 246.
132 op. cit., p. 178.
133 op. cit., transl., pp. 246–247.

that the artificial flowers which a woman wears in her hat can have got there without design.¹³⁴

Mivart makes similar observations regarding the minute contrivances by which the visits of insects are utilized for the fertilization of orchids—structures so wonderful that nothing could well be more so, except the attribution of their origin to minute, fortuitous and indefinite variations.¹³⁵

Through this quotation Butler's own (still controversial) position is rigourously stated and in conclusion, he reiterates it in the same sardonic manner that he has found in Mivart:

> I can no more believe that all this has come about without design on the part of the orchid...than I can believe that a mousetrap or a steam engine is the result of the accumulation of blind minute fortuitous variations in a creature called man, which creature has never wanted either mousetraps or steam engines.¹³⁶

Larbaud translates:

> Je ne peux pas plus croire que tout cela s'est fait sans qu'il y eût intention de la part de l'orchidée...que je ne peux croire qu'une souricière ou une locomotive sont le résultat de l'accumulation de petites variations aveugles et fortuites chez un être appelé l'homme; lequel être n'aurait jamais désiré avoir ni souricières ni locomotives.¹³⁷

Fourteen: Mr. Mivart and Mr. Darwin (M. Mivart et M. Darwin)

This chapter brings Butler's observations within the specific context of the evolution debate of his time, a debate which had been attracting public attention continuously since the publication of Darwin's *The Origin of Species* in 1859. It points toward a statement of his position as it was after he had assimilated and supported the work of St. George Mivart. However, Butler does not neglect to reiterate his admiration for Darwin "who makes other people accept the main conclusions, whether on right grounds or wrong ones."¹³⁸

---

134 op. cit.p. 180.
135 op. cit., p. 181.
136 Ibid.
137 op. cit., transl., pp. 250–251.
138 op. cit.p. 185

Butler points out, however, that Darwin had stressed that "we know nothing of the causes from which the vast majority of modifications have arisen."[139] He concludes: "But to the end of time, if the question be asked, "Who taught people to believe in evolution? " there can be only one answer—that it was Mr. Darwin."[140]

The debate over the success in survival of certain insect species through mimicry, that is by apparent imitation of other life forms, is the subject of much of this chapter. Mivart is quoted as opposing the notion that natural selection would be enough to explain such results over time, invoking the immense amount of time required in order to succeed in initiating such a phenomenon merely by chance, and the implication that other insects in a given region would have to have similar incentives and have reached various stages of "disguise" in order to make the system work through breeding.

Butler provides his own view on this phenomenon. He had pointed out in the first paragraph of the chapter that what was needed was that "intelligence and memory" should come into play. Thus, with respect to Mivart's "objection," Butler develops his own position in greater detail:

> A strong impression is left on my mind that without the help of something over and above the power to vary, which should give definite aim to variations, all the "natural selection" in the world would not have prevented *stagnation* and *self-stultification*, owing to the indefinite tendency of the variations....Grant *"a little dose of judgement and reason"* on the part of the creature itself—grant also continued personality and memory—and a definite tendency is at once given to the variations. The process is thus started, and is *helped forward* through every stage by "the little dose of reason."[141]

This amounts to a manifesto of Butler's position.
Larbaud translates:

> Mais j'ai l'impression bien nette que sans l'aide de quelque chose de plus que la faculté de varier, de quelque chose qui donnerait un but défini aux variations, toute la "sélection naturelle" du monde n'aurait pas pu empêcher que la vie ne

---

139 Ibid.
140 Ibid.
141 op. cit. pp. 188–189.

> fût tombée dans *la stagnation* et *l'hébètement*, à cause de la tendance indéfinie des variations....Car, si on admet "*une petite dose de jugement et de raison*" chez l'être qui varie,—et si on admet la continuité de la personnalité et la mémoire,—une tendance définie est aussitôt donnée aux variations. Dès lors *l'évolution est mise en marche*; et *elle est maintenue dans la bonne voie*; et elle est *poussée en avant* à chaque phase par "la petite dose de raison."[142]

One small point of detail in this translation demonstrates a typical way in which Larbaud improves the original: the translation of the colloquial phrase "*self-stultification.*" The phrase has an awkwardness that suggests that it was already doomed (in Butler's time) to drop from colloquial English. (Larbaud was no doubt well aware of such trends as a result of his sojourns in both literary London and in other English cities and towns as well as the Warwickshire countryside.) For this translation he chooses the French substantive *hébètement* from *hébéter* (with its slightly mocking connotation). Such improvements, in which the translation is clearer than the original, could also be taken as emblematic of the improvements brought about by Larbaud throughout the translation. It is an example of something somewhat "rough hewn" in Butler's prose which becomes a challenge for Larbaud, whose French version could once again be described as more appropriate and precise than the original. This could also be said of the translation of "helped forward" by "*maintenue dans la bonne voie*" in which there is a strengthening of the concept "helped forward."

It is difficult to avoid the impression that Butler, in the autumn of 1877, was anxious to see his book published without delay. It could also be inferred that the painstaking and more leisurely process of translation means that Larbaud's translation represents the finished form of the work.

Concluding Remarks (Conclusion)

In the first pages of this final chapter, Butler sums up his position on evolution and places himself firmly in the lineage of thought established by Lamarck. He also makes an important statement which qualifies much of his work:

> Life is that property of matter whereby it can remember. Matter which can remember is living; matter which cannot remember is dead. *Life, then, is memory.*[143]

---

142 op. cit., transl., pp. 259–260.
143 op. cit., p. 199.

> La vie est cette proprlété de la matière en vertu de laquelle la matière est capable de se souvenir. La matière qui peut se souvenir est vivante, la matière qui ne peut pas se souvenir est morte. La vie, donc, c'est la mémoire.[144]

Butler then discusses the book with his reader, acknowledging the possibility of inaccuracies. As he puts it: "I have been trying to paint a picture rather than to make a diagram,"[145] thus invoking the creative aspect of his work and suggesting that the sort of hypothetical demonstration he has been writing is as much an art as a science:

> So the greatest musicians, painters and poets owe their greatness rather to their fusion and assimilation of all the good that has been done up to, and especially near about, their own time, than to any very startling steps they have taken in advance.[146]

Larbaud translates:

> C'est ainsi que les plus grands d'entre les musiciens, les peintres et les poètes, doivent leur grandeur plutôt à la fusion et à l'assimilation qu'ils ont faite de tout ce qui a été composé. peint ou écrit jusqu'à eux, et particulièrement tout près d'eux, qu'à aucun pas sensationnel qu'ils n'aient pu faire en avant.[147]

This conversation with his reader seems to betray some uncertainty on Butler's part concerning whether the book has responded fully to its aim. However, it does also clearly express his intention of a continuing involvement in these matters. There is also a suggestion that he is expecting reader reaction, possibly debate, when the book appears. The mere fact that he was challenging the great man of the time, Darwin, seemed certain to lead to a reaction. But as it happened this reaction was somewhat muted: to a great extent he found himself confronted once again with the "conspiracy of silence."

However, Butler's sense of his work being in an unfinished stage would soon produce such further publications as *Evolution Old and New* (1879), *Unconscious Memory* (1880), and finally *Luck or Cunning* (1886).

---

144 op. cit., transl., p. 275.
145 op. cit., p. 201.
146 Ibid. pp. 202–203.
147 op. cit., transl., p. 279.

Paradoxically, however, it is Larbaud's translation, *La Vie et l'habitude*, that constitutes the finished version of *Life and Habit*, given that Larbaud's very scrupulous "weighing of the scales" in order to bring out every shade of meaning, revealing this work in its integrity, means that his translation becomes its most perfect revision.

Chapter 9

Butler: Erewhon Revisited

We have noted that *Erewhon* belonged to a literary tradition that had reached a degree of perfection in France in the eighteenth century as in such *contes philosophiques* as Voltaire's *Candide*, in which the literary form is primarily a device for the expression of certain underlying "philosophical" positions and does not pretend otherwise, even though this genre does also furnish the reader with entertainment value as an adventure novel, and it is clear that many such works were read primarily for that reason. The French expression *roman à thèse* nonetheless remains relevant.

The adventure novel's development in Europe and America, from the late eighteenth century, in the climate of Romanticism, seemed at first glance to have made its "escapist" aspect far more important than the expression of an ideology. From the beginning of the modern novel, it soon became evident that an author's "messages" were more often implicit than explicit, as in the classic example of Defoe's *Robinson Crusoe*. However, the satirical novel tended to reverse matters: in Butler's *Erewhon Revisited*, the adventure aspect is merely a pretext, leaving the impression that the author is making use of the action mainly to bring about situations that necessarily tend to favour the expression of his ideology. Thus *Erewhon Revisited* is clearly more explicit in its expression of Butlerian messages than his earlier fiction, to the point at which it could easily be understood as a *roman à thèse*.

Larbaud's translation of *Erewhon Revisited* (*Nouveaux Voyages en Erewhon*) was published in 1924, some time after the first symptoms of the reaction in France against Zola's "naturalism" (in which *race*, *moment*, and *milieu* determined a character or a situation "scientifically"), and also against Bourget's and Barrès' psychological determinism in which character structures lead fatally to inevitable results. The novel was reinventing itself and in so doing was also reviving certain classical novelistic traits.

Jacques Rivière, who was soon to become the director of *La Nouvelle Revue Française*, published an important series of articles entitled *Le Roman d'Aventure* on one aspect of these new trends in the novel, in the numbers from May to July 1913. The number for July 1913 also contained the first instalment (and first publication) of *Le Grand Meaulnes* by his friend and future brother-in-law Alain-Fournier. This now famous novel illustrates the essential features Rivière found particularly relevant.

Rivière also found these in the novels of Daniel Defoe:

> En d'autres termes la parfaite actualisation d'un roman, c'est sa parfaite activité. Plus aucune place pour le rêve, ni pour les décors immobiles; tous les éléments travaillent. L'oeuvre est pareille à ces machines ou' rien ne dort....L'exemple qu'il faut alléguer ici c'est celui des romans de Daniel De Foe.[1]

When *Nouveaux Voyages en Erewhon* appeared, *La Nouvelle Revue Française* was following this trend by publishing translations of Hardy and Chesterton, as well as Jean-Aubry's Conrad translations.[2]

Butler's *Erewhon Revisited* might well be considered a very good actualization of Rivière's conception of the novel. Furthermore, Larbaud's translation of *Erewhon Revisited* appeared in 1924 precisely at this time when the adventure novel had become firmly re-established as an important literary trend in France.

Butler was, of course, first and foremost a philosopher, and *Erewhon* had resembled the "philosophical" novels of seventeenth and eighteenth-century France in that certain preconceived messages, sometimes political and at other times warnings against what might be deemed fatalistic in human nature, thus tending to promote human well being, found their voice. Cyrano de Bergerac's *Voyage aux états de la lune et du soleil*, a major source of Swift's *Gulliver's Travels*, had established this genre in France, having been published in 1656 and 1662 in *Histoires Comiques*. Larbaud mentions this in his *Avertissement* for the French *Erewhon*.[3] In this sort of novel the message, of course, becomes much more important than the "medium" which is sometimes reduced to the status of a mere device, as in the instance of "The Book of the Machines" in *Erewhon*. Nonetheless the "philosophical" novel as it was practised by Cyrano and Voltaire was at the same time an adventure novel.

Erewhon Revisited is similarly both an adventure novel and one which expresses Butlerian views. These arise naturally from the vagaries of the plot in which the protagonist (whose name is now revealed as Higgs) finds

---

1 op. cit., juin 1913, p. 732.

2 *En Marge des Marées*, the translation of *Within the Tides*, had been published in 1921. *Jeunesse*, the translation of *Youth*, appeared in 1925.

3 Cf. op. cit., p. xxi.

himself caught up. In most respects *Erewhon Revisited* may be taken as a model adventure novel within Rivière's conception, even though Rivière does not directly address the question of "commitment" in a novel to a cause or to various causes (*l'engagement*).

Erewhon Revisited is narrated by one of Higgs's sons who has stayed behind in England. Higgs, fluent in the Erewhonian language, arrives in Erewhon by the same route over the mountain passes which he had pioneered twenty years before. He has taken the precaution of bringing along his old Erewhonian costume so that he will not be recognized as an intruder: this is one of the details that create the suspense, since he does not know that the official costume for men had been changed by decree during the intervening years. (He will discover that just in time.) He also quickly discovers that as a result of his "miraculous" ascent by balloon with his bride Arowhena in the *dénouement* of *Erewhon*, he has been deified as "the Sunchild" and that "Sunchildism," with its "holy" texts (*The Writings of the Sunchild*) has become the official religion of Erewhon.

Butler does not delay the action: the villains (*les traîtres*), the unscrupulous Professors Hanky and Panky, who are scheming to exploit the new religion, happen to be out for a hike and appear on the scene almost immediately, so Higgs pretends to be a park ranger and seems to succeed in overcoming their curiosity. Regarding the characterization of Panky, whom Butler describes as having become "a living lie,"[4] Larbaud translates "un mensonge incarné."[5] Higgs does soon meet a real ranger, a comely youth who much impresses him and who is later revealed as his son by Yram, now mayor of the provincial town of Sunch'ton toward which Higgs is directing his steps.

The reader is thus left with the impression that Butler is thoroughly amusing himself in imagining all the details and complexities of this fictitious situation. However, Butler's bitter satire of the Anglican Church and formal Christianity in general, continued to dismay Larbaud, who, several times in his *Journal* expresses his reluctance to translate *ces pages-là*. An example is Panky's intention to speak before the "Sunchild Evidence Society" and make "an earnest appeal for funds to endow the canonries required for the due service of the temple."[6] Larbaud translates: "Un urgent appel de fonds pour doter les chanoinies nécessaires au service indispensable du temple."[7]

The insinuation here that Panky might himself "benefit" from these funds may not seem quite as clear to a francophone reader until we learn of the box

---

4 op. cit. Everyman ed., ch. 4, p. 219.
5 op. cit., transl., p. 62.
6 op. cit., p. 221.
7 op. cit., transl., p. 65.

in front of the altar where people deposited "coin of the realm according to their will or ability."[8] This incident is one of several which lead Higgs to fully comprehend what has happened in his absence.

Again, like Voltaire in his *contes philosophiques*, Butler takes aim at various forms of casuistry, in this instance, on points of dogma such as whether the "ascension" of the Sunchild had taken place with the help of horses.

This form of satire had been largely developed in French, giving the translation a familiar ring to francophone readers. The university is also satirized with remarkable frequency as when Yram as Mayoress gives a dinner party after she has learned from Professor Panky that there might be a foreigner lurking in the realm. At this point Butler takes aim at the university by attacking historians in very Voltairean language of the cynical kind that Larbaud found somewhat extreme:

> It has been said that God cannot alter the past, historians can; it is perhaps because they can be useful to him in this respect that He tolerates their existence.[9]

> Quelqu'un a dit que, si Dieu ne peut pas changer le passé, les historiens le peuvent; et c'est peut-être parce qu'ils peuvent être utiles à Dieu en cela que Dieu tolère leur existence.[10]

In the scene in which Yram has become aware that the stranger is none other than Higgs and explains the situation to her son, she utters the words: "Higgs coming at this time is mere accident;"[11] Larbaud translates "coming" as simply "l'arrivée."[12]

But there could, of course, be ambiguity in the word "coming" in this context. Would it remind an English speaker of the expression "the second coming"? On balance it seems likely that, given Butler's satirical intentions, the word is indeed meant to suggest that phrase, since this is literally Higg's "second coming" and Butler would be unlikely to spare mainstream Anglicanism when given such an opportunity. However, there is no indication that Larbaud understood the word in that way or attempted to find a French equivalent for this "insinuation."

---

8 op. cit., p. 221.
9 op. cit., p. 293.
10 op. cit., transl., pp. 167–168.
11 op. cit., p. 261.
12 op. cit., transl., p. 122.

Butler's understanding of the word "spiritual" also seems to have been something of a problem for Larbaud. *Spirituel*, of course, normally means "witty" in colloquial French (a much admired quality in French culture) but it does also have a second meaning equivalent to the English *spiritual*. (The words *l'esprit* and *l'âme*, on the other hand, make a clear distinction between "mind" and "soul").

In Chapter 10, in a passage on bringing up children, in which quite ordinary matters are taken to court, a judge, in a summation, says: "all diseases of the moral sense spring from impurities within the body which must be cleansed before there could be any hope of spiritual improvement."[13]

Surprisingly, Larbaud translates the last clause "avant qu'on puisse compter sur une amélioration de l'esprit."[14] It can only be concluded that Larbaud seems to experience a problem with the English notion of "spirituality." The other meaning of *spirituel* occurs in Chapter 14 when Higgs meets one of the citizens who had witnessed the "ascension" of the Sunchild, a "Mr. Balmy." The latter comments:

> A spiritual enlightenment from within…is more to be relied on than any merely physical affluence from external objects.[15]

> Une illumination spirituelle venue du dedans…mérite plus de croyance que n'importe quels afflux purement physiques émanés des objets extérieurs.[16]

As Aldaz has pointed out, Butler liked to refer to biblical verses and then construe them in his own way. A young man whom Higgs meets comments:

> Your heaven will not attract me unless I can take my clothes and my luggage. Yes; and I must lose my luggage and find it again.[17]

> Votre ciel ne me dira rien tant que je ne pourrai pas apporter mes habits et mes bagages avec moi. Oui, et encore, il faudra que je perde mes bagages et que je les retrouve.[18]

---

13 op. cit., ch. 10, p. 264.
14 op. cit., transl., p. 126.
15 op. cit., ch. 14, p. 294.
16 op. cit., transl., p. 169.
17 op. cit., ch. 10, p. 266.
18 op. cit., transl., p. 128.

It is not absolutely clear whether Larbaud recognizes here a parody of the Biblical verse or not, but it may be assumed that it is much more likely that he does. However, the real question becomes whether the French reader in a highly secularized republican society will recognize it. (A footnote seems required.) Another Biblical quotation occurs in this chapter when the narrator begs the reader's permission to allow him to make some editorial comments of his own. In justifying this request he writes:

> The mouth of the ox that treadeth out the corn should not be so closely muzzled that he cannot sometimes filch a mouthful for himself.[19]

Larbaud translates:

> Il ne faut pas lier la bouche du boeuf qui foule le grain de notre aire si étroitement qu'il ne puisse, de temps en temps, en dérober une bouchée pour lui-même.[20]

Both Butler and Larbaud were of course inveterate travellers and interested in the cultural relativity from which one's own culture might possibly benefit. In this respect, too, they resembled the eighteenth-century *philosophes* who had used travel as a means of demonstrating the well-known principle that since customs are different in other cultures, this creates a relativity suggesting that quite possibly things could be different...or even better...at home. Italy appealed to both Butler and Larbaud from this point of view.

The reader of *Erewhon Revisited* also experiences Erewhon in this way: here too we are conscious of being in another culture in which certain things are done differently. This sense of cultural relativity also creates a need to be a little cautious and diplomatic when you are there. In Erewhon, one of the "differences" is that it seems more authoritarian than home, with the possible implication that there may also be certain authoritarian tendencies in one's own culture concerning which one must be on one's guard.

The French version of the dramatic public crisis to which the plot inevitably leads, also has a peculiarly Voltairean ring. The occasion is the inauguration of a new temple in Sunch'ton to which Higgs is invited, and he is seated near the front next to his son George, Yram being among the dignitaries seated in the apse. Hanky "preaches a sermon" whose words are full of the sort of "doublespeak" which Butler expressed by inventing the portmanteau word

---

19 Ibid., p. 267.
20 op. cit., transl., p. 129.

"insinuendo." The situation soon becomes explosive, bringing about the central crisis of the novel which then leads to its very Voltairean *dénouement*:

> Here he [Hanky] again glared at my father, whose blood was boiling....He therefore sprang to his feet. "You lying hound," he cried, "I am the Sunchild, and you know it."
>
> Yram turned pale. Hanky roared out, "Tear him in pieces."[21]
>
> Et de nouveau il regarda fixement mon père, dont le sang bouillait....et il se dressa d'un bond: "Chien menteur!" s'écria-t-il. "Je suis le Filsdusoleil et tu le sais!."...Yram pâlit. Compère hurla: "Mettez-le en pièces!"[22]

However, as in Voltaire's *Contes pholosophiques*, plot is of course merely a pretext in Butler's novels. Themes remain the matter of consequence. The major theme in *Erewhon Revisited* might be taken to be Butler's notion of "counterfeit ideology." When Larbaud's translation (*Nouveaux Voyages en Erewhon*) appeared in 1924, it foretold Gide's famous use of that theme in his major novel *Les Faux-Monnayeurs* which would appear in 1926.

---

21 op. cit., ch. 16, p. 317.
22 op. cit., transl., pp. 200–201.

Chapter 10

Butler: Note-Books

The publication in 1912 of Butler's *Note-Books* by his friend and collaborator Henry Festing Jones was undoubtedly the most important event in Butler's "vicarious life" between the appearance of *The Way of All Flesh* in 1903 and that of the definitive Shrewsbury edition of his complete works.

Festing Jones describes the making of this remarkable collection of thoughts and anecdotes in his Preface, quoting Butler in order to explain their origin:

> "One's thoughts fly so fast that one must shoot them; it is no use trying to put salt on their tails." So he bagged as many as he could hit and preserved them, re-written on loose sheets of paper which constituted a sort of museum stored with the wise, beautiful and strange creatures that were continually winging their way across the field of his vision.[1]

As he points out in the *Avant-Propos du Traducteur* of his translation,[2] Larbaud used the third edition of the book published in September 1915. The translation of this allegory of the hunter demonstrates his usual mastery:

> Nos pensées volent si vite qu'il nous faut les abattre d'un coup de fusil; il est inutile d'essayer de leur mettre un grain de sel sur la queue. Il mettait donc dans sa gibecière toutes celles qu'il avait abattues, et les conservait, transcrites sur des feuilles de papier détachées, qui constituaient une sorte de musée rempli de créatures étranges, belles et pleines de sagesse, qui traversaient sans cesse le champ de sa vision.[3]

---

1 *The Note-Books of Samuel Butler* (London: Fifield, 1912), *Preface*, p. v.
2 Samuel Butler, *Carnets* (Paris: Gallimard, 1936), p. 19
3 op. cit. *Préface*, p. 19.

Festing Jones redistributes Butler's notes into twenty-four chapters (a twenty-fifth being dedicated to Butler's verse). Some of these already had titles but, as Jones explains in his own Preface, he "provided titles for many notes which had none."[4]

In his translation of *Note-Books*, Larbaud continues to understand Butler's work as relating to certain major works in French literature. At first sight they might appear to belong to the same genre as Pascal's *Pensées*. In fact the argument in Chapter 20, concerning free will versus necessity, in particular, is very much in the manner of Pascal the polemicist, whose work, especially *Les Lettres Provinciales*, was among the French classics Larbaud reread in order to immerse himself in appropriate styles for his translation. Thus on January 13, 1919, he writes in the English of his diary: "Going on with S.B. and reading Pascal. It helps me greatly."[5]

Basil Willey also refers to Pascal in his evocation of the metaphysical *angoisse* which he sees in Butler's struggles to define his position on Christianity. They seem to Willey to have caused Butler the sort of inner torment that makes a comparison with Pascal plausible. Pascal and Butler could both be seen as men of the Enlightenment who were facing the ultimate questions posed by Pascal's famous phrase *la condition humaine*.

There is, however, an important difference between the two works. Pascal is far more objective in his exposition than Butler, concerned with matters of pure principle meant to hold true beyond any human subjectivity. Butler, on the other hand, almost always writes from a very personal viewpoint, especially in the *Note-Books*, as though he were discussing his ideas within a circle of close friends. He puts himself on stage and even takes us backstage.

As Larbaud explains in his *Avant-Propos* to his translation of the *Note-Books* (*Carnets*), it is for reasons of this sort that he finds in Montaigne the possibility of a more valid comparison with Butler. He even admits to having created some parodies of Montaigne, for his own amusement, from some of Butler's notes and comments:

> On y retrouvait, tout naturellement produit, cet air de loisir, ce ton de conversation bien assise, ces précautions dans le progrès du discours, enfin tout cela qui…nous attarde si agréablement dans nos lectures de Montaigne.[6]

---

4 op. cit., p. v.
5 Larbaud, *Journal*, p. 473.
6 op. cit. (1936), p. 12.

Montaigne's spontaneity, his sense of leisure and his masterful "conversation" with the reader, its easy flow, and at the same time his discretion, in fact everything that makes reading Montaigne such a pleasure.

Larbaud felt that Butler had read Florio's English translation of Montaigne and that the anecdote of the magpie imitating the sound of trumpets in *Life and Habit* came to him from Montaigne rather than directly from Plutarch.[7]

However, in the translation of Chapter 20 ("First Principles") under the heading "Free Will and Necessity," Larbaud's translation seems to echo both Montaigne and Pascal:

> [Free will] is quite as much a *sine qua non* for action as necessity is; for who would try to act if he did not think that his trying would influence the result?[8]

> Le libre arbitre est donc, tout autant que la nécessité, une condition *sine qua non* de l'action; car qui voudrait seulement agir s'il ne croyait pas que sa volonté influencerait le résultat de son acte?[9]

Another note with the title *Necessity Otherwise Luck* has a closely related subject:

> It is all very well to insist upon the free will or cunning side of living action, more especially now when it has been so persistently ignored, but though the fortunes of birth and surroundings have all been built up by cunning, yet it is by ancestral, vicarious cunning, and this, to each individual, comes to much the same as luck pure and simple; in fact luck is seldom seriously intended to mean a total denial of cunning, but is for the most part only an expression whereby we summarize and express our sense of a cunning too complex and impalpable for conscious following and apprehension.[10]

---

7 Ibid.
8 op. cit., p. 317.
9 op. cit., transl., p. 314.
10 op. cit., p. 320.

It is hardly surprising that Larbaud divides this compound sentence into three shorter ones: Butler's clauses again become Larbaud's sentences. In so doing, and by developing the concepts in order to bring out all shades of meaning, he achieves a maximum of clarity:

La Necessité, autrement dite la chance

C'est très bien d'insister sur le côté libre arbitre, ou adresse, de l'action vivante, surtout en ce moment où on a mis tant d'entêtement à le méconnaître. Mais bien que les hasards de notre naissance et de nos milieux soient tous l'oeuvre de l'adresse, ils la sont indirectement, et c'est de l'adresse ancestrale qu'il s'agit; or cela pour chaque individu en particulier revient à n'être qu'une affaire de simple chance. En fait quand on parle de chance on ne songe presque jamais sérieusement à exclure d'une manière absolue l'adresse; mais ce n'est, la plupart du temps qu'une manière de dire par laquelle nous résumons et exprimons la perception que nous avons d'une adresse trop complexe et trop impalpable pour que nous puissions en suivre les démarches et la comprendre consciemment.[11]

This *pensée* is particularly relevant respecting these two writers since both Larbaud and Butler issued from privileged families, and in their respective works they are comparable in the "cunning" they both brought to bear upon those works, a "cunning" whose results were made possible by their authors' unique situations.

Note-Books also contain references to both the art and the history of translation. For example, at one point Larbaud is confronted with a quotation from Butler's namesake Samuel Butler "the Elder," the author of *Hudibras* (1663), a popular satire in verse composed under the English Restoration, which ridiculed Cromwell's republican cause:

Surely the pleasure is as great

Of being cheated as to cheat.

This poem had been translated into French and published by J. Towneley in 1757, an instance of a successful translation from the maternal language into

---

11 op. cit., transl., p. 316.

a second one. (Voltaire had also attempted a translation.) On this occasion Larbaud uses Towneley's words:

> Le plaisir est bien aussi grand
>
> D'être déçu que décevant.

Although the primary "official" denotation of *décevoir* is still "to deceive," or "to fool," that meaning is no longer understood since in colloquial French it has long meant "to disappoint." Nonetheless, as this is a quotation, Larbaud is able to respond to the challenge of the appropriate rendering of words whose original meaning has become rare.

In *Note-Books* we also find one of Butler's occasional comments on translation. These are valuable because he claimed to have translated Homer in such a way that "it would not be jaded by academic study of the language."[12] Elinor Shaffer points out that this shift toward colloquial language from the artificially archaic forms of William Morris, or the pseudo-Biblical language of S.H. Butcher and A. Lang in their popular Victorian translations of Homer, eventually led to the "trivialization" of *The Odyssey* in the world of Leopold Bloom as he wanders through Dublin in Joyce's *Ulysses*. Butler's translations of Homer are thus understood as representing a trend that leads on to Joyce and it is known that Butler's translation of *The Odyssey* was the only English translation to which Joyce referred while writing *Ulysses*.[13]

In this respect Butler writes:

> A translation is at best a dislocation, a translation from verse to prose is a double dislocation and corresponding further dislocations are necessary if an effect of deformity is to be avoided.[14]

> Une traduction, si bonne qu'elle soit, n'est jamais qu'une dislocation; et la traduction en prose d'un ouvrage en vers est une double dislocation. Si donc on veut éviter qu'elle produise une impression de difformité il lui faut subir des dislocations partielles correspondant à ces dislocations générales.[15]

---

12 op. cit., p. 198.
13 Cf. Elinor Shaffer, *Erewhons of the Eye: Samuel Butler as Painter, Photographer and Art Critic* (London: Reaktion Books, 1988), p. 191.
14 Butler, *Note-Books*, p. 198.
15 op. cit., transl., p. 204.

The translation of this sentence clarifies it considerably and itself contains a "dislocation" in order to achieve this clarification, explaining that the further clarifications in question would have to be "partial dislocations" but corresponding to the "general" ones. Thus Larbaud's considerable experience as a translator allows him, in this instance, to express Butler's meaning in more precise terms than Butler's original does. Butler is setting forth the notion of compensation, which is clearly an important aspect of Larbaud's own technique as a translator, as Aldaz has also pointed out. Further, we now have the notion that the original is being doubly transposed, the first transposition being from poetry to prose, even though the two transpositions may appear as part of a single operation.

In a landmark study in literary translation, Professor Barbara Folkart points out that a translation is a form of "metatext" (as opposed to the "prototext") other forms of metatext being paraphrases, pastiche, and parody, (to which one might add adaptations). Solutions to various problems encountered by translators when confronted with texts which have already been transposed ("métatextualisés") are one important subject of this remarkable study.

As several of the examples she analyses are taken from the first French translation of Joyce's *Ulysses*, which Larbaud revised, we shall return to this study in the forthcoming section devoted to that translation.[16]

Although the "amateur" Butler left relatively few observations on the subject of translation, those he did make are clearly founded on his own considerable experience. One very general and obvious comment in *Erewhon Revisited* is made in a fictitious context by the narrator Higgs, who is about to translate from Erewhonian into English:

> I shall translate with the freedom without which no translation rises above the construe level.[17]
>
> Je traduirai avec cette liberté sans laquelle aucune traduction ne s'élève au-dessus du mot-à-mot.[18]

Indeed, Butler and Larbaud are in agreement on this essential point, and Butler applies it to translations of *The Odyssey*:

---

16 Cf. Barbara Folkart, "Métatextualité et traduction." *Canadian Review of Comparative Literature/Revue Canadienne de Littérature Comparée* (December 1986), pp. 548–584.

17 op. cit., p. 214.

18 op. cit., transl., p. 56.

> If [*The Odyssey*] is ever to be well translated it must be by some high spirited English girl who has been brought up at Athens and who, therefore, has not been jaded by the academic study of the language.[19]
>
> Si jamais nous avons une bonne traduction de *L'Odyssée*, il faudra qu'elle ait été faite par une jeune anglaise qui aura été éleveé à Athènes et qui, par conséquent, n'aura pas eu la peine d'apprendre le grec dans les manuels.[20]

This evocation of a hypothetical "English girl" who has been "brought up in Athens" also takes us into the world of Larbaud's own creative work, in which young people from various parts of the world live in adopted countries, as in the novel *Fermina Marquez* and the "*enfantine*" Rose Lourdin.

Many of Butler's "notes," rather than reminding the reader of the manner of either Montaigne or Pascal, may appear to have an eighteenth-century ring. A note in the latter category might be "Scientists" in Chapter 14 of *Note-Books* ("Higgledy Piggledy"):

> They are of two classes, those who want to know and do not care whether others think they know or not, and those who do not much care about knowing but care very greatly about being reputed as knowing.[21]
>
> Ils se divisent en deux classes: ceux qui veulent savoir et qui ne se soucient pas que les gens croient ou ne croient pas qu'ils savent; et ceux qui ne se soucient pas de savoir, mais qui désirent avant tout passer pour *savants*.[22]

The note "Italians and Englishmen" in Chapter 13 ("Unprofessional Sermons") may likewise seem "eighteenth-century" in its theme of cultural relativity. Its translation brings together these two much travelled cosmopolitans:

> Italians and perhaps Frenchmen, consider first whether they like or want to do a thing and then, whether, on the whole, it will do them any harm. Englishmen, and perhaps Germans,

---

19 Butler, *Note-Books*, p. 198.
20 op. cit., transl., p. 204.
21 op. cit., p. 218.
22 "Au Petit Bonheur," *Carnets*, p. 223.

> consider first whether they ought to like a thing and often never do reach the questions whether they do like it and whether it will hurt. There is much to be said for both systems, but I suppose it is best to combine them as far as possible.[23]
>
> Les Italiens, (et peut-être aussi les Français) se demandent d'abord s'ils aiment, ou désirent faire une chose, et ensuite si, tout bien considéré, cela leur nuira. Les Anglais (et peut-être aussi les Allemands) se demandent d'abord s'ils doivent faire une chose, et souvent en restent là, sans arriver jusqu'aux deux questions: "cela me plaît-t-il" et: "cela me nuira-t-il?" Il y a beaucoup à dire en faveur de ces deux systèmes; mais il me semble qu'il vaut encore mieux, dans la mesure du possible, les combiner.[24]

This passage, among others, also expresses Butler's major concern (as found, for example, in his novels) to promote a greater epicureanism in the English society of his time, as a corrective value that might bring about a much more balanced *modus vivendi*.

---

23 op. cit., p. 207.
24 op. cit., transl., p. 212.

Chapter 11

Butler: Note-Books—Further Considerations

A major, if not obsessive, theme in Butler is the notion of what he calls *"vicarious life"* (which Larbaud translates as *"la vie par procuration"*), the life that may be lived in the minds of others after death, as in the famous example of Shakespeare. This theme is developed in detail in Chapter 1 and recurs throughout *Note-Books*:

> On others, again, death confers a more living kind of life than they can possibly have enjoyed while to those about them they seemed to be alive. Look at Shakespeare; can he be properly said in anything like his real life till a hundred years or so after his death? His physical life was but a dawn preceding the sunrise of *that life of the world to come* which he was to enjoy hereafter. True, there was a little stir....But the true life of the man was after death and not before it.[1]

> Mais à d'autres la mort confère une vie d'une espèce plus vivante que celle dont ils ont pu jouir quand ils paraissaient en vie aux yeux de leurs voisins. Voyez Shakespeare; peut-on dire qu'il ait commencé à vivre de sa véritable vie sinon au bout d'une centaine d'années après sa mort? Sa vie physique ne fut que l'aube qui a précédé le lever du soleil de *sa vie d'outre-tombe* qu'il était destiné à vivre dans l'avenir....Sans doute il y eut un petit peu d'agitation....Mais la véritable vie de cet homme vint après la mort et non avant.[2]

The translation here of *that life of the world to come* by *sa vie d'outre-tombe* is particularly appropriate as it suggests Chateaubriand's famous title, *Mémoires d'Outre-Tombe* (Chateaubriand having insisted that these memoirs should not be published during his lifetime).

---

1 op. cit., p. 23.
2 op. cit., transl., p. 46.

Among all the works whose manner and style Larbaud may have emulated to one degree or another, consciously or unconsciously, in his translations, the *Essais* of Montaigne may be said to have had special relevance. In recognizing this debt to Montaigne, Larbaud is situating Butler as a near equal to a great Renaissance humanist, whose integrity (throughout his "vicarious life") had remained impeccable. Larbaud's intimate familiarity with Butler's work, acquired over many years and resulting from the exposure to it that only a translator can achieve, allows him to honour Butler in this very special way, at a time when Butler's importance was becoming more fully recognized in the English speaking world as well as in continental Europe.

The explanation of the unfortunate fact that in France Larbaud's translations of Butler did not immediately lead to a recognition of Butler's true stature, remains a matter for speculation, but given that many of the societal neuroses of which Butler seeks to create awareness, in the implicit hope that they might thus tend to be overcome, would undoubtedly not have seemed as relevant in France, is at least a possible explanation. French society, seemingly more "epicurean," represents, in many respects, the ideal toward which Butler's critique of Victorian English society points as a cure. However, it is clearly to Italy in particular that Butler prefers to point in his search for the corrective values he needs.

Larbaud's comparison of Butler with Montaigne, however, is an indication that Larbaud saw far more significance in Butler's humanism than its mere potential as a palliative. In the "Notes" of Chapter 2, Butler touches on "anti-Victorian" themes that were also famously and far more flamboyantly to be voiced by Oscar Wilde. Butler's tone, on the other hand, could be better described as that of *le bon sens* (for the sake of avoiding the expression "common sense"):

> The extremes of vice and virtue are alike detestable; absolute virtue is as sure to kill a man as absolute vice is, let alone the dullness of it and the pomposities of it.[3]

Larbaud again translates in the seemingly effortless manner which succeeds in being both classical and modernist:

> Le vice et la vertu, poussés à leurs dernières limites, sont également haïssables. Une vertu absolue tuera aussi sûrement son homme que le fait un vice absolu, sans parler de l'ennui et de l'emphase qui l'accompagnent.[4]

---

3 op. cit., p. 28.
4 op. cit. transl., p. 50.

The theme of moral relativity is emphasized and Larbaud rises to the occasion. Relations between parents and children, one of Butler's major concerns, as in *The Way of All Flesh*, are now developed in the mode of the essay under the headings *Young People* and *The Family*:

> Next to sexual matters there are none upon which there is such reserve between parents and children as on those connected with money....Nevertheless [the father] thinks himself ill-used if his son, on entering life, falls a victim to *designing persons* whose knowledge of how money is made and lost is greater than his own.[5]

> Après les questions sexuelles, il n'y en a pas sur lesquelles il y ait de réserve plus complète entre parents et enfants que sur les questions d'argent....Et néanmoins [le père] se considère comme injustement traité si son fils, en entrant dans la vie, se laisse dépouiller par des *aigrefins* qui savent mieux que lui comment l'argent s'acquiert et comment il se perd.[6]

Chapter 3 is of particular interest because it reprints the two important letters to the editor of the Christchurch (New Zealand) *Press*, the first having been published on June 13, 1863, while Butler was in New Zealand. This letter, "Darwin among the Machines," has been considered the source of the concerns about the rapid development of machines that were later to form the three chapters in *Erewhon* entitled "The Book of the Machines." (These letters had been rediscovered only after a difficult search.)

Here the views of "Cellarius" are summed up in a paragraph toward the end of the letter. Regarding the very rapid development of machines in his time, he writes:

> Our opinion is that war to the death should be instantly proclaimed against them. Every machine of every sort should be destroyed by the well-wisher of his species. Let there be no exceptions made, no quarter shown; let us at once go back to the primeval condition of the race. If it be urged that this is impossible under the present condition of human affairs, this at once proves that the mischief is already done, that our servitude has commenced in good earnest, that we have raised

---

5 op. cit., p. 31.
6 op. cit., transl., p. 53.

a race of beings whom it is beyond our power to destroy and that we are not only enslaved but are absolutely acquiescent in our bondage.[7]

Larbaud translates:

> Pour nous, nous croyons qu'il est urgent de déclarer dès à présent une guerre à mort aux machines. Il faudrait que tout homme qui a souci du bonheur de son espèce détruisît toute machine, de quelque genre qu'elle fût. Pas d'exceptions! Pas de quartier! Retournons aux conditions primitives de notre race. Que l'on objecte que cela n'est pas possible étant données les conditions actuelles des affaires humaines, cette objection même est la preuve patente que le mal est déjà fait, que notre servitude a commencé tout de bon, que nous avons créé une race d'êtres qu'il n'est plus en notre pouvoir de détruire, et que nous ne sommes pas seulement asservis, mais que nous consentons à l'être.[8]

In the translation of this passage, Larbaud seems to echo the tone of oratorical prophecy that Rousseau had adopted in his famous *Discours sur l'Inégalité* (in which Rousseau speculates on the origin of property) and also Montesquieu in the "weeping-king" ("Troglodyte") episode in *Les Lettres Persanes*, weeping during his coronation at the thought of the arbitrary power he will have and its inherent injustice.

Butler is using a similar rhetorical device. There is a parallel fatalism: despite the dire threat of the machines humankind does not have the moral rectitude to acknowledge this threat and give them up as the (hypothetical) Erewhonians did.

Returning in Chapter 4 to his preoccupation with evolution theory, under the heading *Reproduction and Memory*, Butler defends his concept of the importance of memory in evolution, which he appears to consider as equal to that of purposefulness. He writes:

> There is the reproduction of an idea which has been produced once already, and there is the reproduction of a living form which has been produced once already. The first reproduction is certainly an effort of memory. It should not therefore

---

[7] op. cit., p. 46.
[8] op. cit., transl., p. 67.

surprise us if the second reproduction should turn out to be an effort of memory also.⁹

Memory, then, as a factor in evolution, is an important Butlerian concept. Like the Lamarckian notion of "little purposes" it is a fundamental component of his critique of Darwinian evolution theory.

Larbaud translates the subtitle as *La Reproduction et la mémoire*:

> Il y a la reproduction d'une idée qui a été reproduite une fois déjà, et il y a la reproduction d'un être vivant qui a été produit une fois déjà. La première reproduction est certainement due à un effort de la mémoire. Par conséquent il n'y aurait rien d'étonnant à ce que la seconde reproduction se trouvât être due elle aussi à un effort de la mémoire.[10]

As we have noted, Butler also demonstrates interest in principles of language that seem to lead into certain theories of Ferdinand de Saussure, as, for example, in the section "*Thought and Word*" in Chapter 7 ("*The Making of Music, Pictures and Books*") drawing attention to the frequent inadequacy of the word in the expression of its concept:

> We want words to do more than they can….But they are *parvenu* people as compared to thought and action. What we should read is not the words but the man whom we feel to be behind the words.[11]

> Nous demandons aux mots plus qu'ils ne peuvent donner…. Mais ce sont des *parvenus* en comparaison de la pensée et de l'action. Ce que nous devrions lire, ce ne sont pas les mots, mais l'homme que nous sentons derrière les mots.[12]

Larbaud clearly feels able to incorporate the French word *parvenu* into his translation here. Saussure would no doubt have seen such a use of the word *parvenu* as too figurative since he was concerned to establish a science of language. Nevertheless Butler uses an image concerning the word and its limitations that is already on a road that would eventually lead to Saussure and the science of

---

9 op. cit., p. 59.
10 op. cit., transl., p. 80.
11 op. cit., p. 94.
12 op. cit., transl., p. 112.

Linguistics and whose expression had preceded Larbaud's translations, even though there is no indication that Larbaud was influenced by them.

Another aphorism in a similar vein seems to derive from Butler's preoccupation with money matters:

> Coins are potential money as...words are potential language.[13]

> Les pièces de monnaie sont de l'argent en puissance comme les mots sont du langage en puissance.[14]

Since Butler's creativity expressed itself in literature, painting and music (although literature took priority among them) he was in a position to speculate on what principles applied to all three. His comments on this subject become a matter of particular relevance:

> The great thing is that all shall be new, and yet nothing new, at the same time; the details must minister to the main effect and not obscure it.[15]

> L'important est que tout en soit nouveau, et que cependant il ne s'y trouve rien de nouveau; les détails doivent concourir à l'effet général et ne pas l'obscurcir.[16]

Butler continues:

> What is required is that he shall say what he elects to say discreetly; that he shall be quick to see the *gist* of the matter, and give it *pithily* without either *prolixity* or *stint* of words.[17]

> Ce qu'on demande à l'artiste, c'est de dire avec discrétion ce qu'il juge bon, après choix, de dire. C'est d'apercevoir tout de suite *l'essentiel* de son sujet, et de nous l'exprimer *avec force* et sans *prodiguer* ni épargner ses paroles.[18]

This translation is also a very good example in its detail, since terms such as *pithily*, and *stint* (in Butler's sense) were presumably in the process of becoming

---

13 op. cit. p. 95.
14 op. cit., transl., p. 113.
15 op. cit. p. 97.
16 op. cit., transl., p. 114.
17 op. cit., p. 97.
18 op. cit., transl., p. 114.

archaic at the time of Larbaud's translation. Larbaud recognizes this and changes *pithily* into a colloquial phrase (*avec force*) and *prolixity* and *stint* into corresponding verbal forms, so that the French result is precise, an example of the elegance of simplicity which is one of Larbaud's "trademarks."

Hence we have here further evidence that his French style tends constantly to make the translation an improvement of the original, by one means or another. Such qualities become particularly manifest in Larbaud's translation of a "note" titled "Free Will and Necessity" in Chapter 20 ("First Principles")

> We imagine that we must have all free-will and no necessity, or all necessity and no free-will, and, it being obvious that our free will is often *overridden* by force of circumstance while the evidence that necessity is *overridden* by free-will is harder to find if indeed it can be found.[19]

> Nous nous figurons que le libre arbitre exclut la nécessité, ou que la nécessité exclut le libre arbitre et, comme il est bien évident que notre libre-arbitre est souvent *réduit à l'impuissance* par la force des circonstances, tandis qu'il est plus difficile de montrer que la nécessité est *dominée* par le libre arbitre.[20]

It is clear that in this passage Larbaud considers the colloquial term *overridden* inappropriate for a "scientific" demonstration. He also finds a different solution for each occurrence of *overridden*: *réduit à l'impuissance* the first time and *dominée* the second, not only avoiding the repetition but finding, in the process, a more precise expression. The sentence continues:

> Most people who theorize upon this question will deny in theory that there is any free will at all, though in practice they *take care* to act as if there was.[21]

> La plupart de ceux qui bâtissent des théories sur cette matière nieront *absolument*, en théorie, l'existence du libre-arbitre,— bien que, dans la pratique ils *prennent soin* d'agir comme s'il existait.[22]

---

19 op. cit. pp. 316–317.
20 op. cit., transl., p. 313.
21 Ibid., p. 317.
22 op. cit., transl., p. 313.

Here Larbaud strengthens the "denial" by adding *absolument* and sees no reason not to considers "take care" and "prendre soin" as corresponding exactly with one another in this sense. (Thus we have here a minor example of parallel expression in the two languages.)

Finally, Butler is concerned to contribute his own interpretation to the well tempered ongoing debate on the question of free will, which, of course, had many French language participants. The translation means that Butler may now participate in such debates on equal terms. One example might be:

> For if we admit that like causes are followed by like effects (and everything we do is based upon this hypothesis), it follows that every combination of causes must have some one consequent which can alone follow it and which free-will cannot touch.[23]

> En effet, si nous admettons que les mêmes causes sont suivies des mêmes effets,—et toutes nos actions reposent sur cette hypothèse—il s'ensuit que chaque combinaison de causes doit avoir une conséquence certaine qui seule peut la suivre et sur laquelle le libre-arbitre n'a aucun pouvoir.[24]

In translating philosophical passages such as these, Larbaud is upholding Butler's proper place in such debates, as well as demonstrating his sound understanding of the intrinsic merit of Butler's entire work, resulting from his many years of commitment to its diffusion.

---

23 op. cit., p. 317.
24 op. cit., transl., p. 313.

Chapter 12

Other Authors Writing in English: Joyce and Sitwell

For Larbaud, *le domaine anglais* in literature naturally included that of Ireland, for which he had shown a particular interest. Since he was often prospecting for new talent, it is not surprising to learn that he frequented the now legendary bookshops of Adrienne Monnier and Sylvia Beach on the Rue de l'Odéon, resulting in his discovery of James Joyce's *Ulysses* while it was still in gestation, and declaring himself "raving mad about *Ulysses*" ("fou d'*Ulysse*"). A year later, on December 7, 1921, having already translated several passages from *Ulysses*, he gave his lecture on the work of Joyce at La Maison des Amis des Livres, Adrienne Monnier's bookshop. It was Adrienne Monnier who eventually published the French translation of *Ulysses* (*Ulysse*) in 1929, Sylvia Beach having published the original (Shakespeare and Company, February, 1922). Larbaud's final role in its translation was that of a *rédacteur en chef*, although he is remembered in France as the "translator" of *Ulysses*. Even the revision of the translation meant an immense and disinterested sacrifice of his time, his diaries revealing that he sometimes spent ten hours a day on it: a veritable *don de soi*.

The statement on the title page of the Gallimard (Folio) edition admirably simplifies the structure of the team of translators: "Traduction d'Auguste Morel revue par Valery Larbaud, Stuart Gilbert et l'Auteur." It was Stuart Gilbert who produced the guide to *Ulysses* which allowed the reader to identify each of the episodes.

Is it possible to recognize, here and there, the mark of Larbaud's stylistic originality or mannerisms that might have resulted from his revision, in collaboration with Joyce himself? A familiarity with Larbaud's style might encourage such a search, but in order to be on firm ground one would need the hard evidence in his correspondence with Joyce and others. Richard Ellmann, at one point in his biography of Joyce, gives Larbaud's comments (in a letter to Joyce of June 14, 1928) on Morel's translation of the first paragraph of the second part of *Ulysses* (Episode IV, "Calypso"):

Text: "He like grilled mutton kidneys which gave to his palate a fine tang of scented urine."

Morel: "Il aimait les rognons de mouton au gril qui gratifiaient ses papilles gustatives d'un fumet de chaix mâtiné d'un rien d'urine."

"Fumet de chaix" is a cliché, while "a fine tang" is not. "Mâtiné de," another cliché, "d'un rien de" is both recherché and facile. The feeble strain of humour in the French sentence is vulgar; of the commercial-traveller sort; the way they talk when they try to talk "well." I leave "gratifiaient" because it is etymologically right; I accept "papilles gustatives," though the expression is a little *prétentieuse*, more "learned" (cheap science) than the simple "palate" of the text, because it gives equilibrium to the French sentence and arrests the reader's attention on that aspect of Mr. Bloom's physical life. The rest I reject, and translate more literally....

Thus...the phrase stands as follows:..."Il aimait les rognons de mouton au gril qui gratifiaient ses papilles gustatives d'une belle saveur au léger parfum d'urine."

Text: "Kidneys were in his mind as he..."

Morel: "Il songeait à des rognons tout en..."

Of course, this is the meaning, but it is not a literary translation of a literary sentence. The humorous side of the phrase in the text is lost. I translate: "Il avait des rognons en tête tandis qu'il..."[1]

Larbaud's now published correspondence with Adrienne Monnier is another important source for the study of his revisions as editor of the Morel drafts. In a letter to Monnier referring to a *"séance de traduction"* which she hosted, Larbaud comments on Molly Bloom's manner of speaking:

Je faisais des efforts lamentables pour me rappeler des expressions populaires que pourtant je thésaurise dans mon coeur en tout pays. Ma femme de ménage de Paris dit en parlant de sa concierge: "C'est une horreur de femme."

---

1 Richard Ellmann, *James Joyce* (New York: Oxford UP, 1959), p. 614.

> Voyez-vous une place où cela peut aller? Mais Molly Bloom n'est pas aussi plébéienne que l'avait faite Fargue. Je crois que le ton trouvé par Sylvia [Beach] est beaucoup plus juste. Molly a un beau vocabulaire bien vivant et plastique, vulgaire mais pas au point d'exclure les mots littéraires, enfin le vocabulaire de *Mallarmé*.[2]

Léon-Paul Fargue was called upon to suggest French equivalents for slang and colloquial expressions in the original text because of his well-known expertise in that area. However, Larbaud was clearly convinced that both Morel and Fargue had misunderstood the social background of Leopold and Molly Bloom and had consequently not always found colloquialisms he considered appropriate.

Hence, in another letter to Monnier,[3] he stresses the point again:

> Il me semble que [Morel] n'a pas bien saisi le caractère de Bloom, son niveau social, son degré d'instruction. Même chose pour Molly; ils les fait beaucoup plus peuple et grossiers qu'ils ne le sont. Molly a souvent, chez lui, des mots de femme de bordel qu'elle n'a jamais dans Joyce, et Bloom parle ou pense avec des expressions de potache qui ne sont pas dans le texte. Exemple caractéristique:
>
> Joyce: Like to give them the *odd* cigarette. (Mr. Bloom et les cochers de fiacre dans *Les Lotophages*).
>
> Morel: J'aime leur allonger une *vieille* sèche.
>
> Je corrige donc: "J'aime leur passer de temps à autre une cigarette."[4]

Thus, in his work on *Ulysse*, Larbaud constantly demonstrates a sensitivity to tone and to the subtleties of the speech of various social backgrounds. He is also very expert on the positioning of words and phrases for certain effects. For example, one might suspect his intervention in the last words of Chapter 5 (*The Lotus Eaters*) (*Les Lotophages*): "languide et flottante

---

2 Larbaud, *Lettres à Adrienne Monnier et à Sylvia Beach*. Correspondance établie et annotée par Maurice Saillet (Paris: IMEC, 1991), p. 163.
3 October 6, 1927.
4 op. cit., p. 317.

fleur,"⁵ in which the order of the English has been maintained: "a languid floating flower."⁶

This order is a bit unusual in French usage, yet at the same time *languide et flottante* would be too prosaic had they followed *fleur*. As it is, the effect created expresses the notion that we may take for granted that the "lotus" is "languid and floating" rather than giving the concept the needless overemphasis it would have if the adjectives were placed after *fleur*. Larbaud's style is again experimental. Long adjectives coming before the noun they modify are one of his "signatures."

The possibility that this phrasing might be one of Larbaud's editorial improvements is nonetheless hypothetical. To return to his correspondence with Adrienne Monnier, we find his statement of October 1, 1927:

> J'ose autant que possible; néologismes; mots agglutinés (odeurdemusc); je tâche de rendre le *ton*. Stuart Gilbert le demande... chaque personnage a son ton, ses tics, ses exclamations propres (ou sales, mais pas toujours)... et c'est cela quìl faut traduire.⁷

On October 6, 1927, Larbaud returned to what he considered a major problem with Morel's draft:

> Je trouve la touche générale de Morel rude et grosse en présence de ce texte tout en nuances et en finesses....Joyce ne se moque pas de Bloom parce qu'il n'est pas un "Monsieur."....Bloom est un "Monsieur" comme, et plus que, Bouvard et Pécuchet.... Bloom et Molly [ne sont pas] nos inférieurs sociaux.⁸

In a letter to Joyce a year later, quoted in the Monnier correspondence, Larbaud defends a part of his revision in some detail:

> Text: "Two shafts of soft daylight fell across the flagged floor."
>
> Morel: "Deux flèches de jour tombaient moelleuses sur le sol dallé."
>
> Larbaud: "Deux javelots de jour adouci tombaient rayant le sol dallé."

---

5 Joyce, *Ulysse* 1 (Paris: Gallimard [Folio], 1976), p. 128.
6 Joyce, *Ulysses* [1922] Harmondsworth, England: Penguin, 1969), p. 88.
7 Larbaud, op. cit., *Lettres à Adrienne Monnier et à Sylvia Beach*, p. 312.
8 Ibid., pp. 317–318.

I prefer "*javelots de jour*" for several reasons: 1. it is longer; 2. it is uncommon and arrests the attention; 3. the alliteration j...j, gives it more strength; 4. it seems to me that it suggests the word "Apollo" more than "traits de soleil" would do.[9]

Another notable challenge (among many) in this translation, is that there are occasional snatches of popular verse, well known to upper middle class anglophone readers but not integrated into the corresponding francophone culture. Thus in Episode V, *The Lotus Eaters*, an unfinished line from a well-known nursery rhyme that was fashionable at the time in England ("Sing a Song o' Sixpence" from *Mother Goose*), runs through the mind of Leopold Bloom in his interior monologue as he arrives home: "Queen was in her bedroom eating bread and —."[10] The reader supplies the word "honey" from memory and also the word "parlour" for "bedroom," thus putting herself/himself into the novel by collaboration, and creating a major dilemma for the translator. It is likely that Larbaud knew the rhyme since he had taken part in the cultural life of London before the First World War. (Otherwise Stuart Gilbert could possibly have come to his rescue.) However, the reference is not used at all in *Ulysse* although it is clear that *la reine* refers to Molly Bloom: "La reine était dans son lit qui mangeait son pain bis, biribi."[11]

This rhyme, therefore, is an example of an allusion that was clearly considered untranslatable. However, there are other examples of references which are already embedded in both languages and so have a common "*archi-texte*," thus solving the problem of a reference that would be unfamiliar to the reader of the translation.

Professor Barbara Folkart, in a genuinely seminal article entitled "Métatextualité et traduction," to which we have already referred,[12] finds a particularly relevant example in Episode XII, *The Cyclops* (*Le Cyclope*). Here we encounter a blasphemous parody of the Apostles' Creed, as a "floggers' creed," concerning the experience of the unfortunate sailor Jacky Tar and featuring frequent assonance and rhymes with the original English version ("conceived of the Holy Ghost" = "conceived of unholy boast," etc.).

Professor Folkart analyzes the translation of this parody in detail. Since Joyce's word play depends on a familiarity with the Apostle's Creed, known to many anglophones but presumably to relatively few francophones,

---

9 Ibid., p. 342.
10 *Ulysses*, p. 76
11 *Ulysse* 1, p. 110.
12 *Canadian Review of Comparative Literature* 13(4), December 1986, pp. 548–584.

the effect could easily be lost in translation. As Professor Folkart explains, Auguste Morel's solution is found by using the French *Crédo* as his "*prototext.*" It might be assumed to be known to many francophones, and it is derived from the same "*archi-texte*" as the Apostle's Creed. He found it necessary to invent a similar system of assonance and rhyming words in the French version rather than translate the terms of Joyce's parody, while at the same time mimicking Joyce's manner ("né de la Vierge Marie" = "né de la verge marine," etc.) and conveying its suggestiveness.[13]

Since the Apostle's Creed and *Le Crédo* are already translations of an original "*archi-texte*," as Professor Folkart points out, we have, in Joyce's parody, a second stage of transposition (*métatextualisation*) and in its French version a third, which is an independent improvisation rather than a translation. (There is no reference on the part of Larbaud to this passage in his published correspondence with Adrienne Monnier.)

A further challenge presents itself when some of the speech of Leopold Bloom, and other characters in the novel, consists of an actual deformation of English words, for humorous effect, of a kind that is usually not considered permissible in French, even in the transcription of dialect. The effort to find equivalents for onomatopoeia is a case in point. In pursuing various solutions for this problem it did become necessary at times to break up French words or to add extra syllables.

Hence in Episode X, "The Wandering Rocks" (*Les Rochers Errants*), we have pigeons that "roucoucooed."[14] Here Joyce is inventing a word by combining the English "coo" and the French "roucouler." This "hybrid" is therefore already present in the English text and leads to further play on "roucouler" in the translation: "roucoulouhoulaient."[15]

There are, of course, many other onomatopoeic effects in the English text. For example, again in Episode X, "*The Wandering Rocks*"(*Les Rochers Errants*), a wicker basket is embedded with "rustling fibres."[16] Onomatopoeic words such as "rustling" are well known to translators to be more characteristic of English than of French. The French equivalent found here for "rustling": *bruissantes*[17] seems not completely successful despite the retention of the suggestive "s" phoneme.

---

13 *Ulysses*, p. 327. *Ulysse* 1, p. 480. Cf. Folkart, op. cit., pp. 554–557.
14 *Ulysses*, op. cit., p. 227.
15 *Ulysse* 1, p. 330.
16 *Ulysses*, p. 226.
17 *Ulysse* 1, p. 330.

Again in Episode VI, "Hades" (*Hadès*), "the carriage rattled swiftly along"[18] is rendered: "la voiture dinguait le long."[19] *Dinguer* expresses a sound of bells so that the effect is translated even if the meaning is not precisely that of "rattle." Since *dinguer* was originally onomatopoeic this original quality is brought out.

The liberty to compensate for less effective results is taken in various places in which the French is more onomatopoeic than the English. Thus "whispering gallery walls"[20] is appropriately translated as "murs murmurants des corridors."[21] On the other hand, when "the bell whirred again"[22] is rendered merely as "la sonnerie recommença,"[23] the translation shows no corresponding onomatopoeic effect.

At other times, certain formulae in the translation seem to be contrary to Larbaud's own principles. Thus the words "They've gone round to the Oval for a drink"[24] appear in the translation as "partis prendre une consommation à l'Oval."[25] The translation of "drink" as "*consommation*" might astonish students of Larbaud's creative work because of an episode which is important to the plot in his novella *Mon Plus Secret Conseil*. It is one of the incidents that will lead to the separation of the protagonist and his lady when it is concluded that they are incompatible. Here the protagonist observes to her that *consommation* has a pretentious, even vulgar, ring, whereas *boisson* is perfectly correct and corresponds to the English "drink."[26]

It could be suggested that since Larbaud and the narrator in the novella need not be assumed to be the same person, he may have considered *consommation* appropriate at this point in the translation, possibly to maintain a tone of gentle irony. On the other hand, it could merely indicate that Larbaud had missed this passage altogether during revision.

A perfectly clear example of a Larbaldian pattern of speech may be found in the first episode, "Telemachus," at the point at which Stephen is in conversation with an Englishman named Haines, on the subject of nationalities and national identity. Haines remarks: "We feel in England that we have treated you rather

---

18 *Ulysses*, p. 99.
19 *Ulysse* 1, p. 143.
20 *Ulysses*, p. 84.
21 *Ulysse* 1, p. 122.
22 *Ulysses*, p. 130
23 *Ulysse* 1, p. 188
24 *Ulysses* p. 131
25 *Ulysse* 1, p 191.
26 Larbaud, *Mon Plus Secret Conseil* [1923], Pléiade, p. 687.

unfairly. It seems history is to blame."[27] The French version of the last sentence is: "La faute en est sans doute à l'Histoire."[28]

This *tournure* seems to contain an echo of the work of a seventeenth-century Bourbonnais poet to whose poetry Larbaud drew attention in his critical monographs on French literature: Jean de Lingendes. He points out that Lingendes is remembered for only two lines that have since found their way into the *répertoire* of French aphorisms:

La faute en est aux dieux
Qui la firent si belle.[29]

Unfortunate disagreements over matters of interpretation and style among the members of the team of translators eventually turned to personal enmity, although the translation itself was published successfully by Adrienne Monnier in 1929. Seventy-five years later a new French translation of *Ulysses* was created and published by Gallimard in May 2004. This translation was promoted by Stephen and Solange Joyce and Antoine Gallimard. It is the work of a much larger team, having a different translator for each episode, and was directed by Jacques Aubert. In justifying this new translation in a *Postface* appended to it, Jacques Aubert points out that in his view the first translation had appeared too soon after the original work itself, resulting in its complexity not always being properly understood.

He proposed a version that would be closer to Joyce's original and to his readers today and also able to take into account the mass of analytical studies that had been published on it since the 1920s, as well as such developments as *le nouveau roman* and *nouvelle critique*, which could now enrich a new translation. However, he pays due respect to "la culture et la sensibilité également remarquables" of Valery Larbaud and Auguste Morel.[30]

Specifically, Aubert expresses the need to respect Joyce's original word order wherever possible so as to convey the effect of "direct sensation" which Joyce so successfully and uniquely sought to reproduce, "l'effet de réalité caractéristique du cinéma."[31] He adds: "rendre la diabolique habileté de Joyce et l'évidente jouissance qu'il tirait à mimer et parodier, jusqu'à en rendre le timbre, ces modes d'être cristallisés en parlers et en phrases typiques, par le respect notamment de la ponctuation, des distortions, des onomatopées, des registres de tons."[32]

---

27 *Ulysses*, p. 27.
28 *Ulysse*, p. 34.
29 Larbaud, "Jean de Lingendes," in *Ce Vice Impuni La Lecture: Domaine Français*. OC 8 (1953), p. 163.
30 op. cit., p. 972.
31 Ibid p. 973.
32 Ibid.

He also points out that meaning is frequently expressed in ways that take priority over the strict definition of words in the dictionary, the frequent use of such effects as those created by alliteration being an example, and that these effects must also be "translated."[33]

Finally he adds: "Il n'y a pas toujours une seule interprétation fixe mais plutôt un flux...on trouve en filigrane des variations stylistiques. Ainsi le sens lui-même est mis en cause."[34]

The Translation of a Modernist Poem: Edith Sitwell's "An Interview with Mars" (Une Entrevue avec Mars)

Larbaud's translation of this poem is to be found in *Commerce* 7 (Printemps 1926) along with the original.[35] The poem no doubt seemed highly experimental in its time although its rime scheme is traditional and may in some places be construed as a parody of traditional rime. The whole matter of the translatability of poetry is never discussed by Larbaud in his writings on translation so that he leaves the impression that, in his view, translating poetry is perfectly legitimate. One might agree that there is, in this instance, a strong impression of the original.

There is no doubt agreement that in translating verse, a particularly successful line in the original cannot necessarily be rendered a success in the translation. An example might be a line on page 118: "The sirens play their harp-strings all the day."[36]

Larbaud seems primarily intent on rendering the meaning here (as throughout the translation) and so resorts to prose: "Les Sirènes tout le jour font chanter les cordes de leurs harpes."[37]

However, other attempts are more rewarding as in this expression of a great celebration when the two languages already overtrace one another:

> And on lone crags nymphs bright as any queen
>
> In crinolines of tarlatine marine[38]

This last line becomes

---

33 Ibid., p. 974.
34 op. cit., p. 977.
35 Cf. pp. 114–123
36 op. cit., p. 118
37 op. cit., transl., p. 119
38 Ibid., p. 118.

En crinolines de tarlatine bleu-marine.[39]

There are many internal rhymes (or repeated vowels), as, for example:

Like sunburnt haycocks in a summer dream.

Here Larbaud manages a line with a similar approximate rime within his translation:

A des meules de foin brunies de soleil dans un songe d'été."

In this example, both the English and the French translation imply a reference to Shakespeare's title "A Midsummer Night's Dream" (*Le Songe d'une nuit d'été*), which is also relevant to the whole atmosphere of the piece, as Larbaud clearly understood. Larbaud seems to manage this with the greatest of ease, possibly a sign that in this translation he may be recognized as having reached his maturity as a master translator.

---

39 Ibid., p. 121.

Part III

Translations from Other Romance Languages

Chapter 13

Translations from Spanish

Concerning the works Larbaud translated from Spanish, we have detailed published accounts of the praxis of translation only in his correspondence with the Mexican diplomat and poet Alfonso Reyes. In both Spain and the Spanish-speaking countries of Latin America, a literary Renaissance was in progress at the time of the peak of Larbaud's career (1918–1935). As we have seen, he lived in Spain for almost four years and read a vast number of works in Spanish, while encouraging Latin American writers to find not only their subjects but their literary formulae within the context of their own traditions, rather than emulating European models. In short, he encouraged them to bridge the gap which in North America was discerned between the works of Poe and Whitman.

This is exactly what was beginning to happen at that time. Borges was one of the great innovators of the 1920s, and Larbaud seems to have been the first to write about Borges in France, in an article in *La Revue Européenne* in 1925.[1]

Ramon Gomez de la Serna

One of Larbaud's enthusiasms in Spanish was the work of the Spaniard Ramon Gomez de la Serna whom he knew personally, sometimes meeting him at the Café Pombo in Madrid (1917) where Ramon held readings during which he would present his latest creations. Ramon's *Gregarias* are sometimes provocative short epigrammatic utterances and at other times highly personal extended commentaries often inspired by his surroundings. Larbaud translated and published a selection in Paris in 1918 and later a larger one, in collaboration with Mathilde Pomès, in 1923, entitled *Echantillons*. The title of one section of the latter work, *Criailleries*, reflects an effort to approximate the Spanish *Greguerias*. (*Piailleries* was also considered.)

Like Eliot, Larbaud was not less a classicist for being one of the artificers of modernism. Actually this trend was seen as one of the more important aspects of modernism. It is expressed in words that Perse used to honour Fargue

---

[1] Larbaud, op. cit. 1 Décembre 1925. "Lettres Argentines et Uruguayennes."

and which apply just as well to Larbaud: "Faire un jour figure de classique parmi les écrivains d'un ancien modernisme."[2] Larbaud's own observations of human nature had led him to fashion a number of slightly exaggerated epigrams and aphorisms which are occasionally reminiscent of the manner of Ramon. He was able to do this by attributing them to such fictitious characters as Barnabooth and the adolescent *collégien* Joanny Léniot in the novel that remains a masterpiece: *Fermina Marquez* (1911). However, these novels were published before his discovery of the *Greguerias*.

In *A.O.Barnabooth* we find such examples as:

> Il y a des choses qu'il faut savoir saisir au vol.[3]

In *Fermina Marquez*, the ever-unfolding world of the ambitious *collégien* Joanny produces similar thoughts:

> Deux heures de l'après-midi est prosaique, presque vulgaire; mais deux heures du matin est un aventurier qui s'enfonce dans l'inconnu.[4]

> Nous survivons à nos sentiments comme nous survivons aux saisons.[5]

The translations of *Greguerias* have a curious resemblance to such creations:

> Les rues sont plus longues la nuit que le jour.[6]

> Les sourires s'éteignent comme les lumières.[7]

> Dans les bibliothèques publiques, nos propres livres nous renient, nous traitent avec dédain....Enfants dénaturés.[8]

It was during his visit to London in September and October 1919 that Larbaud first discovered Logan Pearsall Smith's *Trivia* in which he thought certain epigrams resembled Ramon's *Greguerias*, in particular those that are

---

2   Léon-Paul Fargue, *Poésies*. Préface de Saint-John Perse (Paris: Gallimard, 1963), p. 11.
3   Larbaud, *A.O. Barnabooth*, op. cit., Pléiade, p. 39.
4   *Fermina Marquez*, op. cit. Pléiade, p. 382.
5   Ibid., p. 383.
6   Ramon Gomez de la Serna, *Echantillons* (Paris: Grasset, 1923), "Les Cahiers Verts," p. 24.
7   Ibid., p. 54.
8   Ibid., p. 61.

more developed. Smith's conception of reading as a "vice" was to inspire Larbaud's titles for his two volumes of critical studies: *Ce Vice Impuni La Lecture*. Smith's original words occur under the sub-heading *Consolation*:

> Then I thought of reading—the nice and subtle happiness of reading. This was enough, this joy not dulled by Age, this polite and unpunishable vice, this selfish, serene and lifelong intoxication.[9]

Ricardo Guiraldes

In Argentina, Larbaud was able to count among his close friends an influential associate of Borges, Ricardo Guiraldes, who supported and contributed to Borges' new literary review in Buenos Aires: *Proa*. One of Guiraldes's novels, *Don Segundo Sombra*, had become the object of a cult. It is one of the last of the *gaucho* novels and among the first to celebrate life on the pampas for its intrinsic interest. It is also a fine example of the "spiritual father" relationship between an older man and a very young man, in that respect like Stevenson's *Kidnapped*, Kipling's *Kim* and even Joyce's *Ulysses*.

To return to Larbaud's own friendship with Guiraldes, it may be said to have a certain symbolic resonance, since Guiraldes, like Saint-John Perse, may be seen as a Barnabooth of real life, another instance of "life imitating art," as if he had been invented by Larbaud: a poet and novelist working from an independent base (his vast *estancia* at San Antonio de Areco) and able to transcend national boundaries with the greatest of ease, a *cosmopolite* and *"un vrai Parisien."*

The French translation of *Don Segundo Sombra* by Marcelle Auclair, who had been brought up in Chile, was encouraged by Larbaud. He had in fact been encouraging a whole program of translations of Latin American literature and facilitated the translation of *Don Segundo Sombra* by arranging introductions for her to French and Argentine specialists who could assist her on technical points, since this translation was considered a particularly challenging venture.

Don Segundo Sombra is the portrait of a mature gaucho, a man of few words, who is an absolute master of his vocation. He is seen from the point of view of his inexperienced apprentice as they ride together over the pampas. Various situations and episodes test the latter's endurance on his way to becoming a gaucho, in this *bildungsroman*. However, the novel still belongs to a traditional genre, indeed to the lineage of *Don Quixote*, since, like the latter, it presents a series of episodes and does not betray any hint of the experimental "novelty" in the South American novel in Spanish which, in the next generation,

---

9   Logan Pearsall Smith, *All Trivia* (New York: Harcourt, Brace and Co., 1921), pp. 68–69.

was to be realized so remarkably in the work of Borges, Gabriel Marquez and Mario Vargas Llosa among many others. Its originality resides in its manner of projecting the pampas, which are seen in a mode of everyday realism as opposed to earlier "romantic" representations.

After Guiraldes's premature death, Larbaud translated some of his poetry as a tribute. *Poemas Solitarios* (*Poèmes Solitaires*) appeared in *Commerce*.[10] The text and the translation are presented on opposite pages and the translation reflects the original very closely.

However, Larbaud expressed misgivings on the translatability of Guiraldes's poetry, which he valued very highly, and feared that its true qualities, such as the refinement that is peculiar to the Spanish texts, could not be properly conveyed in French:

> Cette poésie…me produisit une très vive impression, et j'essayai d'en traduire quelques morceaux: mais les sons y jouent un si grand rôle que, de "Tango fatal" par exemple, il ne me resta rien, en français, qu'un plat et pauvre mot à mot, tel que le montrer, le publier, c'eût été trahir le poète.
>
> Text: Me he acostumbrado a estar solo
>
> Como el ombu se ha acostumbrado a la pampa.
>
> Translation: Je me suis habitué à être seul
>
> Comme l'ombu s'est habitué à la pampa.[11]

Alfonso Reyes

The Larbaud-Reyes correspondence has been published in a very detailed critical edition by Paulette Patout.[12] In this work, a major contribution to Larbaud studies, we have the exchanges of two peers. They were alike in many respects, the Mexican diplomat Reyes himself being a translator who, again like Larbaud, also wrote about translation.[13] They also shared an interest in Chesterton, some of whose work Reyes translated into Spanish. The intentional "Englishness" of Chesterton's English style, however, must be presumed to present a huge challenge to translators.

---

10 *Commerce* 15 Printemps, 1928, pp. 89–107.
11 op. cit.
12 Valery Larbaud–Alfonso Reyes, *Correspondance* (Paris: Didier, 1972).
13 Alfonso Reyes, "De la Traduccion" in *La Experiencia Literaria* (Buenos Aires: Losada, 1941).

Larbaud particularly liked Reyes's incantation on the Tarahumara Indians entitled *Yerbas del Taraumara* and undertook to translate it for *Commerce*.[14] The Tarahumara Indians live in particularly remote valleys of the Sierra Madre Occidental of north-western Mexico.

Paulette Patout reproduces the translation opposite the original[15] as well as giving a later French translation by Guy Levis-Mano (1952). The latter, however, is not necessarily an improvement since it often uses Larbaud's phrasing. The poem is seventy-nine lines in length.

As Paulette Patout points out, Larbaud's translation respects the length of the lines of the original and also the pauses.[16] A descriptive line referring to the Tarahumara Indians might serve as an example, although there is a slight difference in interpretation between these two translations: *duros en la lustrosa piel manchada*[17]

Larbaud: leur peau tachetée et luisante durcie[18]

Levis-Mano: durs sous leur peau luisante et souillée[19]

A problem in the names of tropical plants arose when Larbaud was unable to find a French equivalent for *sangre de grado*[20] in any of the specialized dictionaries ("*les livres consulaires*") to which he referred. It then occurred to him that "grado" must be an anagram of "drago" and that *sangre de drago* corresponds to the French *sangdragon*, a red resin given off by the tropical tree known as *le dragonnier*. (*Drago* is archaic in Spanish.) This had been one of the trees described by Humboldt in his study of the flora of the tropical regions of the Americas.[21] (Humboldt described the immense "dragon tree" he encountered on the west side of Teneriffe, in the Canaries, on his way to Venezuela.)

Reyes's position on the translation of poetry in *La Experiencia Literaria* (1941) and *Mallarmé Entre Nosotros* (1938) is that the translator of a poem must herself (or himself) be a poet in order to maintain the "flavour" (*la saveur*)

---

14 Cf. *Commerce* 19 (Printemps), 1929.
15 op. cit., pp. 182–191.
16 op. cit., p. 181.
17 op. cit., p. 182.
18 op. cit., p. 183.
19 Ibid.
20 op. cit., p. 188.
21 Alexander Von Humboldt, *Personal Narrative* [1834] (London: Penguin, 1995), pp. 28–29.

of the original, adding another term to the qualities of *le contenu* that must be expressed by *le contenant*. This notion of the "flavour" might not appeal to a linguist but it is nonetheless highly significant in the writings of these two *connaisseurs*.

This expression also underlines a problem in the translation of Larbaud's own work into other languages since such qualities, like Coleridge's implicit conception of poetry as drug, can of course represent major problems to the translator. Proust's possibly exaggerated comment on the effect on him of reading Larbaud's *Enfantines*, namely that they made him feel "un peu malade," likewise raises the question of how the translated text can be made to express effects of that order.

Hence both Larbaud and Reyes struggle with the conflict between very free translation on the one hand, which nonetheless might succeed in rendering the essence, and on the other the very literal and "correct," but sometimes "flat" translation, that might betray it.[22]

---

22 op. cit., pp. 192–193. Notes for Letters 39 & 40.

Chapter 14

Translations from Italian

Italo Svevo

Larbaud translated a number of works from Italian, sometimes collaborating with others including his spouse Maria Nebbia who was of Italian origin. His translation of a series of extracts, which he particularly liked, from Italo Svevo's novel *Senilità*, appeared in Adrienne Monnier's journal *Le Navire d'Argent* in February 1926, as part of a tribute to Svevo following his tragically premature death. Larbaud had discovered Svevo through Joyce, who had known him and admired his work during his years in Trieste. He liked Svevo's use of interior monologue, especially in his greatest novel, *La Coscienza di Zeno* (1923). *Senilità* (1898) belongs to the earlier of the two major phases of Svevo's novels.

An uproarious comedy in its satire of Triestine "high society," *La Coscienza di Zeno* was also to make a significant contribution to the development of the novel by demonstrating a very early literary effect of Freudian psychoanalysis, being in the form of an autobiography requested by a psychiatrist.

Senilità, however, is clearly pre-Freudian but has undercurrents in its view of alleged human weaknesses and strengths, in fact challenging that very notion as highly arbitrary. (Svevo was reacting to Nietzsche.) The French translation of *Senilità* by Paul-Henri Michel, published in 1930, reflects the "launching" of Svevo's work in Paris due to the persistent efforts of Larbaud, who strongly promoted it on its intrinsic merit, even in the face of considerable adverse criticism.[1] This novel has much more recently been translated into English by Beth Archer Brombert as *Emilio's Carnival* (2001).[2]

Svevo has also been rediscovered as an important playwright, as a result, in part, of Guido Lucchini's two volume edition of the plays[3] so that Svevo's "vicarious life" has at last assumed the form of his recognition as a classic.

---

1 Cf. Ortensia Ruggiero, *Valery Larbaud et L'Italie* (Paris: Nizet, 1963), pp. 229–235.
2 *Times Literary Supplement*, January 4, 2013. p. 23. Cf: Carmine di Biase, "Work of a Golden Sunset."
3 *Commedie*: Edizione di Storia e Letteratura, 2012.

Larbaud had many correspondents among Italian writers and his sojourns in Italy became more frequent during the 1920s, so that his Italian "domain" was becoming a very significant theatre of his work. And under the auspices of his friend and patron, Marguerite Caetani, Princesse de Bassiano, it had become possible to publish in Paris in the cosmopolitan review *Commerce*, which was described on the title page of each number as: "Cahiers trimestriels publiés par le soins de Paul Valéry, Léon-Paul Fargue, Valery Larbaud." Larbaud published several of his translations and presentations in the field of Italian literature in *Commerce*. The name of this prestigious journal had been taken from a line by the poet and diplomat, later winner of the Nobel Prize for literature in 1962, St. John Perse, who is sometimes considered the greatest poet of the French language in the twentieth century: "ce pur commerce de mon âme parmi vous."[4]

Emilio Cecchi

Larbaud's translation into French of Emilio Cecchi's essay "Kaléidoscope" in *Commerce* 8[5] evokes the intense "power" that resides in such jewellery as a ring, so that the ring becomes capable, as it were, of recapturing its owner or former owner, causing her or him to experience it as a charm that won't go away, hence as having a life of its own. This theme is clearly classical since it is intended to express a permanently valid truth.

Bruno Barilli

Another short translation from the Italian of Bruno Barilli, by Larbaud and his spouse (of Italian origin) Maria Nebbia, in *Commerce* 10 (Hiver 1926) evokes, under the title *Bottesini*, an old-school travelling musician and clown, Giovanni Bottesini, performing during a carnival to a very select audience, on his bass viol. (He was famous for having spontaneously transposed Paganini on this instrument.) He is an expert at popular farce of a kind normally reserved for the marketplace, but in this story he is highly successful in his role as musical clown and brings his distinguished audience to tears with a performance of his uncensored farce on the bass viol.[6]

This piece is a vivd evocation of an intimate scene in Italian life which Larbaud can reproduce as a result of his many sojourns in Italy, Italy being virtually a second homeland. An example, among several others, of this aspect of Larbaud's work, is to be found in such shorter works as "Deux Artistes

---

4   St. J. Perse *Anabase* (Paris: Gallimard [NRF], 1924), p. 2.
5   Eté 1926, pp. 135–147
6   op. cit., p. 147.

Lyriques" in *Aux Couleurs de Rome*[7] concerning the lives of two travelling theatrical performers, whose art the narrator is able to observe twice during his travels in Italy.

Ricardo Bacchelli

Again, a further short translation by Larbaud of Ricardo Bacchelli's *Trois Divinités sur les Apennins*, published in *Commerce* 12,[8] attains such perfection in Larbaud's style that there is virtually no indication that it is a translation:

> Bacchus est capricieux comme ce mince tourbillon de poussière sur la calme route de Volterre et après Sienne et San Giminiano il sourit à Certaldo, ou Boccace est né. Et si tout à coup il franchit les Apennins, j'imagine qu'il descend en Romagne par Rocca San Casciano, là ou une vallée toscane s'allonge jusqu'aux portes de Forli. Là, je me l'imagine, le dieu riant et rêveur, énamouré de l'idée d'un architecte qui, devant tracer le plan d'un bourg et d'une forteresse pour un des Médicis, copia la forme de l'enceinte sur l'ombre que projetait sur la campagne un nuage qui passait. C'est ainsi qu'est née Terre-du-Soleil avec son beau nom.[9]

Marguerite Caetani

The publication of *Commerce* depended on the generous support of Marguerite Caetani, Princess of Bassiano. as explained in detail in the recently published biography by Laurie Dennett, *An American Princess. The Remarkable Life of Marguerite Chapin Caetani*.[10]

This biography explains the circumstances surrounding the publication of *Commerce* which published significant translations into French from several languages. The first issue of *Commerce* had appeared in August 1924 and it continued until 1932.[11] Writers whose work was published in *Commerce* include Joyce, Eliot, Archibald MacLeish, Faulkner, Edith Sitwell, Virginia Woolf, Hardy, Meredith, Hawthorne, Poe. Roy Campbell, Rilke, Hofmannstal, Buchner, Kasner, Nietzsche, Kafka, Holderlin, Kierkegaard. Pasternak. Mandestraum, Rosanov, Pushkin, Leopardi, Ungaretti, Cecchi, Bruno Barilli, and Ricardo Bacchelli.

---

7   Cf. Larbaud, *Oeuvres* (Pléiade), pp. 986–987.
8   Eté 1927, pp. 145–151.
9   Ibid., pp. 150–151.
10 Montreal and Kingston: McGill-Queen's University Press, 2016.
11 *Commerce* Eté 1924–Hiver 1932, no. 29.

Chapter 15

Translations from Portuguese

Larbaud's sojourn in Portugal during the winter of 1926 resulted in the Portuguese sequence among the essays of *Jaune Bleu Blanc*. One of them, "Divertissement Philologique,"[1] relates his impressions of the Portuguese language and of his efforts to learn it, which he eventually does. This trip soon became another voyage of literary exploration. He did discover many works that were relatively unknown beyond the boundaries of Portugal and Brazil. (Creative writing from Angola and Mozambique and other Portuguese colonies and former colonies, was still virtually unknown.)

From our present perspective, it seems unfortunate that Larbaud's literary contacts in Lisbon were not able to put him in touch with the work of the already very promising Fernando Pessoa. However, in 1926 Pessoa had still published very little and only in very obscure journals. One can only speculate on what Larbaud's reaction to Pessoa's mass of unpublished poetry might have been, attributed as it was to a number of "heteronyms," and whether the technique of the heteronym might have come to Pessoa (at least in part) as a result of possible assimilation of Larbaud's *Poésies de Barnabooth*, given that Pessoa began inventing them in 1914, a year after the appearance of Barnabooth's *Oeuvres Complètes*.

Nevertheless, Larbaud did become interested in the novels of the cosmopolitan diplomat of the late nineteenth century, Eça de Queiroz, which reflected the realist and naturalist movements of his day. Queiroz, now recognized throughout the Western world as a significant novelist, was then already a classic in Portugal but almost totally unknown beyond its borders. He is sometimes called "the Portuguese Dickens" and also compared with Zola and Proust with respect to the themes of *dégénérescence* and *régénération*.

In his essay *Ecrit dans une Cabine du Sud-Express*, Larbaud provides a résumé of an early novel by Queiroz, *A Capital (La Capitale)*.[2] He was soon to investigate the work of Queiroz in a very thorough manner and recognized

---

1 op. cit. in *Jaune Bleu Blanc* (Pléiade), p. 934.
2 Ibid., p. 951.

the need to promote it in France, a cause which he adopted by encouraging French translations.

One of the volumes in Larbaud's *Bibliothèque Luso-Brésilienne* is a novel by the Brazilian writer of the late nineteenth century, Machado de Assis (1837–1908), *Dom Casmurro*.[3] It is a reminder of the thorough study of Brazilian literature Larbaud had made as a young man as related to his friend (later the diplomat) Marcel Ray, in their correspondence. The French translation of this novel, first published in 1920, was the work of Larbaud's associate Francis de Miomandre, one of the many fellow translators who surrounded him in the 1920s in the extended workplace revealed by Paulette Patout.

Machado was an *autodidacte* who created the dialogue in this novel in the local vernacular. Miomandre, whose name lends itself to being pronounced in either French or Portuguese, and who was from Touraine, finds a French equivalent in the dialects of francophone parts of the Caribbean and French Guiana. An example from among many might be: "aucun de nous deux n'a envie de s'amuser."[4] The fact that the first part of the novel is an *enfantine* might have interested Larbaud since his own *Enfantines* could be related to many other works whose protagonists are children, among them a number of Daudet's *Contes*, Charles-Louis Philippe's *Charles Blanchard*, Jules Vallès' *L'Enfant* and LeClézio's *Mondo et autres histoires*.

Machado is probably best remembered today for his short stories and in particular for the wit and humour of his novella *The Psychiatrist* (1881), in which we have a vivid satire of nineteenth-century South American revolutions, this one at the municipal level. A flurry of interest in the work of Machado occurred in the 1970s when his three major novels, including *Dom Casmurro*, were reissued in English translation. One important characteristic of these novels is that the author-narrator involves his reader in their actual progression, at certain points, in the manner of Sterne and Fielding. *Dom Casmurro* is both romantic and realistic in its Othello theme, which is brought to bear only in the *dénouement*.

On one occasion, Machado challenged Queiroz in the Brazilian press, taking exception to the latter's occasional adoption of naturalist theory: "Je ne peux que conseiller aux jeunes écrivains de nos deux pays de ne pas se laisser séduire par une doctrine caduque."[5]

---

3 Cf. *Cahiers des Amis de Valery Larbaud*, No. 34, 1997, p. 79.
4 Joaquim M. Machado de Assis, *Dom Casmurro* (Paris: Albin Michel, 1956), p. 117.
5 Eça de Queiroz, *Le Cousin Bazilio* [1878]. Traduction Française et Introduction de Lucette Petit (UNESCO, 1989), p. 9.

In 1933, just two years before the severe stroke that tragically terminated Larbaud's active career, he worked with Georges Raeders, who was translating another Queiroz novel, *A Reliquia,* into French.[6] Paulette Patout stresses the importance of Larbaud's collaboration:

> Le texte dactylographié de la traduction...porte à chaque page des annotations de Larbaud, ses suggestions au traducteur."

She then quotes a letter from Raeders:

> Que de soirées prolongées tard dans la nuit....Il n'était pas rare que, le lendemain...je reçusse, à un des premiers courriers, un petit mot de lui... dans lequel il revenait sur un détail de traduction, s'excusant presque auprès de moi de son interprétation.[7]

This vivid image of Larbaud's active role in the translation, working at it with great enthusiasm, since it represented the revelation of a major novelist whose work had remained virtually unknown in the francophone world, utterly engrossed in the project until well into the night and then again, first thing in the morning, is possibly the last image we have of Larbaud the translator.

---

6 Eça de Queiroz, *La Relique* [1887]. Traduction de Georges Raeders. Préface de Valery Larbaud (Paris: Sorlot, 1941). Cf. Larbaud, op. cit. (Pléiade), p. 1272.
7 Valery Larbaud–Alfonso Reyes, *Correspondance,* op. cit., p. 289.

Chapter 16

Conclusion

The translations of Valery Larbaud thus bring important work from four other world languages into French at a time when the translator could experience his mission as responding to an urgent need: "expliquant un peuple aux autres peuples, unifiant la conscience de l'humanité."[1] He is referring here to the forgotten French cosmopolitan novelist John-Antoine Nau, but given his significant tendency to identify with the works of his favourite writers, he is at the same time defining his own role, and in his deeply committed activity as a translator he is cultivating the garden of the new Europe that is now coming into being.

A recent work that frequently stresses the importance of Larbaud's influence during the most active period of his career (1918–1935) is Pascale Casanova's *La République mondiale des lettres*,[2] which was translated into English in 2004 as *The World Republic of Letters*.[3] It is dedicated to Henry James and Valery Larbaud.

It is clear that Larbaud's work is never explicitly committed (*engagé*) to a cause. However, Pascale Casanova, in referring to the overarching effect of Larbaud's creative and critical work, as well as his translations, sees Larbaud as "erasing the boundaries assigned by literary nationalism."[4] She also quotes Larbaud directly, clarifying her perspective on an important aspect of Larbaud's work:

> Every French writer is international; he is a poet, a writer for all of Europe and for a part of America as well....All that is "national" is silly, archaic, disreputably patriotic....It served a purpose under certain circumstances, but that time has passed. There is now a country of Europe.[5]

---

1 In *La Revue Européenne* (1er Septembre 1924).
2 Paris: Editions du Seuil, 1999.
3 Cambridge, MA: Harvard University Press, 2004
4 Pascal Casanova, op. cit., transl., *The Wold Republic of Letters*, op. cit., p. 5.
5 Casanova, op. cit., p. 87.

She further quotes Larbaud on the difference between the political and intellectual maps of the world:

> The one changes its look every fifty years; it is covered with arbitrary and uncertain divisions, and its major centers are constantly shifting. The intellectual map, by contrast, changes slowly and its boundaries display great stability.[6]

She even envisions cosmopolitan writers like Larbaud as foreign exchange brokers "responsible for exporting from one territory to another texts whose literary value they determine by virtue of this very activity."[7] The French translation of Joyce's *Ulysses*, to which Larbaud greatly contributed, might be taken as a case in point. In the context which Pascale Casanova very firmly establishes, Larbaud is admired for having dismissed chauvinistic trends in French writing as being insignificant.

Valery Larbaud's unflinching commitment to translation brought important work from four other "linguistic domains" into French. Despite the trauma of the First World War, he was an undaunted believer in Europe, and his work as a translator could be considered an implicit manifestation in favour of the cause of a united Europe.

Since translation is, in effect, a means of creating greater understanding and appreciation between between diverse cultures, and since Larbaud himself participated not only in important literary activities of his native France but also in the literary lives of Britain, Spain, Italy, and Portugal, the question of the role of translation in the evolution of a more united Europe inevitably arises. Could translation itself be understood in this context as a form of *littérature engagée*?

Such an interpretation would immediately seem controversial since Larbaud insisted on several occasions, especially in the diaries he kept toward the end of his creative life, that literature must never be "exploited" in the interest of any particular ideological cause, whether political or cultural.

He strongly opposed the concept of *littérature engagée* as it was debated during the 1930s. However, his own work does implicitly manifest certain positions, which might more properly be termed "conceptions."

Thus he takes a stand in favour of what has been called literary "cosmopolitanism," and it could be said that the study of Larbaud's work inevitably leads toward a distinction between "explicit" and "implicit"

---

6 op. cit., p. 10.
7 op. cit., p. 21.

commitment. The very nature of his work is often an expression of cultural commitments. His fictitious character Barnabooth, a South American in Europe, is as much at home in Russia as in Italy or anywhere else in Europe. The mere fact that this novel was published in 1913—that is, at a time of acute chauvinism—seems in itself to make a significant statement, yet this work is not explicitly "*engagé*."

Further, Larbaud's conception of Europe is not merely a Europe of nation states but may rather be said to favour a return of the smaller nations which, because of various historical processes over centuries, had been swallowed up, as it were, by the "powers." Thus he drew attention to the time before the evolution of nation states toward their present form and made a very careful study of his own province, Bourbonnais, which, in the early sixteenth century, had allied itself with the Austrian Empire, yet without any thought of "treason" being implied by the parties concerned. This is the subject of his work on Bourbonnais titled *Allen* (1927) after the motto of the independent Bourbonnais of history. Within this context lies the presumption that Catalonia, Scotland, Tuscany, Brittany, Burgundy, and many more such former polities long since absorbed by the "powers," might eventually recover their former autonomy. Larbaud's non-political vision of the future Europe points toward the hope of just such an eventuality.

However, Larbaud's work is never explicitly *engagé*. What is most remarkable about his translations is simply their integrity. As can be seen particularly in the translation of Butler's *Life and Habit*, they amount to a collaboration with the author of the original text and bring about what is in effect an improvement of it by constantly seeking greater clarity, so that it is paradoxically the translation that becomes the finished form of the work.

Bibliography

A. Oeuvres Complètes de Valery Larbaud

Tome Deuxième (*Fermina Marquez, Enfantines*). Paris: Gallimard NRF, 1950.

Tome Troisième (*Ce Vice Impuni la Lecture: Domaine Anglais*). Paris: Gallimard NRF, 1951. (This volume was edited in 1998 by Béatrice Mousli and more than doubled in length through the annexation of studies first published in periodicals.) Cf. *Ce Vice Impuni la Lecture: Domaine Anglais Suivi de Pages Retrouvées*. Edition Revue et Complétée par Béatrice Mousli. Paris: Gallimard NRF, 1998 (676 pp.).

Tome Septième (*Ce Vice Impuni La Lecture: Domaine Francais*). Paris: Gallimard NRF, 1953.

Tome Huitième (*Sous L'Invocation de Saint Jérôme*). Paris: Gallimard NRF, 1953.

Oeuvres (Bibliothèque de la Pléiade). Paris: Gallimard, 1961.

Journal. Edition Définitive. Texte Etabli, Préfacé et Annoté par Paule Moron. Paris: Gallimard, 2009 (1601 pp.).

B. Major Monographs on the Life and Work of Valery Larbaud

Jean-Aubry, Georges. *Valery Larbaud: Sa Vie et son Oeuvre*. Vol. 1: "La Jeunesse" (1881–1920). Monaco: Rocher, 1949.

Delvaille, Bernard. *Essai sur Valery Larbaud* ("Poètes d'Aujourd'hui" 100). Paris: Seghers, 1963.

Ruggiero, Ortensia. *Valery Larbaud et l'Italie*. Paris: Nizet, 1963.

McCarthy, Patrick. *Valery Larbaud: Critic of English Literature*. Oxford: 1968. (unpublished doctoral thesis, Oxford University)

Brown, John L. *Valery Larbaud*. Twayne World Authors Series, 597. Boston: G.K. Hall & Co., 1981.

Cahiers de l'Herne 61, "Valery Larbaud." Dirigés par Anne Chevalier. Paris: Editions de l'Herne, 1992. Edité avec le Concours du Centre National des Lettres.

Mousli, Béatrice. *Valery Larbaud.* Paris: Flammarion, 1998.

C. Editions of Works Translated by Valery Larbaud and Quoted in the Present Monograph

Coleridge, Samuel Taylor. *The Rime of the Ancient Mariner.* London: Folio Society, 1963.

Landor, Walter Savage. *The Complete Works of Walter Savage Landor*, vol. 10 (ed. T. Earl Welby). New York: Barnes & Noble Inc. & London: Methuen & Co., 1912.

Whitman, Walt. *Leaves of Grass.* New York: Modern Library (Definitive Edition).

Butler, Samuel. *Erewhon or Over the Range* (1872). New American Library Signet Classics, 1960.

Butler, Samuel. *Erewhon Revisited* (1901) (Everyman's Library). London: Dent Ltd., 1965.

Butler, Samuel. *Note-Books.* Selections Arranged and Edited by Henry Festing Jones. London: Fifield, 1912 (Original ed.).

Butler, Samuel. *The Way of All Flesh* (1903) (New American Library). New York & Toronto: Signet Classics, 1960.

Butler, Samuel. *Life and Habit* (December 1877). Champaign, IL: Book Jungle Reprints.

Joyce, James. *Ulysses* (1922). Harmondsworth, UK: Penguin, 1969.

D. Valery Larbaud's Butler Translations

Butler, Samuel. *Erewhon ou De l'autre côté des montagnes.* Paris: Gallimard, 2 juillet 1920.

Butler, Samuel. *Ainsi va toute chair.* Paris: Gallimard, 16 mars 1921.

Butler, Samuel. *La Vie et l'habitude.* Paris: Gallimard, 3 juillet 1922.

Butler, Samuel. *Nouveaux Voyages en Erewhon.* Paris: Gallimard, 22 mai 1924.

Butler, Samuel. *Carnets.* Paris: Gallimard, janvier 1936.

E. The Shrewsbury Edition of the Works of Butler Translated by Larbaud

Butler, Samuel. *Erewhon.* Ams Press Reprint, vol. 2. 1923 ed. (London & New York, 1968).

Butler, Samuel. *Life and Habit* Ams Press Reprint, vol. 4. 1923 ed. (London & New York 1968).

Butler, Samuel. *Erewhon Revisited.* Ams Press Reprint. vol. 16. 1925 ed. (London & New York 1968).

Butler, Samuel. *The Way of All Flesh.* Ams Press Reprint, vol. 17. 1925 ed. (London & New York, 1968).

Butler, Samuel. *Note-Books.* Ams Press Reprint, vol. 20. 1926 ed. (London & New York, 1968).

F. Translations into French from Italian by Valery Larbaud

Svevo, Italo. Choix de textes de *Senilita* in "Hommage a Svevo." *Le Navire d'Argent.* Paris: La Maison des Amis des Livres 9 (Février 1926).

Cecchi, Emilio *Kaléidoscope. Commerce* 8 (Eté 1926).

Barilli, Bruno. *Trois Essais.* Traduit de lItalien par Maria Nebbia et Valery Larbaud. *Commerce* 10 (Hiver 1926).

Bacchelli, Ricardo. "Trois Divinités des Appenins." Traduit de l'Italien par Valery Larbaud. *Commerce* 12 (Eté 1927).

Barilli, Bruno. *Vieille Parme.* Traduit de l'Italien par Valery Larbaud. *Commerce* 19 (Printemps 1929).

Mazzini (Gianna). *La Femme du Sourd.* Traduit de lItalien par Henri Marchand et Valery Larbaud. *Nouvelle Revue Francaise* (Juillet 1934).

Fiumi, Lionello. "Poème." Traduit de l'Italien par Valery Larbaud. *Cahiers du Sud* No. 171 (avril 1935).

Cecchi, Emilio. *Poissons rouges.* Traduit par Jean Chuzeville, B. Crémieux, Valerio Jahier, et Valery Larbaud. Paris: Gallimard, 1936.

De Sanctis, Francesco. Pages traduites de *Studio su Giacomo Leopardi.* In Valery Larbaud. *De la Traduction.* Cf: Larbaud, *Sous l'invocation de St. Jérome.* Deuxième Partie: "L'Art et le Métier."

Oeuvres Complètes, Tome 8. Paris: Gallimard, 1953. pp. 78–84.

G. Translations into French from Spanish by Valery Larbaud

Gomez de la Serna, Ramon. *Pages Choisies.* Traduction de Valery Larbaud en collaboration avec Madame B.M. Moreno. *Hispania* (Paris). juillet-septembre 1918.

Gomez de la Serna, Ramon. *Echantillons. Criailleries.* Traduction de Mathilde Pomès et Valery Larbaud. Paris: Grasset (Les Cahiers Verts), 1923.

Miró, Gabriel. *Semaine Sainte.* Traduite par Valery Larbaud et Noémi Larthe. Paris: Sagittaire, 1925.

Guiraldes, Ricardo. *Poèmes Solitaires.* Traduits de l'Espagnol par V. Larbaud. *Commerce*, Cahier XV Printemps 1928.

Guiraldes, Ricardo. *Poèmes Mystiques.* Traduits de l'Espagnol par V. Larbaud. *Chroniques*, No. 6, 1928.

Reyes, Alfonso. *Les Herbes de Tarahumara.* Traduit de l'Espagnol par Valery Larbaud. *Commerce*, Cahier XIX (Printemps 1929).

D'Ors, Eugenio. *Au grand Saint-Christophe.* Traduction de Tissier de Mallerais avec trois natures mortes traduites par Valery Larbaud. Paris: Corréa, 1932.

H. Translation into French from Portuguese by Valery Larbaud

Queiroz, José Maria Eca (de). *La Relique.* Traduit du Portugais par Georges Raeders avec la collaboration de Valery Larbaud. Préface de V. Larbaud. Paris: Sorlot, 1941.

I. Other Translations from English by Valery Larbaud

Hawthorne, Nathaniel. *Idées et germes de nouvelles.* Traduit de l'anglais par Valery Larbaud. *Commerce* 18 (Hiver 1928).

Browne, Thomas. Chapître V de *Hydriotaphia* Précédé d'Opinions de S.T. Coleridge sur Thomas Browne. Traduit de l'anglais par Valery Larbaud. *Commerce* XXI (Automne 1929).

J. Published Correspondence of Valery Larbaud Quoted

Valery Larbaud. *Lettres à André Gide.* La Haye, Paris: Stols, 1948.

Valery Larbaud–Jean-Aubry, Georges *Correspondance* (1920–1935). Introduction et Notes de Frida Weissman. Paris: Gallimard, 1971.

Valery Larbaud–Léon-Paul Fargue *Correspondance* (1910–1946). Texte établi, présenté et annoté par T. Alajouanine. Paris: Gallimard, 1971.

Valery Larbaud–Alfonso Reyes *Correspondance* 1923–1952. Avant-Propos de Marcel Bataillon. Introduction et Notes de Paulette Patout. Publié avec le Concours du Centre National de la Recherche Scientifique. Paris: Marcel Didier, 1972.

Valery Larbaud–Marcel Ray *Correspondance* (3 vols.). Paris: Gallimard (NRF), 1979, 1980.

Valery Larbaud–A.A.M. Stols *Correspondance*. Paris: Editions des Cendres, 1986.

Valery Larbaud. *Lettres a Adrienne Monnier et a Sylvia Beach*,1919–1933. Paris: Institut Mémoires de l'Edition Contemporaine (IMEC), 1991. Correspondance établie et annotée par Maurice Saillet.

K. Thesis

Aldaz, Anna-Marie. *Valery Larbaud as Translator of Samuel Butler*. PhD dissertation. University of Oregon, 1969.

L. Other Relevant Works

Bergson, Henri. *L'Evolution Créatrice* (1907). Paris: Presses Universitaires de France,1948.

Bohr, Niels. *Physical Science and the Problem of Life*. New York:Wiley, 1958.

Butler, Samuel. "The Deadlock in Darwinism." In *The Humour of Homer and Other Essays*. Freeport, NY: Books for Libraries Press, pp. 253–254.

Casanova, Pascale. *The World Republic of Letters*. Cambridge, MA: Harvard University Press, 2004. (*La République Mondiale des Lettres*. Paris: Editions du Seuil, 1999.) English translation by M.B. DeBevoise.

Chamfort, Nicolas Sébastien Roch (de). *Maximes et Pensées*. Le Monde en 10/18. Présentation de Claude Roy. Paris, 1963.

Coleridge, S.T. *La Ballade du Vieux Marin et autres poèmes*. Choix, Présentation et Traduction de Jacques Darras. Paris: Gallimard, 2007.

Connell, Allison. Forgotten masterpieces of liteary translation: Valery Larbaud's "Butlers." *Canadian Review of Comparative Literature*, 1974, *1*(2), 167–190.

Darwin, Charles. *The Origin of Species* (1859). New York: Modern Library Paperbacks, 1998.

Delisle, Jean, & Woodsworth, Judith. *Les Traducteurs dans l'histoire*. Ottawa: Presses de l'Université d'Ottawa, 1995.

Dennett, Laurie. *An American Princess: The Remarkable Life of Marguerite Chapin Caetani*. Montreal and Kingston: McGill-Queen's University Press, 2016.

Ellmann, Richard. *James Joyce*. New York: Oxford UP, 1959.

Fargue, Léon-Paul. *Poésies*. Paris: Gallimard, 1963.

Fodor, Jerry, & Piatelli-Palmerini, Massimo. *What Darwin Got Wrong*. New York: Farrar, Strauss & Giroux, 2010. Great Britain: Profile Books Ltd.

Gide, André. *Les Faux-Monnayeurs*. Paris: Gallimard, 1926.

Gilbert, Stuart. *James Joyce's "Ulysses."* New York: Vintage Books, 1930.

Goldmann, Lucien. *Pour une Sociologie du Roman*. Paris: Gallimard (Bibliothèque des Idées), 1964.

Guyard, Marius François. *La Grande Bretagne dans le Roman Français (1914–1940)*. Paris: Marcel Didier, 1954.

Hardin, Garrett. *Nature and Man's Fate*. New York: Holt, Reinhardt & Winston, 1959.

Jones, Henry Festing. *Samuel Butler, Author of "Erewhon," 1835–1902 A Memoir* (vol. 1 to 1885; vol. 2: 1885–1916). London: MacMillan & Co., 1920.

Joyce, James *Ulysses* (1922). Harmondsworth, UK: Penguin Modern Classics, 1969.

Joyce, James. *Ulysse*. Traduction d'Auguste Morel. Revue par Valery Larbaud, Stuart Gilbert, et l'Auteur. Paris: Gallimard 1929, 1957. Collection *Folio*, 1976.

Joyce, James. *Ulysse*. Paris: Gallimard, 2004. Postface par Jacques Aubert.

Landor, W.S. *Hautes et Basses Classes en Italie*. Traduction Française de Valery Larbaud. Paris: Victor Beaumont, 1911.

Landor, W.S. *The Complete Works of W.S. Landor* (ed. by T. Earle Welby). Vol. 10. New York: Barnes & Noble, 1912. London: Methuen & Co. Ltd.

Lima, Vianna de. *Exposé Sommaire des Théories Transformistes de Lamarck, Darwin et Haekel*. Paris: Delagrave, 1885.

Machado de Assis (Joaquim) *Dom Casmurro*. Traduit du Portugais par Francis de Miomandre. Paris: Albin Michel, 1956.

Margulis, Lynn, & Sagan, Dorion. *What is Life*. New York: Simon & Schuster, 1995.

Margulis, Lynn. *Symbiotic Planet*. Amherst, MA: Science Writers, 1998.

Maupertuis (Pierre L.M. De). *Le Système de la Nature*. In *Les Oeuvres de Monsieur de Maupertuis*, II. Lyon: Bruyset, 1756.

Mumford, Lewis. Introduction to Butler, S. *Erewhon*. New York: Modern Library, 1927.

Mumford, Lewis. *Values for Survival*. New York: Harcourt, Brace & Co., 1946.

Mumford, Lewis. *The Human Prospect*. Boston: Beacon Press, 1955.

Pergnier, Maurice. *Les Fondements Socio-linguistiques de la Traduction*. Presses Universitaires de Lille, 1993. (Cf. pp. 17–19).

Perrier, Edmond. *La Philosophie Zoologique avant Darwin*. Paris, 1884.

Perrin, Noel. *Giving Up the Gun (Japan's Reversion to the Sword 1543–1879)*. Boston: David R. Godine, 1979.

Quatrefages, Armand Bréau de. *Ch. Darwin et ses Précurseurs Français*. Paris: Baillère, 1870.

Queiroz, Eça de. *Le Cousin Basilio* (1878). UNESCO, 1989.

Reyes, Alfonso. *De la Traduccion*. In *La Experiencia Literaria*. Buenos Aires: Losado, 1941.

Reynolds, David. S. *Walt Whitman's America: A Cultural Biography*. New York: Knopf, 1995.

Ribot, Théodule. *L'Hérédité. Etude psychologique sur ses phénomènes, ses lois, ses causes, ses conséquences*. Paris: 1873, 1882.

Rivière, Jacques. *Le Roman d'Aventure*. La Nouvelle Revue Française (mai–juillet 1913).

Shaffer, Elinor. *Erewhons of the Eye*. London: Reaktion Books, 1988.

Smith, Logan Pearsall. *All Trivia*. London: Doubleday Doran & Co. Inc., 1917.

Steiner, George. (Ed.). *Homer in English* London: Penguin, 1996.

Whitman, Walt. *Leaves of Grass* Following the Edition of 1891–2. New York: Modern Library.

Whitman, Walt. *Oeuvres Choisies*. Paris: Gallimard, 1918.

Whitman, Walt. *Complete Poetry & Collected Prose* (including complete prose). New York: The Library of America. Distributed by Viking Press, 1982. Series: Literary Classics of the United States.

Willey, Basil. *Darwin and Butler: Two Versions of Evolution*. London: Chatto & Windus, 1960.

About the Author

Allison Connell was born in 1931 at Sioux Lookout in northwestern Ontario, Canada where his father was District Forester. In 1941 the family moved to his father's original home in Woodstock, New Brunswick. His childhood experiences in the forest and lake country of the north left a deep impression and he eventually returned over many summers for extended canoe and camping excursions.

Allison Connell is a graduate of Mt. Allison University where he specialized in French Literature. This led to teaching fellowships at French lycées, which were renewed twice. He returned to France in 1956 and completed his doctoral programme at the Sorbonne in 1959. During this time he developed a deep and continuing interest in Valery Larbaud and the art of translation.

Back in Canada, he taught for five years at the University of Winnipeg. In 1964 he conducted a summer school course in 17th century French Literature at the University of Alberta. He subsequently became a Professor of French and Comparative Literature at the University of Alberta where he taught from 1965 to 1980. During this period he published a number of papers in The Canadian Review of Comparative Literature, including one on Larbaud's translations of Samuel Butler.

Retiring from university teaching in 1980, Allison Connell returned to Woodstock, New Brunswick. He continued his literary work as an independent scholar. During this time he completed a translation of *Mondo and Other Stories* by Le Clézio. He continued his study of Larbaud, which has now been brought to completion with the publication of *The Translations of Valery Larbaud*.

Since returning to Woodstock, Allison Connell has been active in heritage preservation. He initiated and conducted a three-year project that documented the town's architectural heritage. He is the author of *A View of Woodstock: Historic Homes of the Nineteenth Century*, which is now in its second edition. He has long been active in New Brunswick movements to conserve and protect the province's natural environments and to advance its transition to renewable energy.

www.ingramcontent.com/pod-product-compliance
Lightning Source LLC
Chambersburg PA
CBHW020526080526
44583CB00013B/760